THE
BIG
WATER
FIGHT

THE
BIG
WATER
FIGHT

Trials and Triumphs in Citizen Action on Problems
of Supply, Pollution, Floods, and Planning across the U. S. A.

The League of Women Voters

Education Fund

1966
THE STEPHEN GREENE PRESS
BRATTLEBORO, VERMONT

ACKNOWLEDGMENTS

This book represents the cooperative effort of many persons, groups, and agencies. These include the state and local Leagues which have worked on water problems and the League members who have carefully and promptly supplied the necessary detailed information; the leaders in other citizen organizations; the academic specialists and the many local, state, and federal officials throughout the nation who, with unfailing courtesy and friendliness, have shared their knowledge and creative ideas; and Resources for the Future, Inc., which made possible, through a grant to the Education Fund, the research and compilation.

All photographs not otherwise credited were furnished through the courtesy of the Federal Water Pollution Control Administration.

Project Director and General Editor . Suvia Paton Whittemore
Researcher and Editor . . . . . Elizabeth Duffy Hawkins
Consultant . . . . Lois Kremer Sharpe

Table of Contents

PART II

BROAD STRATEGY

PART III

A GUIDE TO TACTICS

Preface

WATER PROBLEMS plague and alarm the world. In some countries, women stand in line at the village well to bring home a wretchedly inadequate daily ration. Health crises in parts of Latin America are traced to open sewers. Hong Kong's bay may be the last hope for that desperately crowded city's water supply. A fighting war over water has been threatened in the parched Middle East.

In the affluent United States, however, at the flick of the tap, we are accustomed to getting all the water we want, piped directly to our homes or factories or farms. It is clean enough to drink, hot or cold as we choose, and plentiful enough—most of the time—despite industrial and municipal use, to enable us to sprinkle our lawns when we like and fill our swimming pools. We take water as much for granted as the air we breathe. Pay for it on a supply-demand basis, like any other commodity? Certainly not! Water is considered part of the American heritage, almost an inalienable right.

This, of course, is woefully outdated, wishful thinking. Why are plans for more water discussed by every political candidate in our southwestern states? Why must New York City adopt a save-every-drop campaign? What are these reports about millions of fish being killed in our major rivers? Why can't we go swimming any more at our favorite beach or lake? Why don't we have a park nearby, where our children can learn to sail a boat and fish and watch ripples and reflections? Where shall we find enough water to satisfy the population explosion, increased use per person, and burgeoning industrial demands?

These are some of the questions that have led the League of Women Voters of the United States to study the universal and intricate problems of water resources and how they can be solved. Long before 1956, when the national League chose water resources as a major subject for study and action, local and state Leagues had already investigated and acted upon such problems as local sewers and water supply, state programs for pollution control, coordination of state water agencies or state construction programs.

From these experiences came an awareness that few local or state water problems are unrelated to regional or national ones. For two years, League members devoted their attention to federal organization and federal procedures for planning, authorizing, administering, and financing the development of water resources. By the spring of 1958, they were ready to concentrate their study on coordinated administration, equitable financing, and regional or river-basin planning. Using their own river basins for field study, League members undertook "Know Your River Basin" surveys, often joining with other Leagues in the same basin. This brought together urban and rural, downstream and upstream points of view. The findings have been widely distributed for general enlightenment, and several have been published. One is reproduced in Chapter 6.

In the spring of 1966, League members throughout the country voted to retain water resources as a major field of study and action. They are continuing their research, keeping abreast of new problems and new proposals, attending hearings and meetings, testifying before local, state, and national groups, and working to stimulate better community understanding of current and future water needs.

The purpose of this book is to broaden public awareness of the nation's water requirements and to stimulate the participation of informed citizens in the making of wise choices. Decisions involving water resources are being debated right now by hundreds of town councils, by state legislatures, and by the United States Congress. Our environment and future are being shaped. What these governing bodies decide to do—or not to do—about water resources today is often irrevocable and always significant. An informed public should dare to help make the decisions.

Final choices on water problems must, of course, be made in the light of engineering, medical, economic, and other technical information, supplied by experts. Without their guidance, officials and public alike would flounder. But . . . which technical plan shall be accepted? Which project is socially feasible? Which will best satisfy citizen needs? Which should have priority? How shall we resolve conflicts of interest? How will the projects be financed? These questions call for political and social decisions—value judgments, in many cases—and are the legitimate prerogative of the informed citizen.

The problems are vastly complex. But, like most problems, they can be solved by a combination of wise planning and intelligent, persistent, cooperative action. The national League of Women Voters in the course of the past 10 years has learned a great deal about both of these essential means of solving water problems. This book contains accounts of many of its instructive experiences along the way and the productive results. It is published in the hope of stimulating and guiding to purposeful action all citizens who share the League's growing concern about the nation's dwindling water resources.

PART I

Seeds of Conflict

Accepting water so high in mineral content that it is barely tolerable for human purposes is already a necessity for some farmers in the Southwest.

CHAPTER 1

The Problems of Supply

"Last year, for the first time, New Yorkers learned the price of a glass of water."

The speaker was the Governor of Arizona, Samuel P. Goddard, Jr., head of a water-shy and thoroughly water-conscious state. He was referring to one of the great ironies of 1965—the fact that the nation's largest city, flanked by two rivers and within sniffing distance of the inexhaustible Atlantic, found itself perilously short of water.

Arizona is hardened to this sort of predicament, but still understandably nervous about it.

"Available water supply," Governor Goddard continued, "conditions the utilization of all our other resources."

New York's unprecedented drought-stricken plight of 1965 was but a well-publicized example of a hazard that is creeping upon nearly all parts of the nation, stealthily but steadily.

As Americans carelessly go on drinking as much water as they like, washing themselves and their clothes and their dishes and their cars in it, cooling and heating themselves with it, sluicing away their garbage and other wastes with it, sprinkling their lawns, filling their pools, irrigating their crops, and using water extravagantly for a thousand industrial processes, they are flirting with disaster.

The rapidly growing nation is already consuming 350 billion gallons of water a day. In less than 35 years, it will be demanding a trillion gallons a day—if, indeed, the water is there to consume.

The problems of increasing our supply of clean water are nationwide, though they take many forms, depending on locality. Everywhere they are becoming increasingly complicated. Water supply involves storage, distribution, quality regulation, and financing. It requires good planning, improved technology, and new construction. For the future, it will involve increasing regulation to prevent misuse of surface and underground sources. It will require increased sharing of water among communities and states and even among countries, the desalination of sea water, and, of course, greater reuse of water from all sources.

It has been said that 1965 may turn out to have been the year in which this country finally woke up to the vital importance of water. Prior to 1965, however, there had been ominous reports from the Senate Select Committee on Water Resources, and other studies, warning that we shall be critically short of water by the year 1980 in five of the 22 water-resource regions of the U.S., and by the year 2000 in three additional regions. Resources will by then have been developed to their limits, water economies will be in effect, and the arid regions will need additional water if their economic growth is not to be halted.

Feeling the Pinch

In 1965, northeastern U.S., which is supposed to be well-watered, found itself in trouble because of a string of three dry years. This required strict limitations on use and emergency transfers to water-destitute communities from those that had either been more forehanded or more lucky. The pinch was felt not only by the homeowner, who could not save his shrubs, but by the developer and the businessman. Some towns were forced to stop building permits.

In Illinois, the Department of Business and Economic Development will no longer help a community to attract new industry unless it can show that it has adequate water supply for expected growth. Water shortage in southern California is tending to force land out of agriculture, a heavy consumer of water, and devote it to industries which can provide at least 10 times as many jobs with the same amount of water. New Mexico, according to the U.S. Bureau of Mines, will be hard put to continue its major industry, mining, even with water-saving methods, unless more water is found.

Lakes and rivers provide the simplest and most accessible storage. As these natural storage places have proved inadequate, the rivers have been dammed to prevent runoff and hold the water back for later use. Underground sources near the surface have been tapped by wells. When the water table has been lowered, wells have been driven deeper and deeper, thus mining water that may have taken hundreds or even thousands of years to store. As the easy sites for reservoirs have been used up, the construction of additional ones has become increasingly difficult and expensive. While the need for water storage has been growing, our rapid development has been destroying many of the features that used to provide natural storage. Swamps have been filled, sandy hills have been bulldozed away, forests have been cut, grass has been replaced by pavement or buildings.

As costs rise, it often becomes economic to put into effect water-saving devices such as the recycling of industrial cooling water, through use of cooling towers, and of water in the airconditioning systems of apartment buildings. Industries in regions where water costs are high, or water is scarce, have shown themselves able to cut their water demand to a fraction of that required by the same industries in states where water is still cheap and plentiful. As the cost of domestic water supply grows, home water use may also be reduced through recycling. For example, by recycling, water used for washing can later be used for waste removal.

Water is something we cannot do without—in our homes, in producing our food, and in making the products we buy. To maintain our standard of living, we shall need to develop additional water sources, increase our reuse of water, and turn to additional water-saving procedures. All citizens have a vital interest in obtaining a water supply adequate to our needs.

The following case studies deal with various efforts by concerned citizens to obtain a safe and sufficient water supply and to support long-range plans for new sources.

CLEAN ENOUGH TO DRINK?

(SALT LAKE CITY, UTAH)

When airlines and railroads threatened to bypass Salt Lake City, in the 1940s, because of its impure drinking water, the community began to wake up.

Many a region bordering a major U.S. river now looks to that source for its future water supply, but an idyllic surface often belies the water's quality. (PENNA. DEPARTMENT OF HEALTH PHOTO)

Since 1938, health officers and medical authorities had been warning of the potential hazards of the local water supply, but few paid any attention. Without public pressure for improvements, city officials were hesitant to make proposals that might raise taxes. State health authorities were powerless to intervene, because, at the time, Utah had no laws requiring standards for water or sewage treatment. Only when the U.S. Public Health Service declared Salt Lake City's drinking water substandard and unfit to be used on public interstate carriers did local action begin.

In 1948, after the Metropolitan Water District had hired an engineering firm to study the water supply and make recommendations, the U.S. Public Health Service agreed to give conditional approval to the city's water. The city, in turn, was required to protect the watershed from further pollution, give complete treatment to the water supply, and cover the reservoirs.

This was a big assignment and would cost money. Would the public understand the need and agree to pay?

In 1951, the League of Women Voters took the initiative and asked the Utah Medical Association and the Utah Engineering Council to join with it in a full-scale campaign to inform the public. After careful study, discussion, and agreement on what would constitute an adequate system of water purification for the city, the three groups started their joint publicity drive.

A leaflet entitled "Is Your Drinking Water Safe?" was printed and distributed to give the facts, the proposed solutions, and the estimated costs. Newspapers cooperated in the campaign. The League devoted its weekly radio program to discussions on water. Doctors explained the dangers of a substandard drinking supply; engineers described the various systems of water purification; health officials reported on present conditions; financial experts pointed out several methods of paying for improvements; city officials were interviewed as to their intentions. In January, 1952, a public meeting was held at which the Mayor proposed a pay-as-you-go plan for financing the program. Then the League put its speakers' bureau into operation. Members spoke and showed movies to any group who would listen and look.

Local officials asked that a bill be presented in the 1953 state legislature to enable cities to levy a tax for water and sewage disposal. The bill was written and passed—but for two years only.

However, each time since then that it has come up for renewal, civic groups have lobbied successfully for its extension. This taxing power has been vital for financing improvements. The state legislature also passed a clean-water bill and approved a revision of the State Health Code. At long last, the State Health Department was able to set and enforce standards for water supply. Salt Lake City, in turn, drew up a 10-year water-improvement program that met the approval of Utah health agencies and the U.S. Public Health Service. Since then, purification plants have been built and all of the reservoirs have been covered.

The local plan called for a purification plant at the mouth of Little Cottonwood Canyon, to be financed by an $8 million bond issue. Several citizen groups, including the League, worked hard to alert the public. In 1958, the bond issue was approved by the voters, because they had been given the facts and had recognized the need. With the construction of another plant at Parley's Canyon, finished in 1965, and the covering of two remaining reservoirs, Salt Lake City's water-purification program was completed. In addition, a new dam, Little Dell, which will increase the city's water supply, is under construction. A purification plant to handle Little Dell water as well as the present supply is already in use.

If future Winter Olympics should be held in Salt Lake City, or if the ski resorts at nearby Alta are to be developed more fully, new sewage disposal lines will probably have to be constructed. But as far as supply of clean water goes, Salt Lake City has more than adequately protected itself.

PREPARING TO TAP A GREAT LAKE

(ONONDAGA COUNTY, N.Y.)

As long ago as 1959 Onondaga County, in central New York, knew that it was headed for water trouble, and soon. The county's biggest city is Syracuse, but also there are 19 towns, suburban and rural, and they were all developing a growing thirst as their population expanded. Available supplies were fast becoming inadequate.

A County Water Agency, created that year, was charged with the specific responsibility of presenting to the Board of Supervisors a proposal for an additional source of water for the county. Already most of the major organizations in the area—Chamber of Com-

When communities tap a new source of supply, water purification facilities are part of the overall plan.

merce, Junior Chamber of Commerce, League of Women Voters, Syracuse Governmental Research Bureau, Manufacturers' Association of Syracuse, and the Metropolitan Development Association (MDA)—had been discussing the need for more water. Members had learned from their city and county officials that the 68.5 million gallons a day being drawn from Skaneateles Lake, Otisco Lake, and from local springs and wells was just barely keeping ahead of the 66 million gallons a day being used. Use of water had begun to be curtailed in some areas, and population projections chillingly showed that in a little more than a decade, 90 million gallons a day would be needed, and by the year 2000, about 140 million gallons a day.

At the suggestion of the MDA and the League of Women Voters, representatives of the above organizations, together with other business, labor, and civic leaders, met to exchange views and form a study group.

With the publication, late in 1960, of an interim report by the County Water Agency, this study group set out to develop a consensus on the Agency's proposal. Members visited officials, talked with specialists, looked into alternative methods of financing. In the process, they gained the respect of those who were responsible for final plans, and built an atmosphere of cooperative give-and-take. Then, having ironed out their own differences, the members of the civic study group were ready to return to the various city, county, and Agency officials to suggest certain modifications and changes. Several of these proposed revisions were incorporated into a revised plan in 1962, and members of the study group then urged their respective organizations to endorse the plan and work for public support.

Core of the unusual and dramatic plan is the tapping of Lake Ontario. It includes the construction of about 30 miles of transmission mains of large diameter from Oswego Bay, on the lake, to the town of Clay, at the northern edge of Onondaga County. The entire county (Zone 1) is to pay for this part, at a cost of $22 million. A branch line will run from Clay to the northern boundary of the city of Syracuse, to be paid for by Syracuse and the 10 northern towns, including Manlius and Cicero (Zone 2), at a cost of $3 million. A third line is to run east directly to the northern towns, and will be paid for only by those 10 towns (Zone 3), at a cost of $20 million. A purification plant will be constructed at Oswego, near the lake, so that all water coming into the county will be treated and ready for consumption. The whole project will be financed by annual assessment on the equalized assessed valuation of properties in the three zones, based on degree of benefit.

Convinced that the plan merited their support, members of the study group turned their attention to convincing the voters of the county, who would decide the matter at a public referendum on July 10, 1962. The $45 million bond issue was the largest ever placed before the county, and proponents of the plan realized that if it were to pass, an extensive educational program would first be necessary. Since no public funds were available, civic organizations had to provide the necessary leadership to mobilize community support. The task was made more difficult by two aspects of the referendum: first, it called for higher taxes; second, it was a special election, held in July, a difficult time of year to assemble voters. Leaders agreed that bipartisan political support was essential, but would have to be augmented by a broadly-based citizens' committee. This committee, it was hoped, would serve the dual purpose of providing a non-political vehicle to lead campaign activities and of mobilizing a widespread volunteer effort.

By May 15th, arrangements for a full-time staff were made. Negotiations for office space were undertaken and tentative campaign plans outlined.

In preliminary discussions of the composition of the citizens' committee, it was decided to ask representatives of both major political parties to participate. Two goals were stressed in drawing up an invitation list for the organizational meeting: one, to reach every community organization that could help in some specific way to publicize the referendum and gain support among its own members; two, to have someone from each of those organizations participate in campaign activities. Consideration was also given to geographic as well as political balance.

A Crucial Campaign Opens

The organizational meeting, held on May 28, 1962, was the official opening of the campaign—six weeks before the referendum. Officers were elected to head the new Citizens for Water Committee, and finance and steering committees were appointed. The latter met regularly once a week during the campaign. A second general meeting was held midway through the campaign, to distribute materials and make a progress report.

A tentative budget of about $12,000 was authorized by the finance committee, on the basis of projected costs for promotional material. No allowance was made for paid advertising, except for the rental of billboard space. Initial pledges of up to $5,000 each were made by the MDA and the Chamber of Commerce; the balance was to be solicited from other organizations and individuals. Actual campaign costs were under $10,000.

In planning the campaign, two assumptions were made; namely, that the larger the total vote, the greater the chances of an affirmative decision; and that, while an attempt should be made to counteract negative reaction where it occurred, it was better to concentrate major effort on those areas most likely to approve the proposal.

Some groundwork in explaining the need for an additional water supply had already been done, with the circulation of a prize-winning documentary film, "The Prosperity of Water." This film, financed principally by the General Electric Company, had been shown to many community organizations in the 18 months preceding the campaign.

Prior to final preparation of campaign literature, a limited telephone survey was undertaken to determine opinions and attitudes among city, suburban, and rural residents. Results, three weeks before the referendum, indicated a small margin in favor, but enough "undecided" citizens to swing the decision either way. Most objections were directed toward source, costs, and doubt of actual need.

A major share of time and money was allocated to a simplified, one-page summary of the proposal, of which 111,000 copies were mailed, one to practically every registered voter. Though handling and addressing services were donated, cost of this item alone amounted to almost 50 percent of the total campaign expenditures. The necessity for condensing the complex financial aspects of the proposal limited the usefulness of the mailer as an educational tool, but it served its primary purpose of creating awareness of the issues and of the special election.

Supplementing this were a more detailed printed brochure (about 20,000 copies) and a mimeographed statement (about 10,000 copies). These were distributed at meetings, through special mailings by organizations and business and labor groups, and, in some cases, door-to-door. Flyers (about 90,000) were included in regular mailings by banks and department stores. Posters (1,600) and billboards (12) also served to remind voters of the July 10th referendum.

Campaign activities proceeded simultaneously on two levels, through community organizations and on an area (ward or town) basis. Through their representation on the Citizens for Water Committee, community organizations were asked to participate in as many of the following ways as they could: endorse the plan; hold a meeting; circulate information among their members; contribute money; provide volunteers for various committee activities. In many instances, these efforts had a multiple effect, because business and professional firms affiliated with member organizations were stimulated to circulate campaign information among their own employees. At the same time, an attempt was made to organize volunteers in each ward and in each of the 19 towns. These activities of organizations and of area volunteers were coordinated through committee headquarters which was located downtown and kept open during the last four weeks of the campaign.

Headquarters also served as center of operations for a speakers' bureau. Over 40 speaking engagements were filled in a five-week period. In addition, "The Prosperity of Water" was shown throughout Syracuse high schools during June.

News Media Help

An outstanding feature of the campaign was the massive support offered by the county's news media. Daily and weekly newspapers, and television and radio stations gave unusual amounts of space and time to the subject and much editorial backing. Only one radio station opposed the proposal. Both daily newspapers prepared their own series explaining the issues in depth. The fact that the late Alexander ("Casey") Jones, chairman of the Water Agency, was also the nationally known editor of one of the daily papers was a factor of importance in the excellent press support. In fact, part of the county's new water facility will be named after him, as a tribute to his leading role in promoting the referendum. Both dailies worked closely with campaign headquarters to keep up with the questions most frequently asked by the public. Interviews were held on various radio and TV programs. Both TV stations gave half-hour shows and later repeated them. Half-hour programs were also presented by several radio stations as a public service.

Closing activities of the campaign included saturation telephoning by League members and volunteers from the Junior Chamber of Commerce in those areas where a favorable vote seemed most likely. Arrangements were made and publicized to transport voters to the polls. Headquarters remained open on Referendum Day to handle last-minute questions.

The proposal passed by an impressive margin—36,414 votes in favor, 21,649 opposed. It was majority approval in every city ward and in 11 of the towns. The latter figure included the 10 towns in Zone 3, the area of highest assessment. The total vote cast represented almost 30 percent of the eligible voters, relatively high for such a referendum.

Soon after passage of the bond issue, the newly named Metropolitan Water Board found itself in the midst of a lawsuit, brought by the towns of Skaneateles and Spafford. The two towns won the suit and therefore are no longer part of the water plan or its financing. This has disappointed leaders of the campaign, but the county has decided, in order to get on with the project, not to appeal the case.

Meanwhile, the water crisis is becoming more severe. Supplies that were adequate a year or two ago are already being used almost to their maximum capacity. In the villages of Fayetteville and Manlius, the limit has already arrived. The Fayetteville League of Women Voters had warned of this approaching crisis in a booklet issued in May, 1963. Manlius has had to hunt for an additional water source to serve adequately those areas to which it is already committed. The Water Board has recently changed its original plans to include an additional reservoir at Manlius.

The Onondaga County Water Authority, already drawing from Otisco Lake the maximum 20 million gallons of water per day allowed by the New York State Water Resources Commission, had to request permission to increase its take to 25 million gallons per day. This request was granted in October, 1963.

With present sources stretched to the limit, Onondaga County would have been in for very serious trouble had not officials and civic groups pushed for a solution when they did. As of December

31, 1965, the Ontario Project, now called "Water Unlimited," was 55 percent completed, and 1966 plans are still aimed at achieving the target completion date of June 1967, when, barring unforeseen difficulties, water will flow from Lake Ontario to Onondaga County. The Metropolitan Water Board has also initiated for 1966 a comprehensive water survey, to be financed by New York State, to provide the basis for a step-by-step program to supply water to all portions of Onondaga County where there will be a demand in the next 50 years.

THE BIG PIPE DREAM?

(KERN COUNTY, CALIFORNIA)

"Being a voter out here is a full-time job," recently exclaimed a Bakersfield, California, resident who has been trying to comprehend and judge intelligently the multitude of decisions in which he, as a voter, has been asked to participate.

In addition to having his say at the polls on an array of candidates for national, state, and county offices, and on a host of state and county issues of conventional nature, he has had to vote on weighty questions of water resources. He has been asked, first, to vote on the Water Bond Act (1960), which established the State Water Project for bringing northern waters via aqueduct to southern regions of California. Then he had to vote on whether to set up a Kern County Water Agency to negotiate with the state for purchase of Project water. Then he had to vote on the complicated contract itself. And the end is not in sight. He may possibly be asked to return to the polls in 1966 to determine whether to establish a Greater Bakersfield Water District to plan and finance future water supply for his local area.

Before State Project water actually reaches the farms and homes in Kern County, many irrevocable decisions will have been made, decisions that test the citizen's objectivity, tax his pocketbook, and force him to look at long-range implications and needs.

Fortunately for the future of the area, a Kern County Water Association had been formed as early as 1956. A non-profit, nonpartisan group interested and knowledgeable in water problems, it has spent money, time, and energy in educating the public about the significance of an adequate water supply. Other citizen groups, as they have become interested in the problem, have turned to the Association for facts and speakers.

Water Agency is Approved

The vote on the Water Bond Act went through in Kern County without much difficulty, chiefly because the voters felt that they were making no irrevocable commitment. Even voting for the Kern County Water Agency didn't bind local citizens to any rigid agreement. There was, however, considerable opposition to the idea. The people were well aware of the need for more water; in an area almost totally dependent on wells for its supply, the serious drop in the water table was obvious to all. But the idea of adding another unit of government to the already existing structure met with resistance. "Why should money be siphoned off to a new bureaucracy?" "If I need more water, I'll hire someone to dig a deeper well. I don't need 'government' to supply me with water." "Why can't the existing water and irrigation districts dicker independently with the State for this new water? Free competition among districts is bound to bring us more water in the end." So went the arguments against establishing the County Water Agency.

The State of California, however, encouraged formation of larger agencies where feasible. It prefers to deal with such sizable units as the Metropolitan Water District of Southern California, formed in 1928. This MWD, because of its size, its experience, and the presence of a well-informed public to insist on its rights, is also in a better bargaining position with the State than a smaller group would be.

The Kern County Board of Supervisors also supported the idea of a County Agency that could concentrate its efforts solely on water problems, but it refused to give up its own ultimate authority over water. The Board of Supervisors insisted that it have the final word on any major decisions, especially financial ones. This veto role of the Supervisors turned out to be unique among the various agencies formed throughout the state. Another unique feature written into the legislation was that the entire voting population of the County would be called upon to approve the contract to be drawn up between the Water Agency and the State of California. Some said, prior to the vote, that this meant the officials were scared to make their own decisions; others said this was a technique for transferring to the public the onus of a wrong decision. Recriminations were plentiful. But in 1961 the Kern County Water Agency was voted through, and work began on the all-important contract.

The Agency committee and its consultants entered immediately into negotiations with officials from the State Department of Water Resources, but it took two difficult years before agreement could be reached.

The Contract Squabble

The Metropolitan Water District of Southern California had signed its contract with the State even before the Water Bond Act was actually passed, and this contract served as a model for future contracts for metropolitan regions. But the State had decided from the outset that agricultural areas should also be able to participate in the new plan for water supplies. It therefore looked to Kern County to set the pattern for agricultural water contracts. Kern County Water Agency was potentially the largest contractor for agricultural water in the State, and the second-largest water contractor of any kind. Ninety-five percent of State Project water was scheduled to go for agricultural uses in Kern County, an area that had about reached its peak for farm production unless it could get more water for irrigation. The area was an ideal one for mass farm output. Many argued, in fact, that the contract was the only way to increased economic prosperity, and that without more water the area would begin to decline.

City people in Bakersfield, the only large urban center in the whole county, were not convinced. "Why should I pay for water that will help only the farmers? I still drive a cheap old car, and I know farmers who are riding around in Cadillacs!" one protested, voicing a common complaint. Proponents of the contract had the difficult task of showing the city voter that it was to his long-range advantage to pay for secondary benefits. This meant that while he himself might not use the State Project water, the surrounding farm area would prosper from it, his own property values would thus go up, and what was good for the county and the state was good for him. For many citizens, this broad, long-range point of view was an entirely new concept. Governmental rather than pri-

California's Central Valley Project has brought water to this formerly uncultivated land in the Sacramento Delta.

vate development of local water resources was a new idea. Upping taxes now for something that might not "pay off" during a man's lifetime was also hard to swallow. Even some of the established farmers who would benefit from the new water supply asked themselves why they should support a project that would inevitably bring new competitive farmers into the area.

To answer such queries and to organize and direct the overall campaign in support of the contract, a Citizens' Campaign Committee was formed. Its job was to get the facts to the people and the people to the polls to vote for the contract. Being a non-political-action organization, and thus unable to take sides in any campaign, the Kern County Water Association served by disseminating the facts only.

The League of Women Voters in Bakersfield, the only League in the county, worked as an independent group, clearing its activities with the official Campaign Committee to avoid duplication and to be sure of its timing for maximum effect. It printed a fact sheet, obtained radio and television time, held meetings, and printed "Yes for Water" lapel tags to draw attention to the contract election. Its fact sheet was printed originally for the benefit of those League members who had been unable to attend unit study groups on the State Water Project and the Kern County contract. Guided by the proposition that no contract should be signed without a thorough reading and understanding, the fact sheet was drawn up in great detail. It turned out to be of considerable benefit to the entire community and was distributed in the mailings of both the Chamber of Commerce and the Campaign Committee.

The Voters Decide

The vote on the Kern County contract was crucial. It would commit the area; the county's future hung on the decision. Earlier votes on the Water Bond Act and on formation of the Agency had also been important, but not to the man in the street. This contract vote, however, he understood (from publicity sponsored by the Citizens' Campaign Committee and other groups) would really commit him.

Proponents of the contract emphasized that approval of the contract did not actually determine the means of financing. The proposed property tax was likely, but would be a separate and later decision, based on final information on costs and on prices to member units. It was the property tax, however, on which many based their opposition to the contract. Some were willing to risk losing the needed water in their efforts to force the Agency to promise not to use such a tax. The opposition mailed to every voter a four-page flyer capitalizing on the incipient split between urban residents and farmers. It was violent and extravagant; so much so, in fact, that it defeated its own purpose.

On Election Day, Nov. 12, 1963, League members helped by telephoning in each precinct. Forty-five percent of the eligible voters turned out, and the contract was approved, despite a possible 50-cent jump in the tax rate and despite the newness of the concept of regional planning and cooperation. It passed, however, by the very narrow margin of 589 ballots. "Yes" votes totaled 22,418; "No" votes numbered 21,829.

If construction continues to proceed on schedule, the first year of delivery for agricultural water will be 1968; for urban water, 1970. Planning is based on the needs of 1990, when maximum delivery of 1,153,400 acre-feet per year is scheduled to begin. The contract terminates after 75 years; capital costs and interest are to be paid off in 70 years.

Burgeoning Battles

Ever since the 1963 election on the contract, two major conflicts have been brewing in the county, which keep concerned citizen groups alert sorting fact from fancy. One is the growing antagonism among urban residents to paying for the secondary benefits of agricultural water, which they do not use. Many also object to the Kern County Water Agency's use of a uniform tax rate for all secondary benficiaries, without regard to differing degrees of benefit. One group, in fact, has brought suit against the Water Agency. The Agency Act provides for a tax on all property in the service area, including mineral rights, so this group, in which oil interests are prominent, is not especially happy.

The second bone of contention is whether to form a Greater Bakersfield Water District to plan for and handle future water supply on a wholesale basis. All other areas in Kern County are already organized into districts, which are coordinated by the County Water Agency. Greater Bakersfield is not organized, and if the City Council in office in 1966 has its way, no Water District will be created.

The crux of the problem is that Greater Bakersfield has no political, jurisdictional unity. The incorporated city of Bakersfield covers only about one-third of the area, and includes about one-third of the population. Nearly one-half of the assessed valuation, however, is within city limits. The City Council seems to fear that if the water needs of the unincorporated areas outside are met through a Greater Bakersfield Water District, the City will lose its control of growth in the region and of possible future annexations. The unincorporated areas will be less dependent on City Council decisions about water supply. On the other hand, it is doubtful whether the city alone can handle an adequate water program for the whole area.

The problem would be simpler if there were a single purveyor of water for the whole metropolitan area, but in the course of time approximately 30 purveyors of various sizes and kinds have developed.

Four of the largest, while stating that they could not finance the necessary waterworks for imported water, have said they could undertake jointly to contract for a total of 60,000 acre-feet of State Project water for the year 1990. However, a reputable engineering firm estimates that the area will need 100,000 acre-feet of supplemental water by the year 1990.

Some leaders in the area have come to the conclusion that a public agency with taxing powers is needed to finance the amount of water recommended and to pay for the waterworks needed. The water purveyors, as a group, advocated such a water district, but felt they were not the ones to promote it.

Late in 1964, some businessmen and other interested people held a few meetings to discuss promoting a water district, but nothing definite came of them. The normal leadership of the community was split by the controversy, and no one group felt confident enough to oppose the City Council's point of view.

The Council, meanwhile, along with the Property Owners Association, was being very vocal about its opposition to the idea of a water district. These opponents have argued that the amount of water the purveyors could contract for would be enough for now. They have suggested that a district would only mean more government and more taxes. There have even been some unwarranted statements about poor quality of State Project water. In spite of their general opposition to the Kern County Water Agency for taxing urban property owners for secondary benefits, these opposing forces have proposed that the Agency take on the responsibility of handling imported water for Greater Bakersfield.

The Agency itself claims that this is not its function, and that a local water district should be established. The Agency, its directors pointed out, is a county-wide coordinating agency, responsible for affairs that affect more than one district. It is already busy representing Kern County in water matters at the state and national level. It would be improper, the directors argued, to divert Agency attention from such matters to problems that a local district could and should handle. They pointed out that any matter as important as water supply should be controlled by the people concerned.

Early in 1965, the LWV of Bakersfield finished a two-year study of the water situation in Greater Bakersfield. Members concluded that a local water district was needed. This was consistent with the League's earlier position of support for the Water Agency "as a means to coordinate the water resources development of Kern County." A water district, the LWV decided, was necessary to facilitate comprehensive, long-range planning for Greater Bakersfield's water supply.

In February 1965, the League's local Board of Directors decided to take action against the City Council's stand. They formally requested the Kern County Water Agency to refuse to consider assuming responsibility for Greater Bakersfield water supply until the question of forming a local water district had been brought to a vote of the people. (The only way to force a decision on forming a municipal water district is to have 10 percent of the voters sign a petition asking the County Board of Supervisors to call an election for that purpose.)

The Board of the Water Agency responded by adopting a policy of not making any long-term contract for water except with a duly constituted public agency. In other words, if the people of Greater Bakersfield wanted to secure what amounted to a permanent right to State Project water, they would have to form a local district.

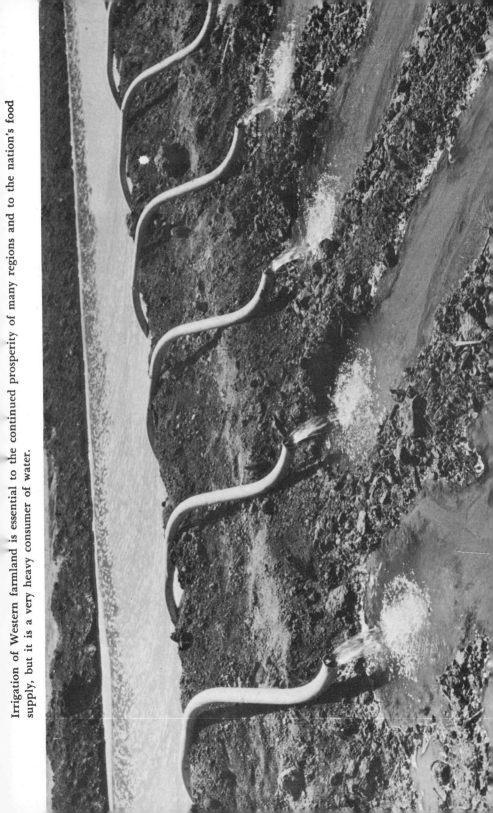

Irrigation of Western farmland is essential to the continued prosperity of many regions and to the nation's food supply, but it is a very heavy consumer of water.

The LWV was immediately accused of being a tool of the Water Agency, but League members saw their cause as in the public interest. Their action, with attendant publicity, served as a catalyst and also defined a larger area of agreement. Even those opposed to the district could agree that it would be fair to have the election. (They *do* love to vote in Bakersfield!)

A citizens' committee to circulate the necessary petitions was formed (though not by the LWV), and enough money collected to open an office in April, 1965. With the exception of the Labor Council and the LWV, however, few community organizations came out with a formal statement of support for the district. None, on the other hand, took a stand that the people should not have an opportunity to vote on the issue.

League members undertook to secure 1,000 of the approximately 8,000 signatures needed. They went to friends and acquaintances, "sat" at supermarkets with petitions, and conducted door-to-door drives that brought TV and newspaper publicity. Other interested individuals helped collect signatures during the following 11 months, and finally there were enough to justify certifying the petition to the Board of Supervisors.

But the petition did not immediately come before the Board, and no one is predicting when the desired election may be held. It seems that when Kern County's Local Agency Formation and Annexation Commission approved the proposed district, it did so on the condition that an existing, small, but never active district of the same kind be dissolved. The directors of that district had said they would dissolve it, but political pressure to preserve its existence could possibly hamper the whole election.

So the pot continues to boil. If this story proves nothing else, it does show clearly that water is basically a political problem, requiring wise and well-informed voter decisions. When the expected election campaign gets under way, the LWV of Bakersfield will doubtless participate by preparing and circulating an information sheet providing background information on the water-supply situation and an objective presentation of the pros and cons of a local water district.

This local dispute should not cloud the fact that the State of California is embarked on a bold solution to its complex water problems and is breaking new ground in the field of water supply management.

COUNTING ON THE SCOGGIN

(TUALATIN BASIN, OREGON)

It is feast or famine for water users in Oregon's Tualatin River Basin, on the outskirts of Portland, in the northwestern part of the state. In summer months water supplies dip dangerously low, just when demand is greatest. In the rainy winter and spring, water comes rushing into the valley from the surrounding hills in such overabundance that it inundates hundreds of acres of farmland bordering the river. Although some of this runoff is caught in private farm ponds, there are no reservoirs to conserve water for public use. Municipal supply in most of Washington County is adequate for only eight or nine months of the year; potential industrial development and an estimated doubling of population by 1980 will tax the supply still further.

Local farmers are especially hard hit by this fluctuation in supply. Cramped by the spread of residential development from the nearby Portland area, they want to increase their use of irrigation to get a higher economic yield per acre. Of crucial importance to farmers is the fact that their non-irrigated fruits and vegetables cannot compete in size and uniform quality with crops from irrigated lands. The Birdseye plant in Hillsboro has already curtailed freezing of local beans and corn; the company prefers to contract acreage in counties where full irrigation assures high-quality crops. Increasing competition at the wholesale markets of Portland also makes Tualatin Valley farmers insistent on more water for summer irrigation. Being flooded out in winter and dried out in summer is a farmer's nightmare.

The basin has other water problems. Washington County has no lakes, so the demand for water-related recreational sites is putting an additional burden on the Tualatin and its tributaries. Yet pollution is on the increase. In recent summers, parts of the Tualatin River have been designated as unsafe for swimming, and the State Sanitary Authority is alarmed. In a report released in May, 1965, it recommended immediate, basin-wide planning for better disposal facilities.

When the Department of Interior's Tualatin Project is approved by the U.S. Congress, some relief for the area will be in sight. The Bureau of Reclamation plans to construct a dam on Scoggin Creek, which flows directly into the Tualatin. The dam will create a storage reservoir about four miles long and a mile wide, with a capacity of 61,000 acre-feet. The active capacity of this reservoir (53,800 acre-feet), coordinated with available inflows below the dam, can be utilized to meet annual requirements of 89,100 acre-feet. These requirements include 14,000 acre-feet for municipal and industrial water supply; 33,800 acre-feet for water quality control and fishery purposes; and 41,300 acre-feet for irrigation.

On the Right Track

This plan to supply water from one reservoir for several different purposes fulfills most of the major criteria that the League of Women Voters looks for in a wise development policy. Members from the local Leagues of Hillsboro, East Washington County, and Forest Grove, formed for the first time into an Inter-League Committee, had studied the complex needs of the Tualatin Basin for over three years. They had developed yardsticks against which to measure any new proposal. When the Bureau of Reclamation's report was issued, the Committee agreed to support the proposal, chiefly because it follows the multiple purpose approach and does not fly in the face of larger, regional plans.

In outlining to its general membership the many advantages of the project, the Inter-League Committee was obliged to note that the project will not—nor does it claim to—solve all water problems. Pollution, for example, may be lessened, but it cannot, through this project alone, be totally controlled. Maintaining minimum flow standards for pollution abatement purposes on unappropriated waters is regulated by the Oregon State Water Resources Board. But all local streams in the Tualatin Basin are already over-appropriated. This means that more water rights have been granted than can be satisfied during the summer months. Interior's new Tualatin Project will permit release of waters ample to satisfy presently developed rights, but the minimum flow levels are still not expected to be up to the standards desired by the State Board. The U.S. Public Health Service has also studied the plan, and, while agreeing that the project will certainly contribute to pollution abatement, it concludes that quality control that cannot be met by the Scoggin Reservoir will need to be incorporated in future development planning or satisfied by local means. The Oregon State Sanitary Authority has already raised the level of treatment required at all sewage-disposal facilities in Washington County that are located or proposed for location on Tualatin River tributaries, and warns that requirements can be expected to go even higher in the future.

Flood-control benefits from this project will be only incidental. After a disastrous statewide flood in December, 1964, Oregon's Senators obtained approval from the Senate Committee on Interior and Insular Affairs for certain flood-control revisions, but extensive channel improvements would also have to be made, according to surveys conducted earlier by the Army Corps of Engineers and independent engineering firms. At the county level, a flood-plain study has been made and a flood-plain zone may be established. But farmers seem willing to run the risk of floods. What they want is adequate water for irrigation.

Irrigation Needs Long Discussed

In its background study, the Inter-League Committee learned that the Scoggin Dam proposal is by no means the first to be offered. For almost 30 years local farmers have been meeting to discuss the type of irrigation development best suited to their needs. In 1948, the Bureau of Reclamation made suggestions on water-resource development in the area. In 1954, it offered an irrigation plan in cooperation with a Corps of Engineers flood-control proposal. Again, in 1956, an irrigation plan was suggested by the Bureau of Reclamation, in which the Scoggin site was proposed as the most feasible. Each time, however, a combination of general public apathy, high costs, and organized minority opposition forced the plans to be shelved. As conditions in the area changed, so did the thinking about solutions. The present Tualatin Project is a revision of earlier plans.

Drumming Up Home-Town Support

Knowing that even a federally-sponsored project cannot go through without local citizen support, the Inter-League Committee has helped to keep the public up to date. It wrote a series of seven articles about the background and needs of the Tualatin Basin, which local newspapers throughout Washington County have carried. The Committee has followed progress of the proposal in Congress.

On April 3, 1964, the Feasibility Report from the Secretary of the Interior was sent to both the House and Senate, was printed as House Document 295, and was sent to committees for study and recommendation. In the first session of the 89th Congress, both Senators Neuberger and Morse introduced the bill to authorize construction of the project, and Representative Wyatt introduced it in the House.

In February, 1965, the League of Hillsboro issued a "Time for Action" bulletin asking informed members to write their Congressmen and urge that committee hearings be scheduled. An Inter-League statement of support was sent to the Senate Subcommittee on Irrigation and Reclamation for the hearing in March, 1965. An updated version was sent to the House Committee in July. The Inter-League Committee has also encouraged local editors and other influential citizens to contact the Congressmen. The state Chamber of Commerce alerted its members to send supporting letters. A metropolitan planning agency in Portland has given its backing to the Tualatin Project, because it offers a recreation plan providing fishing, boating, and developed park acreage conveniently close to the metropolitan area.

In anticipation of Congressional passage, local farmers, who worked so hard on the project's behalf, have organized into a Tualatin Valley Irrigation District. They are prepared to contract with the government and assume their share of the repayment responsibility. They have signed up large numbers of farmers who express firm intent to purchase irrigation water from the project.

Each city and the Lake Oswego Corporation have written letters to the Bureau of Reclamation expressing interest in use of the municipal water-supply allocation. Construction of the project is estimated to take approximately five years, so, in most cases, local planning and financing are only now getting under way. However, the City of Hillsboro, while still supporting the project, has already been forced to make additional plans for its municipal water supply. Construction designs are under way to divert water from the Trask River, so that Hillsboro could have a new source of water by 1968. It is still interested in allocation of Tualatin Project water, however.

The County Planning Department, despite a heavy prior workload and serious budgetary limitations, is conducting preliminary studies for park and recreational facilities in the Tualatin Basin.

Interest is running high in the valley, and public discussion of the project has stimulated other steps toward development of the basin's water resources. In cooperation with the Soil Conservation Service, planning is under way for two dam projects in the McKay Creek Water Control District, an area not included in the irrigation acreage of Interior's Scoggin Creek plan. One of these projects, at Rock Creek just 20 minutes from Portland, will be devoted chiefly to recreation. Recent state legislation permits formation of county special-service districts, and the State Sanitary Authority is strongly recommending a Washington County Sewage Disposal District. Already the City-County Joint Planning Advisory Board is working toward a master plan for municipal and industrial water supply and waste disposal for all parts of the county. The Bureau of Reclamation, along with other working members of the Willamette Basin Task Force, is continuing investigations for the orderly development of the basin and plans to issue its report in 1969.

The much-discussed dam on Scoggin Creek has thus started a chain reaction of water-resource improvements and will be an important first step toward controlling the irregular supply of water in the Tualatin River Basin.

MORE RESERVOIRS ARE ONE ANSWER

(NEW JERSEY)

In the early 1950s, urban and industrial development were booming in the State of New Jersey, but the public had not yet become aware that such growth would inevitably call for increased water supplies. Land that might be available for reservoir sites was fast becoming scarce, land prices were steadily increasing, some groundwater sources were being curtailed by salinity in wells, and expansion costs for existing private and municipal suppliers were becoming almost prohibitive. Yet a strong conviction that the state should not enter the "water business" still persisted in the public mind.

The League of Women Voters of New Jersey decided to study the facts and to stimulate greater public awareness of New Jersey's water needs.

Members made a survey of the source, adequacy, and control of existing water supplies. They learned how these supplies were developed, distributed, and sold to users in the state. They evaluated the advantages and disadvantages of existing methods of development. They checked on past proposals for handling state water problems. This information was printed in a booklet, "Water for New Jersey," and distributed to League members and the general public. It was also used as reference material by state water agencies, state legislators, and organizations interested in water resources. Some newspaper reports were based on the League booklet.

Their study convinced League members of the need for state acquisition of reservoir sites—the sooner, the better, before costs might become prohibitive. When a statewide referendum to acquire and develop a reservoir site at Chimney Rock, in Somerset County, was put before the voters in 1955, League members suggested its passage. This site in the Raritan River Basin had the approval of the state water agencies and was recommended by an engineering study authorized by the Legislature. However, the proposal was rejected at the polls. Opposition came from home owners and a large factory near the site, as well as from those who resisted the idea of state participation in an area traditionally considered in New Jersey to be a private or municipal matter.

Though the vote was negative, the campaign sparked fresh concern about the state's water problems. More organizations began to offer active support, and the League capitalized on the new citizen interest by issuing thousands of copies of a flyer called "Water Makes The Wheels Go Round," which gave the highlights of the state's dilemma.

New Jersey officials continued to seek new ways of meeting the problem. In 1956, the Commissioner of the State Department of Conservation and Economic Development appointed a Water Resources Advisory Committee, composed of representatives from labor, industry, agriculture, and recreation, to devise a fresh plan for increasing New Jersey's water supply. In cooperation with the state water agencies, the committee proposed acquiring reservoir sites at Spruce Run and Stony Brook. The League of Women Voters testified before the New Jersey Senate Committee on Revision and Amendment of Laws in support of the plan, and endorsed also the purchase of the Round Valley site, in Hunterdon County, near Clinton.

In 1958, a detailed plan was compiled, and a $45,850,000 water-bond referendum was presented to the voters. Its proposal included the construction of two multi-purpose reservoirs—a big one at Round Valley, with a capacity of 55 billion gallons, and a smaller one at Spruce Run with a capacity of 11 billion gallons—for water supply and other uses not inconsistent with this main purpose. Provision for minimum stream-flow regulation, recreation, development of additional supplies when authorized, and a 10-year study of ground water, to be made jointly by the state and the U.S. Geological Survey, were also included in the proposal.

A statewide committee of civic organizations and individuals helped to publicize the referendum and to get out the vote. This time, the proposal passed by a sizeable majority. The broad information campaign, plus the impact of a severe drought in the summer of 1957, had finally created a climate favorable to state participation.

After the referendum, League members followed each stage in the development of Round Valley and Spruce Run: mapmaking, soil-testing, geological investigations, engineers' plans, and land purchases. Each step was reassurance that before long one of the League's favorite projects would become a reality.

In September, 1963, members saw at first hand the culmination of their years of work and support. At the invitation of the Commissioner of Conservation, 180 members from all over the state went by bus on a tour of the two new reservoirs, already well on the way to completion. The Commissioner and leading engineers of the project went along as guides.

Although the main purpose of Round Valley Reservoir is to increase the water supply, it will also be a valuable recreational asset, providing boating, picnicking, and swimming. Actual development of the recreational sites has been left to local governments, however, and League members are devoting close attention to this phase of water-land use in their local communities.

Round Valley probably will not be completely full until 1968, but Spruce Run was filled about on schedule at the beginning of

1965. Because of a long dispute over the price of water from these two reservoirs, however, relief for drought-stricken municipalities in 1965 did not materialize. The rate was finally set at $32 per million gallons, and water companies can now make provision to distribute the water to various parts of the state.

Looking Farther Ahead

These two important new reservoirs are only part of the larger water-development picture in New Jersey. Recognizing that strict protection of existing water supplies is a logical corollary to finding new sources, the New Jersey LWV in 1963 actively supported passage in the Assembly of the Surface Water Control Bill, which became law in 1964 and gave the State Water Policy and Supply Council jurisdiction over the private use and diversion of surface waters of the state.

League members also continue to follow proposals and plans for more reservoir sites and for optimum development of the Raritan River Basin and underground water supplies.

They are also giving particular attention to the pollution problem. Members see clearly that reuse of water is an important way to increase supply and are supporting measures for improvement of water quality.

State workshops and area meetings have been held to stimulate membership thinking on the subject of regional planning, with special emphasis on the regional nature of water supply and quality control. State aid of $1 million for the planning of regional sewer systems, authorized in July, 1965, has to be increased considerably ($5 million was originally requested), in view of the possible need for tertiary treatment throughout the state. Costs of this added step in the treatment process will be so great that municipalities may be more inclined than before to support joint facilities. Careful planning is a prerequisite.

League study has led to increasing recognition of the need for a truly coordinated plan for all water-resource development and protection for the next 50 years. Letters have gone to state officials urging completion of a comprehensive long-range water-resources plan. Support is also being given to the Inter-Agency Water Resources Committee, formed in 1965, and consisting of representatives from all departments concerned at state, regional, county, and municipal levels.

In view of the fact that New Jersey's population density in 1964 was 880 persons per square mile, the highest in the nation, and that between 1960 and 1964 state population increased by 8.8 percent, estimates may be on the low side which claim that by the year 2000 municipal water needs there will double and industrial needs will quadruple. Continuing cooperation from an informed public will be needed if officials are to succeed in providing a plentiful, clean water supply for the highly industrialized state of New Jersey.

CHAPTER 2

The Problems of Pollution

WHEN AMERICANS were fewer, and cities and industrial plants were smaller and farther apart, our stream and river systems could carry off waste materials and still provide satisfactory water for people downstream. The great capacity of flowing water to clean itself made it simple, natural, and reasonable for people to use streams and rivers to dispose of domestic and industrial waste.

That situation is no longer tolerable, or even feasible, for water pollution is not so much a water problem as it is a people problem. As people multiply, their multitudinous wastes inevitably increase. As people buy more and more products to satisfy their needs and desires, pollution from agriculture and industry mounts. Ironically, new technology and the increased demand for more clean water bring with them increasing pollution problems. As towns and cities expand, sewer outfalls are beginning to line the river banks side by side with water-intake pipes. Mining poisons, farm fertilizers, pesticides, and silt from bulldozed lands are seeping into our water supply. New industrial processes are creating pollutants unknown 20 years ago. Pleasure-boat owners are polluting their own lakes and rivers. Runoff from certain types of composition roofs, from tarred highways, from roads treated with salt to remove snow is adding to the pollution problem.

"No Swimming—Water Polluted" signs are posted all over the country. Odors and chunks of filth deliver their own precise message. In some waters, even the fish give up. On the lower Mississippi alone, fish kills by pollution between 1960 and 1963 totaled nearly

7 million. Our waterways are estimated to be six times as polluted today as they were 60 years ago.

Pollution is a natural process; no surface or ground water is pure H_2O. But man is the great polluter, and modern man the greatest polluter of all. His multiple and varied pollutants are entering U.S. rivers, lakes, and groundwater, increasingly limiting the water's usefulness.

Use is not the same for every lake and river in the United States, nor for all parts of a river system, nor even for every section of mainstream or major tributary. Therefore, a single national standard of stream quality cannot be set as it has been for drinking water, a single use. The present goal of those primarily concerned with water quality is that it be suitable for all legitimate uses: public water supply, industry, agriculture, recreation, and propagation of fish and wildlife.

To have enough water for all these purposes, it is obvious that Americans must reuse it. "Water is not a sometime thing, destroyed by one-time use," declared the Calgon Corporation's 1964 annual report. In some of the country's river basins the dependable flow is reused, often several times, during low-flow periods. Repeated reuse of water is forecast by all estimates of water needs in 1980 and 2000, for only with reuse will supply meet demand. Waste water is this country's most immediately available water supply; it need not be pumped over divides or up from deep below the surface. The cheapest, quickest, most flexible way to increase the quantity of usable water is to reduce water pollution.

With increasing awareness throughout the nation that water must be reused many times, and therefore protected, pollution control by municipalities and industry is making some headway. Improvements are barely keeping up with needs, however, though it is heartening to note that there has been a decided upsurge in the number of communities attacking the pollution problem by building sewage-treatment plants or enlarging former ones. Federal grants alone for this purpose have risen from a total of 1,146 in mid-1958 to 6,200 as of July 1, 1965, according to the Federal Water Pollution Control Administration.

New industrial treatment plants are required on a comparable scale. Better methods of treatment, effects of "exotic" chemicals, underground water pollution, atomic wastes, and many other related problems need to be thoroughly explored. Any all-out effort to clean up the nation's waters and keep them reasonably clean will also call for effective laws, good administration, strict enforcement, money, intergovernmental cooperation, and citizen understanding and determination.

The following cases reveal some of the obstacles along the path to cleaner waters, as well as several solutions that officials and citizens together are putting into effect.

WHAT WE NEED ARE FACTS

(SCOTTSDALE, ARIZONA)

On July 10, 1962, a hundred irate citizens of Scottsdale, Arizona, appeared at the doors of City Hall wearing gas masks, waving petitions signed by other neighbors, and carrying placards that twisted Scottsdale's publicity slogan, "The West's Most Western Town," into "The West's Most Stinking Town."

It was an aroused public, all right. Women cried about the health danger to their children. Men protested that the sewer was overloaded. All wanted to know what had happened to the bond-issue money voted by the city back in April, 1961. Rumor was king, and facts—like fireflies—lit up the skies only fitfully that July night. As these citizens saw it, the problems were the following:

(1) The odor from the sewer plant was sickening. In an area noted for its outdoor living, residents near the plant could not use their patios or other outdoor recreational facilities. When they retreated indoors, the awful stench followed them, sucked in through the cooling systems commonly used during Arizona's searing summer temperatures.

(2) The numerous mosquitoes in the area were alleged by some to breed at the sewage plant. It was claimed that nine out of ten of these mosquitoes were carriers of encephalitis. Deaths were reported.

(3) Devaluation of property was occurring. People could neither sell nor rent their homes or apartments.

(4) The digestor at the plant was inadequate. It was built to care for sewage from 1,200 families, but was in fact carrying the burden of 5,900 families.

In addition, all new tract homes in this fast-developing area were

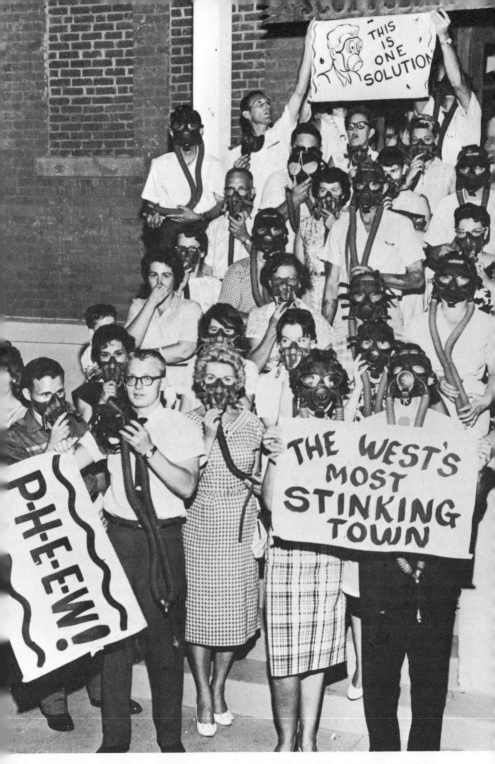

A dramatic protest launched a campaign in Scottsdale, Arizona, that has brought remedial action to end a malodorous sewage problem.

added to the sewers as soon as they were built, and the city seemed to be encouraging even more hookups.

(5) It was conceded that the city had tried to build another treatment plant, but no one had wanted it in his particular backyard. The land intended for this purpose had since been annexed by nearby Tempe, which objected strongly when bonds were floated for construction, and even instituted legal action to forbid the plan's going through. Thus Scottsdale had to pay $10,000 to a construction firm for breach of contract. The only open space left for the treatment plant was an elegant area of homes costing $50,000 or more. Obviously no sewage was going to be permitted there, either. This was the picture as seen by the citizens, and what they saw—and smelled—caused the protest of July 10th.

Members of the local League of Women Voters, also endowed with a keen sense of smell, knew that their town needed facts. They had already been at work studying water resources, sanitation, and health facilities in the area. Confident that it had the womanpower and techniques required for helping to inform the citizens in an objective manner, the League held a special meeting to map its approach.

With copies of the petition in hand, a telephone committee started by calling the signers to inquire into their specific complaints. The spokesman for the protest group was also interviewed at length.

Next day, members of the League interviewed the city manager. He was aware of and concerned about the residents' plight, but pointed out that the city was looking ahead to a five-city plan for joint sewage treatment. Steps taken now, he said, would necessarily be only temporary. He also stated that the situation could be aggravated if the city permitted septic tanks on small lots, that the sewage plant was there before most of the people bought their homes, that engineers had been hired to make further studies, and that such protests as this only hurt the good name of the city.

Pity the Poor Mosquito

The local newspaper printed the mayor's views, in which he outlined various steps taken recently to meet the sewage problem. After analyzing complaints and statements of the mayor and city manager, the League decided more information was needed if the ballooning rumors in town were to be either killed or substantiated. At least three questions had yet to be answered:

(1) Is the sewage plant actually a health hazard?
(2) Do mosquitoes breed there?
(3) Do they carry encephalitis?

The mosquito rumor had bitten the town the hardest, so members of the sewage committee of the League started first to cope with that one. They eventually tracked down a veterinarian who was currently making a study of encephalitis in the county, under the sponsorship of the U.S. Public Health Service. His study had included investigation of the bird, mosquito, and human populations of the County in relation to encephalitis, he reported, but sewer ponds were not considered a source of the disease—and never had been.

The veterinarian also supplied the League with statistics from 1950-1961 on cases of infectious encephalitis in both the county and the state. Considering the tremendous growth of population, as well as better reporting methods, there appeared to have been no increase in the incidence of encephalitis.

The League was beginning to make progress. In answering "Is our sewage plant a health hazard?" the committee found that the digestor at the treatment plant was no longer in use, but raw sewage was being dumped into special ponds, called oxidation ponds, located in the Salt River bed. The ponds were high enough so that sewage would not be washed down the river in event of a minor flood, and they were not close to drinking-water sources, so they were no danger to the public health. The ponds were deep, steep-sided, and under constant surveillance by the Sanitation Department and the County Health Department. The pond water was devegetated, sprayed, and disinfected when necessary. Such ponds were not a breeding place for mosquitoes. Having learned that under proper care the ponds could not breed mosquitoes, the League members had to ask themselves where the mosquitoes did come from. They found that other breeding places were numerous. Recent aerial photographs had disclosed shallow pools not previously known to the Sanitation Department. Steps were taken to eliminate them as breeding spots. The photos also showed that on private property old tires, cans, and buckets were left filled and allowed to stagnate; drainage ditches were obstructed. These were additional breeding spots for mosquitoes.

Five-City Exercise

In trying to plan for immediate and future needs, the city had the choice of relying on the present ponds, which were minimally adequate but could be a health hazard in the event of a major flood and were admittedly malodorous, or of joining the Five-City Plan. This plan provided that a treatment plant for the sewage of the five neighboring cities be centrally located in Phoenix, with each community bearing a metered share of the cost. The League came out publicly in favor of this plan, and, despite some local opposition, the City Council endorsed it in April, 1963.

When the League realized there was more to do, it recommended that no more residential zoning near the sewer ponds be permitted and that only "clean, garden-type I-1 industrial zoning" (industry free from odor, dust, noise, or anything else offensive to a residential neighborhood) be allowed in the plant area. Both the Planning and Zoning Board and the City Council have agreed to the limited industrial zoning. Citizens now support this point of view.

In the fall of 1963, when a bond issue was floated to finance repair of the present digestor for temporary use and to begin the construction of two trunklines to carry sewage into Phoenix, League members worked for passage. Two members served on the City Sewer Bond Committee, one acting as chairman. A fact sheet was prepared for the local paper, and 9,000 explanatory leaflets were folded, labeled, and mailed to the citizens of Scottsdale. Voter response was overwhelmingly in favor of the bond issue, and the Five-City Plan facilities have gone into operation. Property values have been upgraded in the previously affected subdivisions, and sewer lines are replacing cesspools and septic tanks all over Scottsdale.

DON'T KNOCK THE SEWER BOND ISSUE

(St. Joseph, Kansas City, and St. Louis, Missouri)

"Keep taxes down!"
"Why clean up for the town below?"

"Stop picking on us! The river was dirty long before we built our plant."

"This city hasn't had an epidemic for years."

"We just can't afford the facilities!"

Such pleas are more than familiar to enforcement officials charged with carrying out the provisions of the Federal Pollution Control Act, passed in 1956. They have held numerous conferences and formal hearings, and each time the refrain of procrastination is heard at least once. The fact remains, however, that in 10 years Step 3, court action by the U.S. Attorney General, has been used only once—in 1960. When it was applied, cities and industries all across the country began to realize that "it could happen here."

How did it come about that St. Joseph, Missouri, was the city to feel the full force of the law? Chiefly because the citizens kept refusing to pass the necessary bond issues to finance a treatment plant. "We have sewers," they argued. "What more do we need, with the river right here to carry it all off? Besides, treatment costs too much." Meat-packing plants in the area agreed, and continued to clog sewers and the river with disgusting debris. The filth that piled up was beyond tolerance.

State and federal authorities had time and again warned area citizens that even a river can die. A local-state-federal conference (Step 1) in 1957 pinpointed the sources of extreme pollution: the city itself and 18 specific industries. Yet, in March, 1958, despite a citizens-committee campaign, the people voted "No" to a bond issue. Although the campaign failed by only 385 votes out of a total of 15,000, city officials had had enough. They just didn't dare champion a cause that they thought might lose them votes. They showed no inclination to resubmit the bond issue to a referendum.

So the U.S. Secretary of Health, Education, and Welfare called a formal hearing (Step 2) on July 27–30, 1959. On the basis of testimony received, he issued a cease-and-desist notice to St. Joseph and the 18 offending industries. A time schedule was set up; a bond issue was called for prior to June 1, 1960. Again the public refused to vote the funds.

At this point, the Kansas State Board of Health and the Missouri Water Pollution Control Board agreed that the federal government had no choice but to use its full enforcement powers, as granted under the Federal Pollution Control Act. The Secretary of H.E.W.,

Possible Steps

IN THE STATE-FEDERAL ENFORCEMENT PROCESS

UNDER P. L. 660, FEDERAL WATER POLLUTION CONTROL ACT

(AS OF MAY 1966)

Step 1: CONFERENCE** of state and federal agencies
       Held in local area
       Open to the public
       State agencies free to select representatives from industry, municipalities, and civic groups to speak
       Facts presented; testimony heard
       Sources of pollution pinpointed

At conclusion of Conference the Secretary* may recommend remedial action with a time schedule for compliance.

States, localities, and industries involved determine means of financing their share of improvements.

If no reasonable progress is made after six months, the Secretary* may call a . . .

Step 2: PUBLIC HEARING** before a selected board
       Witnesses testify under oath
       Cross examination permitted
       Evidence presented; time schedule reviewed

If Board determines that pollution is occurring and that effective progress toward abatement is not being made, it makes recommendations to the Secretary* concerning measures needed to secure abatement. The Secretary* evaluates and makes recommendations.

If again no reasonable progress is made after six months, the Secretary* may refer the case to the U.S. Attorney General for possible . . .

Step 3: COURT ACTION**
       Hearing Board's recommendations and other evidence reviewed .
       Court enters judgment, with orders enforcing such judgment (daily fines, for example)

* Secretary refers to the Secretary of the Interior. Prior to May 1966 the Secretary of Health, Education, and Welfare had this authority.

** Between January 1957 and March 1966, 36 Conferences, 4 Hearings, and 1 Court Action occurred.

on August 1, 1960, requested the Attorney General to institute court action against the city, and a complaint was filed. After an informal conference, held before the judge of the court, the city agreed to schedule new bond elections, and the people of St. Joseph finally passed a $5,955,000 sewer bond issue on April 11, 1961.

Implications of this action were not lost on cities all along the river. The Attorney General had acted against St. Joseph in August, 1960. Three months later, Omaha, Kansas City, Kansas, and Kansas City, Missouri, all passed sewer-bond issues, totaling over $100 million. Each of these cities had already been through Step 1 of the enforcement process, and Step 2 had been reached in both Kansas City, Kansas, and Kansas City, Missouri. They were not anxious to contend with Step 3.

It takes more than this threat to get bond issues passed, however. Most voters don't even know that enforcement conferences may be going on in their city right at this moment. Civic leaders in Kansas City, Missouri, knew that they would have to get busy and launch a campaign. Sixty-four different organizations agreed to cooperate to get out the "Yes" vote for that city's $75 million bond issue. Among them were the Chamber of Commerce, the AFL-CIO, many women's groups, service clubs, the Jackson County Medical Society, church groups, the conservation council, the Regional Health and Welfare Council, and the Home Builders of Greater Kansas City.

The newspapers gave full support. On November 3rd, just before the vote, the Kansas City *Star* declared, "The only thing this community could get from delay is a bad reputation for fighting to keep a public health menace." Radio and television stations also produced supporting programs.

The League of Women Voters' part in the campaign involved putting out a three-page question-and-answer pamphlet with facts on Kansas City's water costs, as compared with those of other cities. Members also made phone calls (in a room provided by the Chamber of Commerce). They contacted over 500 organizations, took orders for thousands of pieces of literature, placed about 30 speakers, and secured endorsement from many groups.

The Kansas City bond issue passed in November, 1960, by a good margin, demonstrating the ingredients needed for a successful campaign: someone to get it started; hard work by a lot of people; effective use of facts by organizations, newspapers, radio, and tele-

This mountain of pure grease was extracted by a municipal treatment plant from sewage flowing from a Colorado meat-packing plant.

vision; and the cumulative building of community understanding and support.

These successful bond issues were only the beginning of a long-range drive to clean up the Missouri, and there is still much foot-dragging. Under court order, St. Joseph finally got its treatment plant into operation early in 1966. Kansas City has run into financing troubles, and its city council has had to ask for an extension of its construction schedule. Some industries in the St. Joseph area got together and built their own plant in 1963, but conditions there are still far from ideal. Meat packers' pollution from upstream Omaha has not helped the condition of the river.

St. Louis Blues

Where the Missouri joins the great Mississippi, there has been another serious pocket of pollution, the St. Louis area. In 1962, raw sewage and industrial wastes totaling 300,000 gallons a day were being dumped into the Mississippi from this area, and the U.S. Public Health Service had indicated that pollution just below St. Louis was of crisis proportions.

As long ago as 1951, local health authorities had publicized their concern over pollution around St. Louis. A citizens' committee was set up to study the sewer problems in the metropolitan area. Following the citizens' report, petitions were signed for establishment of a bipartisan Board of Freeholders, which in turn drafted a plan to set up the Metropolitan Sewer District.

With other groups in the area, the League of Women Voters endorsed and actively supported the creation of this Metropolitan Sewer District, and it was adopted by St. Louis and St. Louis County in February, 1954. MSD thus became the public agency charged with responsibility for planning and carrying out water-pollution abatement in this portion of the Mississippi River watershed.

A report issued in 1954 by the Bi-State Development Agency, in cooperation with the U.S. Public Health Service, the Division of Health of Missouri, and the Illinois State Sanitary Water Board, also stimulated interest in river-pollution control. The facts it revealed were appalling. Pollution was seriously threatening health, wildlife, recreational facilities, and the future economic growth of the whole area.

When MSD started operations in 1956 it quickly realized that the cost of needed improvement was going to be a major obstacle. Given the power to levy a tax, MSD had proposed a 6 percent property tax, to be levied after assessments had been equalized for the area. When this proposal failed to win public support, MSD, on May 10, 1960, agreed to reduce the rate from six cents to four cents, but cautioned that such action could cause St. Louis to fall one year behind its timetable for river-pollution abatement. Regular checking by the U.S. Public Health Service showed MSD already in default in part of its treatment-plant program.

Day of Reckoning

Part of St. Louis' voluntary timetable for cleanup included a bond issue, to be voted in 1962, for financing actual construction of treatment plants and interceptor sewers. Failure to pass would, without a doubt, bring federal intervention similar to that in St. Joseph. But not until late 1961 did citizen groups realize that hard work, imagination, and a unified front were demanded if the bond issue was to be voted through.

A tremendous citizen drive was mobilized. Newspapers cooperated; local dignitaries made speeches; public meetings were held; both Democratic and Republican leaders spoke in favor of the bond issue. The Real Estate Board of Metropolitan St. Louis urged passage. So did the Building Owners' and Managers' Association, the Labor Council, and the Federated Garden Clubs of Missouri. University officials supported the proposal, as did most state and local elected officials. A "Keep Clean Water Committee" was formed. Posters and reminders dotted the city.

The Leagues of Women Voters in St. Louis and St. Louis County, acting jointly, devised and distributed attractive pamphlets and flyers pointing out the grim facts of pollution and urging passage of the bond issue. These pamphlets were eye-catching, simply written, non-technical. They stressed, for example, that the up-river cities and towns were doing their part to pass along clean water to St. Louis, so it was up to St. Louis to send its water on in, a similarly clean condition. Kansas City was working on a $75 million project; St. Joseph was spending $5,955,000; cities like Omaha and Minneapolis and others had promised effective plans. So must St. Louis. Slogans such as "The Free Ride Is Over," "Pollution

Destroys," and "You Are Guilty!" were used in pamphlets and flyers.

In addition, the League offered its services to other organizations in the area. It wrote hundreds of letters to various groups, offering to supply speakers, a half-hour movie, brochures, discussion-group leaders. It held public meetings, conducted workshops.

A month prior to the vote, several League members took a trip to Cincinnati to visit a clean and efficient treatment plant. When they returned home, their comments were printed in the St. Louis press, with photographs. The chairman of the League group for Metropolitan Sewer District affairs said, "We wish that everyone in the St. Louis area could have shared the sense of shame we felt in comparing this plant with the complete lack of sewage-treatment facilities we have in St. Louis."

Members also attended the enforcement conference held in St. Louis on September 6, 1962, to review progress being made to meet abatement schedules. These conferences are open to the public, and attendance by citizens is an extremely important way to follow and encourage better pollution control.

The St. Louis meeting of the President's Water Pollution Control Advisory Board on September 28th offered another opportunity for citizens to express their points of view. League representatives from Missouri, Tennessee, and Illinois took advantage of this meeting, and, along with other citizens, made statements to the Board.

During the last three days of the campaign, the League set up a telephone brigade in the offices of the MSD and called as many registered voters as possible to urge them to vote and to vote "Yes."

The story of this bond-issue campaign in St. Louis shows what citizen groups can accomplish if they mobilize their efforts toward a common goal. By a dazzling 5-to-1 margin, the $95 million sewer-bond proposal, largest ever passed at the local level, was approved on November 6, 1962.

THE METRO SOLUTION

(SEATTLE, WASHINGTON)

Who should handle a pollution problem that is metropolitan in scope when no metropolitan form of government exists?

Rapid growth of Seattle and its suburbs brought this question to prominence in the early 1950s. Seattle was fast becoming one of the 20 largest cities in the United States (1960 census), and the suburbs east of Lake Washington were doubling their population between 1950 and 1960. They will double it again by 1970, according to estimates.

The city itself is 80 percent surrounded by water. Water recreation is a normal part of everyday living. Yet beaches were being closed, and citizens complained that odors around the lake were becoming unbearable and that the water was too murky to be enjoyable.

As the suburbs grew, so did their sewage problems. Some dumped raw sewage into the lake. Newly incorporated towns found the lake the least expensive place to dump treated effluent. The increase in septic-tank drainage also was fertilizing the algae in Lake Washington.

Citizens in both the city and the surrounding areas began to question whether new urban-suburban problems could be handled efficiently and economically by reliance on the jurisdictional hodgepodge of these individual cities, towns, and special districts. King County had over 130 different units of local government within its borders, yet pollution was getting worse every year. Many looked toward some kind of governmental organization that would enable local governments to cooperate in the planning, financing, and carrying-out of area-wide services.

In 1952, a group of citizens, led by the Municipal League of Seattle and the Seattle League of Women Voters, tried to revise the King County charter, in order to obtain home rule, but the change was defeated at the polls.

Realizing, after more study, that a wider citizen understanding of metropolitan problems was necessary, these citizen organizations formed study groups and stimulated broader interest.

State Permission Needed

This led in 1956 to formation of a Citizens Advisory Committee, appointed by the Mayor of Seattle and the Board of King County Commissioners. This 75-member committee, representative of all parts of the metropolitan region, studied thoroughly such area problems as air and water pollution, transportation, fire and police protection, garbage disposal, planning, and parks and recreation. The group then recommended that the state legislature pass legislation to permit cities and counties to join together in a metropolitan council for the purpose of solving problems beyond the capacity of each to solve by itself. After considerable debate, this Metropolitan Municipal Corporation Act was passed in the 1957 legislature by a single vote.

With passage of the enabling legislation, the metro campaign got under way. March 11, 1958, was set as voting day for citizens of the area. A Metro Action Committee of 400 members was organized to run the campaign, supported by volunteer help from the Municipal League, the League of Women Voters, and the King County Medical Society. Numerous other organizations endorsed the proposition, which included comprehensive planning, sewage disposal, and transportation. Press, radio, and television launched a broad public-information campaign; a speakers' bureau gave 300 speeches in six weeks.

The drive went well in Seattle but met considerable opposition in the outlying areas. Metro was a new idea in modern government. Would it be a "super-government" with unlimited power to tax? Would it be responsive to the will of all the people, or would it be controlled by the Seattle City Council? Was it needed in the first place? Many people outside Seattle were doubtful that Metro was necessary or desirable.

This suspicion was reflected at the polls in March, when Seattle citizens voted for the plan but the county areas outside the city rejected it. Due to a provision in the enabling act requiring that *both* the central city and the suburban area must approve, Metro had been defeated. Ironically, the total vote was 101,947 for and 85,590 against.

Never Say Die

Within a month, citizen groups were again meeting with mayors and sewer-district commissioners to map out a new strategy. Suburban representatives were invited to help prepare the new plan, and those areas too remote to be concerned were dropped from the area to be covered by Metro. The new plan also called for limiting Metro's functions to sewage disposal only, with an option to vote other functions, such as transit, at a later date. Election on the new plan was set for September, 1958.

Waste dumped into a creek was held responsible for this shocking fish kill at the mouth of an Eastern river.

The Metro Action Committee again went into action, and got support from 9 of the 10 city councils and all 10 mayors, as well as the Municipal League of Seattle and King County, the King County Medical Society, the King County Medical Auxiliary, the Leagues of Women Voters of Seattle and Bellevue, the Chambers of Commerce, sportsmen's groups, community clubs, many business and professional groups, and both major political parties.

Opposition groups were also vocal. A special group, called the Metropolitan League of Voters Against Metro, was formed to organize the opposing forces, and was supported by the Washington State Grange and Apartment House Owners and Managers, chiefly on grounds that Metro might be a "super-government" and that its costs were too high.

Proponents continued to work, however, and climaxed their campaign with a Metro March to ring doorbells. Five thousand men, women, and children participated, and 100,000 pamphlets were distributed from door to door.

Other pressures were helping to arouse the public to action. Pollution in Lake Washington was getting worse. Along Puget Sound the discharge of untreated wastes was forcing more beaches to close and was curtailing boat recreation and water-skiing. In the Duwamish River, the excessive organic materials contained in sewage discharge were consuming oxygen needed for fish. In unsewered areas, reliance had to be placed on private septic tanks, many of which could not function properly because of soil conditions. The unusually hot summer that preceded the September election also helped to make people aware of the importance of clean recreational waters.

The September, 1958, election was an outstanding victory. Metro received 58 percent of the vote in the city and 67 percent in the suburban area. Several towns that had cast 60 percent of their ballots against Metro in the spring voted for it by an equal margin six months later. And so the Municipality of Metropolitan Seattle, popularly called Metro, was formed.

Sweet Success

The Metro program, which called for construction costs of nearly $125 million over a 10-year period, got rapidly under way. All four of the new treatment plants (Carkeek Park, Richmond Beach,

Renton, and West Point) are now completed, along with related interceptor lines and pumping stations. The 125 million-gallon-per-day West Point plant is the largest treatment facility in the Northwest. A pamphlet, "The Municipality of Metropolitan Seattle," written in 1963 and revised in December, 1965, by the League of Women Voters of King County, outlines the history and development of Metro, as well as its organizational structure, responsibilities, and methods of financing. It also includes a detailed work schedule for the entire sewerage construction program.

By the summer of 1966, all sewage and sewage effluent had been removed from Lake Washington, making it the largest lake in the world to be rehabilitated after a serious deterioration caused by sewage discharge. All salt-water beaches are also protected except those in Elliott Bay. Construction of the $16 million Elliott Bay interceptor line began in 1964 and is scheduled to be completed in 1970, thus, in effect, ending the pollution of Seattle's commercial waterfront.

Seattle and its citizens were honored in 1960 for the successful formation of Metro by receipt of the All-America City Award, sponsored by the National Municipal League and *Look* magazine. Other praise came at a national conference held in Seattle in October, 1963, when the president of the Water Pollution Control Federation stated that "Seattle is ahead of us, but we are all going to have to undertake a water-pollution control program as aggressive as they have here."

AN UPHILL STRUGGLE

(MAINE)

In Maine, a state known for its abundance of lakes, rivers, and streams, where recreation is the second largest industry, and where five-sixths of the area is covered with forest, one might conclude that water would cause little, if any, concern. Scarcity is certainly not the problem, but pollution is.

Most of the population is crowded into the southern part of the state. So is most of the industry. So is most of the pollution. It's the same old story: the dirtiest water flows where the cleanest water is needed. In what might be called a liquid Gresham's Law, the bad drives out the good. And, with similar inevitability, new industry is not attracted, some property values have declined, certain recreational facilities have had to close down or were impossible to develop, fishing industries have been hampered, sportsmen have been frustrated.

In 1957, Maine was treating only 11 percent of its municipal sewage; the rest was flowing raw into the nearest stream or bay. Statistics for 1965, sad to relate, tell about the same story. Improvements have been made, but simply cannot keep up with increased pollution.

Industrial waste adds another serious burden. Lumber and lumber products, leather goods, pulp and paper, textiles, canned foods, and potato-processing plants are basic to Maine's economy, but each adds a variety of complex pollutants to the streams.

Classifying the Waters

In 1953, a state statute was passed requiring classification of streams. Although some states are working toward outfall, or effluent, standards, Maine's stream classification is based on receiving-water standards. Under this technique, discharge of wastes—even raw sewage —into a stream is permitted, provided the quality of the stream is maintained within certain limits. Quality standards vary from Class A (excellent quality) to Class D (primarily for use in transportation of wastes without creation of a nuisance). One class need not be applied to the full length of a river. The river may be divided into zones, each with a different classification.

In 1941, the Maine Legislature established the State Sanitary Water Board, which in 1951 became the Water Improvement Commission. This Commission is charged with responsibility for classification, but its ratings are only recommendations, and must be voted each time by the state legislature. This is a long process, and one open to political pressures and delay.

The Commission is also charged with enforcement, once the classification has been approved, but up to the present time classification itself has been so time-consuming that little time or staff has been left for the vital job of enforcement. Now that classification is nearly completed, emphasis will presumably shift toward enforcement.

The WIC must also allocate and administer federal and state grants to municipalities. This work will increase as construction requests increase. Lack of funds and manpower also limits the amount of research that the Commission can do on some of the special pollution problems that Maine's tanning, paper and pulp, and food-processing industries create. Little or no money is earmarked for educating the public.

Citizen Group Lends Support

The League of Women Voters of Maine, recognizing the limitations and handicaps under which the WIC is required to operate, determined to strengthen this Commission.

In 1960, state League members gathered background information and issued "Mainestream: A Study of How Maine Uses and Manages Its Water Resources." The booklet outlines Maine's sources of water, uses of water, pollution-control measures, and administrative agencies involved with the state's water-resources program.

With "Mainestream" as basic resource material, local Leagues began to study their own river basins and local pollution problems in detail. The state League set up workshops to stimulate interest among members and to coordinate League efforts. To supply a yardstick by which to judge Maine's pollution-control laws, the first workshop discussed the Suggested State Water Pollution Control Act published by the U.S. Public Health Service and endorsed by the Council of State Governments. A workshop report said, "We are all hoping that our study units will not get bogged down in the usual discussion of how bad the water is, but instead will consider what can actually be done this year and in the years to come to make our laws stronger."

A speakers' list was compiled at the first workshop, and the state League mailed it to all Kiwanis, Rotary, and Lions Clubs in areas near local Leagues. Each League made contact with women's clubs, with garden clubs, and with schools, and held meetings to which were invited members of city councils; public-works, water, or engineering-department representatives; mayors; heads of influential businesses and civic groups; local legislators; and, of course, the general public.

The League also helped to distribute a pamphlet called "Better Waters for Maine," put out by the Water Improvement Commis-

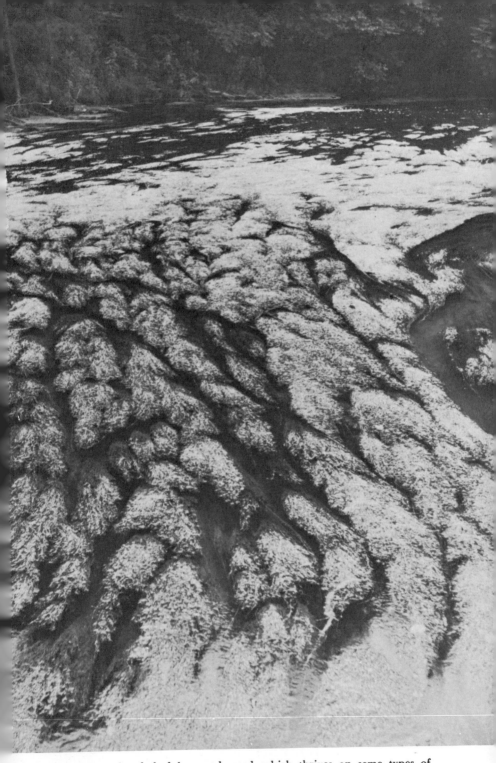

Streams can be choked by pond weed, which thrives on some types of pollution.

sion. In Bangor, the State Water Chairman of the League took a copy of this booklet to radio station WLBZ and talked with one of the executives there. The result was a series of broadcasts on pollution, in which representatives of the League, of conservation groups, of municipalities, of public-health organizations, of industry, and of the Water Improvement Commission were interviewed. These programs were taped and made available to other interested radio stations throughout the state.

To lend further support to the Water Improvement Commission, the League has campaigned for a more adequate staff. It has provided numerous forums for Commission members to speak to the public. It has appeared in support of the requested budget for the Commission each time it was being debated in the Legislature. In 1963, League members put on the desk of each legislator a flyer supporting the WIC request for funds. In the 1961 legislative session, the League testified, either in person or by written statement, on 16 bills having to do with water and support for the Commission.

Classification Triggers Action

Despite its workload, the Commission is proceeding with the classification job, starting with the very smallest tributaries and working downstream.

A major breakthrough was achieved in 1961, when classification of the main stem of the Kennebec River was passed by the Legislature, substantially as recommended by the Water Improvement Commission. This was the first large river to be classified and the first time treatment was required of a major industry.

Classification of the Kennebec required that 10 municipalities and four industries build treatment facilities, and a timetable for compliance was written into the law, chiefly at the insistence of the industries involved. The spokesmen for industry argued that they were ready to recognize pollution abatement as a necessary cost of business if they could get assurance that municipal pollution would be brought under control. Accepting this point of view, the Legislature voted for the following timetable:

October, 1964—Preliminary plans and engineers' estimates.

October, 1968—Arrangements for administration and financing

to be completed, including state and federal grants.

October, 1969—Detailed engineering and final plans completed.

October, 1970—Review of final plans completed and construction begun.

October, 1976—Construction completed.

Such is the plan for the Kennebec. It at least got towns and industries to start making plans, and, in fact, some are ahead of schedule. The city of Augusta, for example, is already treating its wastes.

Recommended classification for the Penobscot River, with a similar timetable for compliance, was passed by the 1965 Legislature without a single voice of protest.

The Androscoggin River has been left by the Commission until last, for the reason that this river is the only one that has had some degree of control since 1942, when a court order was handed down. Under supervision of a "river master," the paper companies along the Androscoggin have been ordered to abate the public nuisance caused by discharges of sulfite waste liquor. But even as recently as December, 1960, a League spokesman was obliged to report at the U.S. Corps of Engineers hearing at Lewiston:

"Pollution from pulp and paper mills equivalent to a population of 1,400,000 reaches the Androscoggin, while waste from other industries equals that of an additional 235,000 people.

"Municipal sewage from a population of 87,000 is also discharged untreated into the river."

League members also attended a federal-state conference on the Androscoggin in September, 1962, called by the Secretary of Health, Education, and Welfare, under powers given him by the Federal Water Pollution Control Act. The federal agency claimed jurisdiction by suggesting that pollution originating in New Hampshire was endangering the health and welfare of the residents of Maine. "New Hampshire was furious and refused to participate," reported a League member. "When the fireworks had died down, everyone seemed to agree that there wasn't much of anything anyone could do to bring about the classification of the Maine section of the river any earlier than 1967."

Meantime, classification of both the interstate and intrastate tributaries has been approved by the Legislature, and New Hampshire and Maine are reportedly working harmoniously now toward the 1967 target date for the main stem of the Androscoggin. By then, the classification job for the entire state will have been completed.

Some Rough Sailing

In addition to its rivers and streams, Maine has a large salt-water coastline to guard from pollution. The old wives' tale that salt water disinfects, and that the tide carries everything away, has been difficult to overcome. The closing of clam flats by the Department of Agriculture helped to bring home to people the fact that salt water, too, must be protected.

By 1963, some steps had been taken to accomplish that. Classification of Lincoln County tidewaters went smoothly, and in Cumberland County those interested in protecting Scarboro Beach initiated a classfication improvement. However, the WIC recommendation that tidewaters in prime recreational areas of Hancock County be made safe for bathing and for shellfish by requiring treatment of all sewage did not pass in the Legislature. In fact, the compromise measure seems to have taken several steps backward. The recommended classification was *lowered* in nine of the 22 communities affected, and the time limit for compliance was *extended* from eight years to 16. The cry from these towns that they simply could not "afford" the cost of meeting the proposed classification had been heard loud and clear in the Legislature. Only a few people dared ask whether these towns could "afford" to lose their recreation-industry potential.

Does the Exception Prove the Rule?

Many citizens think that if Maine's classification system is to be meaningful, if the Water Improvement Commission's program is to be effective, special exceptions and variances cannot be tolerated. Others feel that the whole economy of the state should be considered, even if temporary downgrading of a stream may be part of attracting new industry. There was very little public discussion when the 101st Legislature completely removed two ponds at Blue Hill from the classification system in order to permit mining operations. In contrast, a 1965 bill to lower Prestile Stream from Class B-1 to Class D, in order to accommodate a proposed sugar-beet refinery at Easton, became a hot issue throughout the state.

Recognizing that northern Maine, dependent for generations on the potato crop alone, needed an economic shot in the arm, the state finally obtained a hard-to-get sugar-beet allotment from the U.S. Department of Agriculture, but was required to build a refinery in the area by 1966.

Where to put the plant? Time-consuming debate followed, until Easton, on Prestile Stream, was proposed, next to an already established potato-processing plant. The potato-plant owner encouraged this new neighbor, even offering use of his treatment plant until adequate facilities could be installed. It was agreed, however, that under this setup the stream classification would temporarily have to be lowered to D.

This caused considerable soul searching on the part of legislators deeply concerned with the conflict of interest between a potential new industry and the state's pollution-control effort. Proponents felt that nothing must stand in the way of sugar beets, and that the classification system was meant to be flexible. It was further argued that this lowering of classification was to be temporary, to allow a new industry to work out the problems of waste treatment.

In the eyes of the Governor, retention of the sugar-beet allotment was so important to the state that he called a special joint session of the Legislature to give strong personal backing to the reclassification of Prestile Stream. The bill was passed on March 5, 1965, but without any mention of its being a temporary measure.

Opponents of the lowered classification urged changes in the sugar-beet plant process itself to cut down wastes. They argued for recycling and reuse of water. And they complained bitterly that the potato plant's treatment facilities were grossly inadequate, even for its own wastes, and could never handle anything new. The plant, in fact, has been under WIC "order to abate" for two years, with token improvements noted from time to time.

Maine Sugar Industries has now built a $350,000 dam to impound water for sugar-beet processing. (It is too early to tell whether its proposed treatment facilities will be effective.) The dam, however, is filling, thus holding back the water that would normally flow in Prestile Stream. At present, in fact, about the only water in the stream is what comes from the potato-processing treatment plant, and, in downstream Mars Hill, citizens have signed

Untreated industrial pollution stains and spoils a picturesque stream in North Carolina.

a protest petition because of the stench. Tests made by the WIC in late 1965 and early 1966 verified the seriously polluted condition of the stream.

So the potato plant and the sugar-beet plant are tied together in a confused picture at the moment. Will the Attorney General issue an injunction? Will in-plant processes be tried as long as the D Classification is being met? Will the citizens downstream band together in effective protest? Is anyone willing to oppose the potato-plant owner, who, after all, is providing 10½ months' employment each year for several hundred people who formerly had only a few months a year of seasonal employment? Will both the potato plant and the sugar-beet plant eventually put their houses in order so that Prestile Stream can again become Class B-1? These are knotty questions, involving economics, political decisions, and value judgments. All across the nation similar questions will have to be met, face on.

Getting Ready Takes Time

Classification is only the beginning; compliance takes time. As a matter of fact, in 1956 when federal aid for treatment plants was first offered, many municipalities were simply not ready for it. Funds were allowed to lapse. The towns had done little or no prior planning. Major trunk sewers were nonexistent in almost every municipality. Financial problems were unsolved, and in the early days of the program the maximum federal contribution of $250,000 per project did not attract larger communities. At that time, too, the state contribution was limited to 20 percent of the project cost.

But in 1961, when the federal act was amended to permit a maximum of $600,000 per project, the State of Maine voted to match whatever the federal government spent on any one undertaking. This far-sighted action by the state Legislature seemed to stimulate larger municipalities to begin serious plans for treatment and was considered a big step forward by those interested in clean-up.

Trained not to lose sight of a program once voted through, League members have found it necessary, however, to appear time and again at the Legislature, and to write letters urging that necessary matching state funds be appropriated.

In some cases, state funds have been voted only at a special session, because the Legislature was reluctant to appropriate funds that might not be used. Some of the pressure and expense of special sessions has been lessened, though, thanks to approval in November, 1964, of $25 million in bonds, to be issued over a 20-year period. The first issue of $4.5 million was approved—again as an emergency measure—by the regular session of the 102nd Legislature, thereby salvaging $700,000 in federal funds that were about to lapse. It also provided the state's share of the matching funds for the next two years. "It was a real thrill to see the Maine House rise as a body to vote approval of this $4.5 million investment in pollution control," commented an eyewitness.

Small Beginning on a Big Job

A rough estimate of the total municipal sewage-treatment needs for the State of Maine is 125 plants, at a cost of $125 million. As of July, 1965, 20 projects had been completed, 10 were under construction, and five had reached the formal application stage. For the most part, these are the smaller plants, and still only about 10–12 percent of the estimated total of municipal waste is now being treated.

An encouraging indication of the way the pollution-control program is finally taking hold in Maine, however, is the number of preliminary sewer plans on file with the Water Improvement Commission. Ninety-one preliminary reports were on file as of October, 1965, calling for expenditures estimated at $113.5 million. There is no doubt that the availability of federally-sponsored advance-planning grants or loans has had a great deal to do with this progress. Instead of letting federal funds lapse, municipal officers are now asking "When will our turn come for matching funds? We are ready to go."

Enforcement Is the Key

A classification system without effective enforcement is meaningless. Enforcement is Maine's next major problem. The Water Improvement Commission has been devoting only 15 percent of its time to enforcement, and its annual report for the year ending June 30, 1965, shows the consequences. The only successful prosecution listed is that of an individual farmer who was fined $50 for dumping potatoes into Prestile Stream. Over a dozen "Abatement Orders" were issued, some of which hinge on construction of municipal treatment plants. The majority of violations are by industry, however, the two most worrisome abuses being the tannery at Saco and the potato plant at Easton.

The Attorney General is designated as the one who may institute injunction proceedings to enjoin violation. In the past, however, cases referred to that office have tended to become involved in a legal tangle and have done little to promote the case of clean water. It has been suggested that if a few strategic cases were vigorously pursued by the Attorney General, it would do much to set an example and show that the law has teeth.

As sewage treatment becomes more general in Maine, it is the taxpayers themselves who are going to insist on enforcement to protect their investments. It may take a few more years, but there is reason to expect that before long the full force of public opinion will be ready to back enforcement of established standards.

TROUBLE FROM THE COAL MINES

(PENNSYLVANIA)

"What this country needs is a good anti-acid pill! Not for us, but for our poisoned rivers and streams." So wrote a Pennsylvania League member after studying the acid-mine-drainage problem in her coal-rich state.

This special kind of pollution flows from bituminous or anthracite mines, deep or strip mines, active or abandoned mines. When surface or underground water seeps into the mines, it dissolves pyrites and sometimes harmful amounts of other mineral salts, and then is pumped or seeps out into the nearest stream to begin its journey of destruction. Rivers run red from acid wastes, plant and animal life are choked with "yellowboy" and shrivel up, fish die or move elsewhere seeking food, bridge foundations erode, recreational facilities are barred, and industry finds the corrosive water intolerable. Acid mine drainage completely ruins a river for any other use.

In 1961, the Governor of Pennsylvania stated that "one of the most serious problems we face in Pennsylvania is the fact that some 2,000 miles of our streams are polluted with acid mine drainage." This has been a serious problem ever since miners first cut into the earth. The oldest known strip mine in Pennsylvania dates back to 1815, and is still discharging its damaging chemicals into surrounding streams. Coal mines operate today in 43 of the 67 counties of Pennsylvania, and hundreds of applications to open new mines or reopen existing ones are filed with the state every year.

Controlling this acid mine drainage has become a public responsibility chiefly because many coal operators have not chosen to exercise their private responsibility. Unless we can tackle this problem now and win, say many citizens and officials, our grandchildren in the coal-producing regions will inherit a dead land, land lost to recreation, to industry, to farming—lost to any kind of viable economy.

Keeping Clean What's Clean

During the depression years of the early 1930s, the federal government initiated a program of sealing up abandoned mines to prevent air and water from entering them, but most of these efforts have now deteriorated. Pennsylvania's big stride came in 1937, with enactment of the Clean Streams Law. Under this Act, streams were classified as "clean" if relatively unpolluted, and as "acid" if already impregnated with acid from mines. The aim of this distinction was to establish high standards for the pure streams by forbidding all untreated wastes, from whatever source, to be discharged into them. The acid streams, on the other hand, were more or less written off as hopeless.

In 1965, however, the General Assembly passed a new Clean Streams Act, effective January 1, 1966. Directed particularly toward control of acid mine drainage, this Act contains significant changes in the Commonwealth's approach to cleaning up its streams. First, mine drainage (which may be alkaline as well as acid) is now to be included in the category of industrial waste, and subject to the same regulations as other forms of industrial waste. It had been specifically excluded from this category in the previous Clean Streams Act. Although there is still much to be learned about preventing acid discharge into the streams, and about neutralizing water that is presently acid, the General Assembly believed that enough progress had been made to justify the change in approach.

Second, the new Act prohibits the discharge of mine-drainage pollutant into any stream, thus removing the classification system

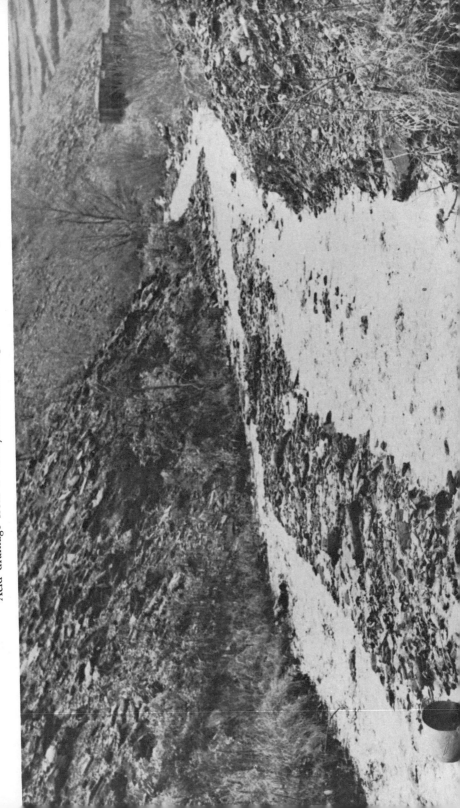

Acid drainage from a Pennsylvania mine begins its destructive journey.

previously used. Under the former system, some progress had been made in upgrading streams. The change in classification of the Lackawanna River, so that it might be salvaged, is a case in point. And the League of Women Voters of Pennsylvania gave strong backing to the 1962 legislative act that prohibited dumping of acid mine waste into those streams that might be rehabilitated. However, it was always a difficult fight, stream by stream, and in general more streams were lost than reclaimed. Pollution violations will now be spotted from the air as well as by the traditional inspections on foot or by boat, and the state seems determined to push for real clean-up.

Controlling the Source

Most states see the wisdom of keeping acid mine drainage out of the streams in the first place. This has meant regulation of the mines themselves, often a ticklish political problem in states where mining interests are powerful. Kentucky has tackled this in strong new legislation. Colorado seems' to have a working agreement with the industry for reclamation of the land after mining.

In Pennsylvania, the basic acid-mine-drainage laws, passed in 1945, initiated a system by which those desiring to open mines or reopen old mines were required to submit applications for permits. These applications had to include maps showing drainage patterns as well as plans for backfill and grading when the coal had been removed. The type of permit issued depended to a great extent on the classification of the stream into which the discharge would find its way.

As the problem of acid pollution grew worse, though, these laws have several times been tightened through amendment. In the summer of 1963, with strong backing from the Governor's office, the Bituminous Strip Mining Bill was strengthened. So were the Bituminous Coal Open Pit Conservation Act of 1945 and the Anthracite Strip Mining Act. These amendments, in general, place firm responsibility on the mine owners by requiring licenses, stricter mapping and planning before operations can begin, higher bonds, and more prompt backfill after coal has been removed. Cover-up of mines used to be required within five years. Now the limit, in most cases, is six months. An interesting sidelight to these regulations is the fact that soil conservationists and other specialists in some circles are discussing the possibility of requiring land developers to adopt similar practices in an effort to cut down one of the most serious pollutants in the country, siltation from land erosion.

Authority to check on compliance at bituminous strip mines was given in 1963 to the Land Reclamation Board, created within the Department of Mines and Mineral Industries. Previously, engineers from the State Health Department had been responsible for checking all mine sites. They still have jurisdiction over the deep bituminous mines, and both the deep and strip anthracite mines. Whether this new administrative setup will improve enforcement or dissipate authority is still being debated, but whether enforcement is within the Health Department or the Mines Department, there is a need for many more trained persons and enforcement officers.

What About Old Mines?

While strict enforcement will help control pollution from going operations, something else is needed to clean up past damage and old acid sources from which the original operators are long gone. This may require new state legislation, and in some of the less wealthy areas it may also take federal aid. West Virginia in 1963 passed a law aimed at this "old business," and while it has discovered some inadequacies due to faulty estimates, it is a beginning. An annual fee is charged for each mining permit. The fee money goes into a fund for rehabilitation of abandoned mine areas for which no rehabilitation was originally required and no bond posted.

Community leaders might want to look into alternative ways of controlling pollution from abandoned operations for which no legally responsible individual can be found. It is estimated that at least half of the acid mine-drainage pollution in the country comes from such old mines. In parts of Pennsylvania and West Virginia, the rate is even higher. Should the state be permitted to set up control operations even though these abandoned mines are on private property? On what basis should present landowners be obligated? These knotty issues and many others need to be investigated and decided soon. Citizen groups can do some of the basic spadework and can perhaps even initiate possible solutions.

Increased Research at the State Level

There are now 12 technical projects being sponsored by the Coal Research Board of the Department of Mines and Mineral Industries of the Commonwealth of Pennsylvania, totaling over $300,000. Some of this is done with financial support from the coal industry (about $81,000 worth), but Pennsylvania is one of the few states that have appropriated large sums of state money for this kind of research. One project is called "Operation Yellowboy," performed by Dorr-Oliver to investigate the acceptability and the economics of the lime-neutralization process for the treatment of acid mine water. Westinghouse Electric Corp. is conducting a research project on flash distillation of acid mine drainage. These both may prove significant in relation to deep mines, especially those that are abandoned. Jones & Laughlin Steel Corp. is also working in the lime-neutralization field, with special emphasis on a new approach to disposal of the voluminous sludge produced.

These are only a few of the research projects being conducted by universities and industry under contract with the Department of Mines and Mineral Industries. For the present, at any rate, the answer seems to be that there is no one answer to the problem of acid mine drainage.

Civic Groups Can Play a Role

Supporting public conferences is one way to stimulate interest. In June, 1962, the LWV cosponsored, along with about 50 other public and private groups, a national symposium on control of coal-mine drainage, organized by the Pennsylvania Department of Health to commemorate the 25th anniversary of the Clean Streams Law. Private-interest lobbyists were present. So were many groups interested in developing effective public support for state enforcement measures. Concerted action on the whole problem is long overdue. At a meeting as long ago as 1911, the Engineering Society of Western Pennsylvania discussed some of the same problems and came up with many of the same recommendations made at the 1962 symposium. The Pittsburgh *Press,* in a June 17, 1962, editorial, did note an important change in public viewpoint: "Perhaps the outstanding conclusion that emerged from the Symposium is this: that so far as the future is concerned it is water, rather than coal, that is our priceless resource."

Stressing clean water as one of its main concerns, the Pennsylvania League has been studying the complex problems of acid mine drainage for several years. It has made a detailed study of the Susquehanna River. It has prepared a report comparing bituminous strip-mine legislation in Pennsylvania with that in the six neighboring states of Indiana, Kentucky, Maryland, New York, Ohio, and West Virginia. Local Leagues have held public meetings on the problem, have testified, written letters, sent telegrams, made numerous personal visits to legislators, and have repeatedly talked with representatives of the State Secretary of Mines and Minerals, the State Secretary of Forests and Waters, and the State Secretary of Health.

In November, 1963, a League member was among those who testified at an Army Corps of Engineers hearing in Harrisburg, urging that a detailed study of acid mine drainage be made for the Susqehanna River Basin. Announcement that such a study will, in fact, take place was made in March, 1964.

League members attended the federal-interstate enforcement conference in December, 1963, called by the Secretary of Health, Education, and Welfare to look into acid drainage problems of the Monongahela River, from its headwaters to the Allegheny County line. West Virginia and Ohio officials were involved, as well as those from the Pennsylvania Department of Forests and Waters and the State Sanitary Water Board. Broader citizen pressure is needed, however, to support these officials and to assure them the political backing they need to be effective.

In November, 1964, the LWV of Pennsylvania served on an Advisory Committee to the Sanitary Water Board on Revision of the Mine Drainage Aspects of the Clean Streams Law. Also on this committee were representatives of coal operators' associations, labor unions, professional engineers, and conservation groups, such as the Western Pennsylvania Conservancy, the Izaak Walton League, and Sportsmen's leagues. The 1965 Clean Streams Act was based, in part, on recommendations made by members of this Committee.

A Federal Concern

This acid-drainage problem exists not only in Pennsylvania but in almost every coal-producing area in the country. It is a national problem, and the federal government has made and is making continuing surveys and recommendations for action. In April, 1962, the U.S. Department of Health, Education, and Welfare issued a report saying that acid mine drainage amounts to an estimated 3.5 million tons of acid discharges into the streams of the United States annually, resulting in major damages to more than 4,000 miles of streams. The report included proposals for a mine-sealing program, stepped-up research, and a stream-flow regulation program.

One of the recommendations of the report, for a demonstration program to try out and evaluate various measures and procedures for control or reduction of acid pollution by coal-mine drainage, is already under way. Under the leadership of the Department of Health, Education, and Welfare, working jointly with the Department of the Interior, one demonstration project on some 30 square miles of coal-mining land near Elkins, West Virginia, has been installed, and another will begin soon in northeastern Pennsylvania.

The Appalachia Program, passed by the 89th Congress in February, 1965, authorizes up to $36.5 million in grants to that area's states to seal and fill voids in abandoned coal mines and to reclaim and rehabilitate existing strip and surface mines. However, these grants, not to exceed 75 percent of costs, may be used for projects on publicly owned land only. The Act also requires the Secretary of the Interior to make a comprehensive, long-range study for the purpose of reclaiming and rehabilitating strip-and-surface mined land areas in the United States, with recommendations to be submitted by July 1, 1967, to the U.S. Congress by the President.

Civic groups in areas plagued with this destructive by-product of coal mining can help to create public understanding and support for strict enforcement of state mining laws, for stronger legislation where necessary, for continuing funds for research, and for federal aid, if needed, to spur and supplement state and local efforts.

FEDERAL ANTI-POLLUTION POLICY AND THE CITIZEN

Any discussion of the citizen's role in water pollution control would be incomplete without a statement of his part in the shaping and adoption of federal programs. Water quality is now recognized as a national problem, requiring the best efforts of all levels of government. The exercise of federal power in the field of pollution abatement, however, is a relatively new concept. Water pollution has historically been considered a matter of local, or, at most, of state concern. Although attempts had been made in Congress since the early 1900s, it was not until 1948 that resistance to federal entry into this field was overcome. The 1948 Water Pollution Control Act (Public Law 845), however, gave little actual control. Modest loans to municipalities were authorized, but no funds were appropriated. The real significance of the 1948 Act was the recognition, for the first time, that water pollution abatement is a legitimate federal concern.

This was a major breakthrough, but progress thereafter was slow. In 1960 President Eisenhower vetoed a federal pollution control bill because he believed that polluted water is "a uniquely local blight" and that the states should have responsibility for its control. There are many reasons for localities and states to have failed in effective action. The local tax dollar is already greatly overburdened, and the pressure of other needs on state funds has been equally adverse to the adoption of costly pollution abatement programs. Private interests resist strong state enforcement; plans are lacking; and citizen interest and concern are not made manifest. Most legislatures have taken only halting steps toward clean-up.

Senate Select Committee Field Hearings

The weakness of the 1948 Federal Water Pollution Control Act was generally recognized, and a considerably stronger bill was passed in 1956. Also called the Water Pollution Control Act, this Public Law 660, though amended several times since, is the basic authority for federal enforcement powers and for incentive payments to municipalities for the building of sewage treatment plants. Funds were appropriated, and under the 1956 Act effective action began. Public Health figures show a 62 percent rise in sewage treatment plant construction during the first five years of the incentive program compared with the previous five years. But those who were aware of the emergency aspects of the problem realized that much more was required.

The Senate Select Committee on National Water Resources held field hearings from October, 1959, through May, 1960, in 22 states. League members appeared at each of these hearings. League statements before this Committee were not in the form of general resolutions; they set out specific examples, well researched, of local pollution abuses and of state and local attempts, often ineffective, at improvements. The statements emphasized the validity of federal incentive payments to stimulate local construction of needed treatment plants. When the Blatnik Bill, providing for an increase in such payments, was vetoed by the President in 1960, protests to legislators poured into Washington from all over the United States. Although the bill received strong support in Congress, the House was 22 votes short of the two-thirds needed to override. The veto stood.

National Conference on Water Pollution

In an effort to make his veto more acceptable to the numerous citizen and conservation groups which had supported the Blatnik Bill, President Eisenhower called a National Conference on Water Pollution in December, 1960. Representatives were present from all levels of government, from private industry, and from civic and professional groups. A member of the LWV National Board served on the steering committee, was a speaker at the Conference, and participated in drafting recommendations from one of the panels.

Most industrialists at the Conference supported the National Association of Manufacturers' stand that industry should have maximum freedom in handling water problems. Many, though not all, of the state agency representatives present also opposed strengthening of federal enforcement powers. They feared that further federal participation in enforcement would weaken state programs and diminish their own effectiveness and significance.

Many municipal representatives at the Conference, however, recognized that federal authority to enforce strict control was of great assistance to them. Representatives from larger cities, especially, knew that they were in trouble and lacked both funds and power to require clean-up. They pointed out that federal authority to enforce compliance tends to bring about voluntary compliance and agreement at the conference table.

Action in Washington, 1961-1963

In January, 1961, with a new administration in the White House and with the newly published report of the Senate Select Committee on National Water Resources available, legislators interested in clean water tried again. Several new bills were introduced to amend the 1956 Water Pollution Control Act. Such bills reflected what legislators believed their constituents and citizens in general wanted. Citizen organizations were in touch with administrative officials and the appropriate Congressional committees during the period in which this legislation was taking shape. There was some contact among organizations with the same goals. Such informal give-and-take among those who are drafting legislation and those who are likely to support it often determines the substance of the bills and their chance of adoption. This process has become increasingly effective.

At hearings on the 1961 bills held by the House and Senate Public Works Committees, League spokesmen supported provisions for more research, for increased grants-in-aid, and for extension of federal jurisdiction over pollution in all navigable waters, not just in interstate streams. To this last proposal to expand federal enforcement powers to all navigable rivers, groups such as the National Association of Manufacturers, the Chamber of Commerce of the United States, the Manufacturing Chemists' Association, and the American Paper and Pulp Association expressed objections. But numerous civic and conservation organizations contended that the new proposal was necessary because experience had shown that the states in most cases were not doing the required job of enforcement.

Among the organizations testifying in favor of strengthening the Federal Water Pollution Control Act were the National Wildlife Federation, Wildlife Management Institute, the Wilderness Society, Sport Fishing Institute, General Federation of Women's Clubs, the National Audubon Society, and the Izaak Walton League of America. Groups such as the Garden Clubs of America, Daughters of the American Revolution, and some state conservation boards and fish and game departments also expressed interest in one or more of the strengthening amendments. There were many supporting letters from citizens to Congressmen while the bill was under consideration.

Following this show of great citizen interest, the proposed bill was passed and was signed by President Kennedy in July, 1961, as Public Law 87-88. One section adds authority for federal action on intrastate streams at the request of the governor of that state.

Other amendments to the Federal Water Pollution Control Act

have been proposed. Some have been adopted. At the 1963 hearings to strengthen P.L. 660, the League testified in Washington, D.C., in support of a higher ceiling on federal grants for sewage treatment plant construction, but with retention of the limit of 30 percent of the total project cost. It favored research and development grants for projects that demonstrate new and improved methods of controlling discharges from combined storm and sanitary sewers. It testified for a proposed 10 percent bonus in federal aid to metropolitan areas which construct a joint sewage treatment plant. It urged that the federal government help to promote complete transition to biodegradable detergents by December 31, 1965, a date which the soap industry agreed it could meet and did meet.

Water Pollution Advisory Board Hearings

Authorized under the 1948 Water Pollution Control Act and reconstituted under the broader 1956 Act, the President's Water Pollution Control Advisory Board holds public hearings at the invitation of Congressmen and state or local officials who want to focus public attention on a particular problem area.

The arrival in town of this Advisory Board, its open meetings, and the on-the-spot field trip it usually takes attract community attention to the pollution problem. Citizen groups who wish to arouse public interest should consider urging their officials to invite the Pollution Advisory Board to schedule locally one of its regular meetings. The Board held a meeting in St. Louis just prior to the big bond issue (see P. 47). Its 1964 Atlanta meeting preceded the big southeastern study now being conducted by the Water Pollution Control Administration.

House Subcommittee Goes on Tour

A recent opportunity to communicate with Congressmen has come through field hearings of the Natural Resources and Power Subcommittee of the House Committee on Government Operations. These were held to determine the effectiveness of the federal program for water pollution control and to get facts about local conditions. This group of Congressmen, known as the Jones Committee (Chairman: Robert E. Jones of Alabama), during field hearings from August, 1963, to May, 1964, heard from League members all across the country.

Most of the statements submitted at these hearings report that although local and state officials are doing all they can with the tools available, pollution in many places, if not in most, is increasing at an alarming rate. Because of this grim picture, the League of Women Voters strongly supports federal enforcement of pollution abatement wherever state action is inadequate.

Federal-State Enforcement Conferences

Public Law 660 provides that an enforcement conference shall be held when serious pollution of interstate waters is brought to the attention of federal authorities. The 1961 amendment extends this authority to intrastate waters on request of the governor. Quick to take advantage of this new provision, the Governor of Washington asked for, and got, an enforcement conference early in 1962 on pollution in Puget Sound, a strictly intrastate problem.

There is some understandable resentment over this enforcement feature of the Act. On the other hand, there is increasing sentiment that enforcement procedures are still too weak and operate much too slowly. It appears that small gestures at compliance are too often accepted as adequate and that federal officials may be overly cautious in their desire to respect state and local authority. Years may pass before any actual clean-up begins. Meantime, water supply is depleted, public health and safety are menaced, fish and wildlife suffer, and recreational needs are unfulfilled.

Water, it is plain, remains a political problem, and, if the processes of government move too fast for some and too slowly for others, perhaps the informed citizen group has the opportunity to be a determining factor in how and when improvements are made.

The League of Women Voters thinks that attendance at these state-federal conferences is important. Its members attend most of them. Between March, 1963, and January, 1966, members have been present at conferences in St. Paul on water quality conditions in the Upper Mississippi and Minnesota Rivers; in Boston on the Merrimack-Nashua; in Hartford on the lower Connecticut and its tributaries; in Denver on pollution of the South Platte; in New Orleans concerning the Pearl River; in Rome, Georgia, on Coosa River conditions; in Detroit on the Detroit River; in New York City on the Raritan Bay problem; in Rhode Island on the Blackstone River; in Illinois on southern Lake Michigan; in Ohio and New York on

Lake Erie; in Minnesota on the Red River of the North; and in New York City on the Hudson.

To speak at such conferences, one must be invited as a witness by one of the states involved. LWV members have been invited to speak at almost every conference. In her statement on the Connecticut River, the League spokesman said that the League supports such enforcement conferences not only as means for stimulating actual clean-up but also as focal points for arousing citizen interest through press and radio coverage of the meeting.

These conferences are held throughout the country and are announced in the local press, though often in an obscure box on a back page. Some League members have found, however, that if asked to do so, their local editors will give a more prominent position to the announcement. The League has also made a contribution by briefing its members and the public on the enforcement conference process and its potential for effectiveness, provided that the states and industry cooperate.

The Water Quality Act of 1965 authorizes substantial increases in financial aid to states and municipalities, and adds a new provision asking each state to submit its own quality standards for interstate streams to the Secretary of the Interior prior to June 1967. LWV members, the Izaak Walton League, and other groups are expressing to their state agencies, state governors, and their state legislatures the various uses which they suggest for sections of their rivers and streams. Setting quality standards is, of course, a complicated process, but informed civic groups can help technicians by suggesting broad guide lines for actual improvement of the waterways and by insisting that when high standards are set by the states they be enforced.

New Proposals

Several bills to strengthen further the Federal Water Pollution Control Act have been introduced into the 1966 Congress. Some ask for much higher federal aid for treatment plant construction. One would authorize $6 billion in federal grants during the next six years.

Other bills call for federal reimbursement to those states which pre-finance local treatment works construction. One bill proposes a permit system for all discharges into interstate or navigable waters. Several bills would allow accelerated depreciation on the cost of industrial treatment works.

Appeals for commitment of more federal tax money for water pollution abatement are heard at every hand. Perhaps the most dramatic example is the suggestion that federal financing of stream clean-up use the same cost formula that is now applied to interstate highway construction: 90 percent federal, 5 percent state, and 5 percent local government contributions.

How fast the country moves toward upgrading its lakes, streams, and coastal waters, and in what ways it chooses to pay the costs, will continue to be a lively and complex challenge to the nation.

Highlights of Clean Waters Restoration Act of 1966

Public Law 89-753, signed by President Johnson November 3, 1966:

• Encourages orderly clean-up of entire stream systems by authorizing grants to broadbased planning agencies.

• Removes the dollar ceiling limitation from federal construction grants.

• Increases annual authorizations for construction grants gradually from $150 million in fiscal 1967 to $1,250 million in 1971; total authorization $3.55 billion for the five-year period.

• Encourages states to share costs and set standards for intrastate waters by offering federal aid in excess of 30 percent of project cost as an incentive.

a) Maximum federal grants increase to 40 percent of project cost if state agrees to match at least 30 percent of cost of all projects receiving grants from that state's annual allocation.

b) Maximum federal grants increase to 50 percent if state agrees to match at least 25 percent of project cost, as above, and if state establishes enforceable water quality standards for waters into which the project discharges.

• Doubles amount authorized for support of state and interstate pollution control programs.

• Strengthens the federal enforcement process by providing that pollutors or those affected by pollution may speak without invitation at the enforcement conference or before the hearing board.

CHAPTER 3

The Problems of Floods

CATASTROPHIC FLOODS have brought tragedy and despair to various regions of the Far West and Middle West in recent years. Yet these floods are only the latest in an irregular series of similar disasters that have taken place, within the memory of most readers, in nearly every part of the nation.

Floods occur when very heavy rainfall or quickly melting snow suddenly produces more water than the ground can absorb or a stream channel can accommodate. There were floods before man began tampering with the countryside, but rapid development of the land has brought many practices that have increased the frequency and the size of floods, as well as the consequent economic loss.

Destruction of natural water-storage areas, such as forest or grass lands and gravel ridges, and their replacement by highways and buildings; the draining or filling of swamps; the straightening and deepening of stream channels have all contributed to moving water faster toward the sea and increasing the volume of flood water. At the same time, houses, factories, and farms have spread along the natural flood plains which are needed to take care of recurring inundations.

Since 1936, the federal government, largely through projects of the Army Corps of Engineers, has carried out a major program to control floods on United States rivers through dams on the tributaries and on the main stems combined with levees to wall off water from developed areas. The U.S. Department of Agriculture also

Construction of dams, storage reservoirs, and levees may greatly reduce the incidence of drowned farmlands and other destruction, but too often an unwise choice of riverside location for farm, residence, or industry has been a careless invitation to eventual disaster.

has built flood-control storage reservoirs and promoted good forest and agricultural practices through its Soil Conservation Service, under the small-watershed program.

Unfortunately, the building of flood-control reservoirs and levees has accelerated industrial, business, and residential development on flood plains, even though the dams and levees, no matter how big, cannot protect those plains against the major floods that periodically take place.

It is encouraging that more attention is now being given to the need for a balanced attack on the problems of flood control. In the spring of 1965, record floods swept down the Upper Mississippi. Yet a crash program to combat floods on that stretch of river would cost many hundreds of millions of dollars and would not benefit the cities in the region until 1973. A more comprehensive long-range program is being drawn up by the Corps of Engineers. Now, in the midst of a comprehensive study of this basin, the Corps suggests that such a program should include storage reservoirs to hold back snow melt and excessive rain on tributaries, local flood-plain ordinances to block construction of buildings on land likely to be flooded, floodproofing of buildings that must be built near the water's edge on a flood plain, levees to wall out high water, and proper use of agricultural land along the tributaries.

The small flood, though it does not make headlines, causes inconvenience by blocking highways and rail lines, damages property, and causes health hazards by backing up sewage in sewers and septic tanks.

It is only in the exceptional case, fortunately, that persons must be rescued from buildings in the path of a rampaging river. The most common problem of flooding that harries the homeowner is water in his basement. Often this is due to lack of local regulation to prevent building on the flood plain of a small stream or on other low land. Once such homes are built, the corrective tendency is to drain the land by ditches or by deepening a stream bed. Such measures may simply pass the water downstream to cause further trouble and may also hurt the first community by lowering its water table.

Interesting new approaches to solving flood problems are being developed. For example, it is possible to lead or pump excess flood water to a natural low spot, or an excavated one, thus storing the water and at the same time making a recreation lake out of land unsuited for other development. Such programs, carried out by farmers, industries, or municipalities, can store flood waters to use for recharging ground water, for recreation, for water supply, or to cope with peaks of hydoelectric-power demand. Cities are discovering that to avoid flash floods they can hold excess water from a heavy rain in very temporary storage on roofs or in parking lots. Such projects can supplement larger state or federal storage reservoirs.

Though several states, with the help of federal agencies, are establishing stream-encroachment lines (sometimes called flood-hazard mapping), it has been left to local communities to pass ordinances to control development on flood plains. If local government fails to take such responsibility for minimizing flood damage, the states and even the federal government may be forced to take action to encourage such regulation. This might be done by withholding flood-control construction until the municipalities to be benefited have acted to stop business or residential encroachment on the flood plains, or it might be done by direct intervention and control.

The various flood-control possibilities and methods for avoiding future flood destruction need to be studied jointly by technicians, officials, and citizens in light of the specific situation in the area. Ideally, flood control should be considered as part of coordinated, long-range planning for future water-supply needs, pollution control, recreational uses, and preservation of fish and wildlife habitats.

The case studies that follow show some of the ways in which localities are attempting to solve their flood problems, and reveal several opportunities available for a citizen organization to encourage and support flood-control programs through coordinated local, state, and federal action.

THE "RURBAN" WATERSHED

(MONTGOMERY COUNTY, MARYLAND)

Metropolitan Washington, D.C., is one of the fastest-growing areas in the United States. Branching out from the nation's capital into northern Virginia and southern Maryland, residential subdivisions are giving an urban flavor to once-open countryside.

The dairy farm of yesterday is the supermarket of today; mammoth housing developments are replacing pastures and woods. The bulldozer does the grazing now, voracious, insatiable.

Such land use and abuse have thrown nature completely off balance in the Rock Creek Watershed, the drainage basin of a stream that begins in the hills of Montgomery County, about 20 miles northwest of Washington, and empties into the Potomac River at Georgetown. The upper third of the watershed is still rich farmland, chiefly dairy and livestock farms, but suburban sprawl is already beginning to push in. The middle third was also a farm area prior to World War II, but today it is transformed into densely populated residential areas, with big shopping centers and even some high-rise apartments. The lowest portion of the watershed, in Washington, has for years been completely urban, except for that part of the flood plain that is in Rock Creek Park.

This gigantic building boom upstream caused a runoff problem that was already serious by the early 1950s. As more and more of the water-retaining vegetation was bulldozed from its roots, heavy summer rains swooshed down the Creek, flooding recreation areas in the park, destroying property, clogging roads with mud, and sweeping so much silt into the Potomac at Georgetown that extensive dredging operations were required. Combination storm and sanitary sewers repeatedly overflowed, turning once-lovely Rock Creek into a sluiceway for sewage. Flood gauges, set up to record water levels, revealed that even small rain storms registered higher than larger storms had done before urban expansion hit the upstream area.

Aroused Citizens Unite

One of the first groups to become aroused by these conditions was the local chapter of the Soil Conservation Society of America. The Interstate Commission on the Potomac River Basin also became interested. As a result, a series of three public meetings was held, in 1955, to seek possible solutions to protect Rock Creek. The League of Women Voters of Montgomery County, at that time in the midst of a study on community planning and development of recreational facilities, participated in each of these meetings.

Discussion there led citizens to form the Rock Creek Watershed Association, and plans were initiated to explore the possibility of obtaining help under P.L. 566, the Watershed Protection and Flood

Prevention Act of 1954. To qualify under this Act, a community first has to demonstrate, support for the project by its citizens and by local government. The League and 12 other civic organizations offered their support and gave full backing to the Watershed Association. The Association, in turn, began to generate interest and support among local officials.

Prior to filing an application under P.L. 566, local sponsorship of the project had to be guaranteed. Sponsorship includes willingness to acquire necessary land, handle contracts for construction, and get cooperation for appropriate soil-treatment measures from landowners above the dam structures. Letters were sent by the Association to the Montgomery County Council (the local governing body) and to the Montgomery Soil Conservation District (formed in 1945), requesting their support as cosponsors. Both groups consented. The Maryland National Capital Park and Planning Commission, the local park and planning agency for both Prince Georges and Montgomery Counties, agreed to handle the land acquisition and to serve as the contracting agency.

With these assurances of local support and sponsorship, formal application was filed in September, 1956, for a P.L. 566 survey. It was approved in January, 1957. In March of that year a survey party from the Soil Conservation Service came to the area and met with interested local and state agencies. A steering committee of these agencies worked along with the survey party to plan, to provide information to the Department of Agriculture, and to keep local citizens up to date on progress. Such federal-state-local cooperation at the outset, it is agreed, helped to avoid potential misunderstandings and frictions.

A Master Land-Use Plan

While plans were being drawn up by this committee and the Soil Conservation Service technicians, housing developers in Montgomery County were drawing up their own plans—schemes for bigger and better developments. It soon became obvious to local officials that if flooding downstream were to be controlled, and if the proposed two dams were to last out their expected lifetime of 50 years without premature silt deposits, plans would have to be made to guide the entire land development of the area. Uncontrolled building could jeopardize the whole flood-prevention program. Yet the

pressure for suburban expansion was becoming increasingly strong
as population in the Washington metropolitan area burgeoned and
land for development became less and less available. The Maryland
National Capital Park and Planning Commission (MNCPPC)
realized that it would have to propose a master land-use plan,
especially in the low-density area above the dams. Only by protecting what open spaces remained upstream could the flood-control
project be effective.

Its master plan for the Upper Rock Creek Watershed called for
two dam sites and a surrounding park of almost 3,000 acres to be
acquired by MNCPPC. At the hearings on the master plan, held
November 11, 1959, the League, among others, testified in favor of
the plan, in favor of the two dam sites, and in favor of controlled
development to preserve the much-needed open space. Interested in
multipurpose use of water projects where feasible, the League also
supported a proposal to build the first dam higher than originally
planned, in order to insure recreational facilities for the area as
well as flood control. The League repeatedly backed the survey
party and the park planners in their efforts to foster cooperation
among farmers, suburbanites, and urban dwellers to make the
whole plan effective. This joining of urban, suburban, and rural
areas into one effort has been called the "rurban" approach.

Two years later, the master land-use plan was adopted by the
Park and Planning Commission. Tax money from the suburban
area was earmarked to pay for the needed land acquisition and
part of the recreational costs. Funds were also obtained from the
Housing and Home Finance Agency, under its open-space program
for metropolitan areas.

The Congressional Green Light

When the work plan for the first dam and for the entire watershed
was completed, it was sent to the Bureau of the Budget and then
on to hearings before the Committees on Public Works in both
houses of Congress. The Montgomery County League wrote to its
representatives in Congress to ask their support for the watershed
plan and circulated newsletters to its members to keep them informed of developments. The plan for the Upper Rock Creek
Watershed was approved by the House and Senate Committees in

June, 1963. A floor vote is not required for this type of watershed project.

After 10 years of detailed attention and patient cooperation by local, state, and federal officials, as well as a decade of persistent public interest, led by the Rock Creek Watershed Association, the project is coming—somewhat tortuously—to fruition. Construction began in November of 1964 and is expected to be completed by 1968. About two-thirds of the park land has been acquired. (When the federal government realized, in 1962, that recreation was a legitimate and valuable part of watershed planning, it amended the Watershed Protection and Flood Prevention Act to include up to 50 percent payment for recreational purposes. As a result, the estimated federal share of the Rock Creek Project will be $1,286,734, and local agencies, chiefly the MNCPPC, will pay an estimated $841,652.) Two dams are incorporated in the plan, both of which will be high enough to permit recreational uses.

Control of flooding, conservation of resources through better soil-treatment procedures, new recreational areas, protection to roads and parks in the lower Rock Creek area, and decreased silt deposits in the Potomac River will eventually result if the project is carried out as planned and pressures for intense development are resisted. But herein lies the rub; herein lies the nub of citizen responsibility.

Who Will Protect the Master Plan?

The County Council that backed the early proposals and gave assurance of cooperation went out of office in 1962. The new Council, much to the dismay of those who advocated a rational plan for area development, granted twice as many zoning requests in its first two years as were allotted by the previous Council during four years. In the Rock Creek Watershed itself, the Council granted several rezoning requests that violate the master plan.

Some citizen groups who were keeping track of the project became alarmed at this seeming indifference to the future of the watershed. So did the Soil Conservation Service. Its spokesman went to the Council in December, 1964, after the first two rezonings had been granted, and raised the question of his ability to pledge federal funds for the second dam without some indication that

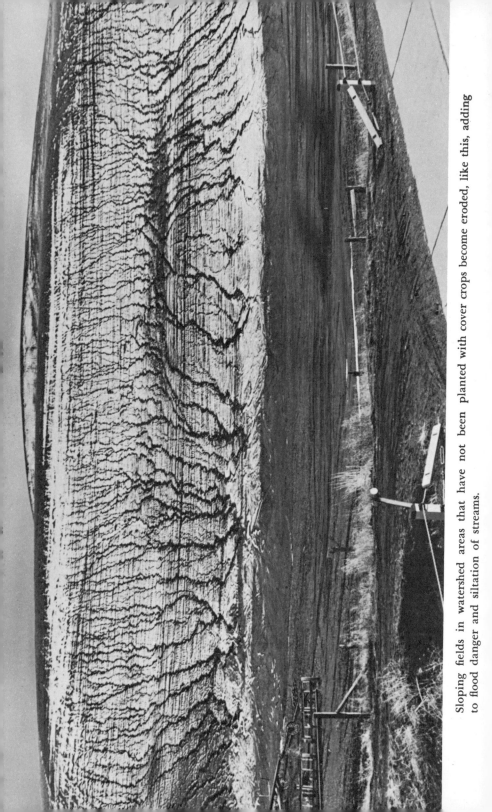

Sloping fields in watershed areas that have not been planted with cover crops become eroded, like this, adding to flood danger and siltation of streams.

Montgomery County would keep its part of the bargain and protect the land above the dams. Despite this warning from the key agency for technical advice and financial aid, the Council, in April, 1965, rezoned still another 88 acres of land just above the first dam, permitting half-acre lots in place of the original provision for two-acre lots only.

The Council did take the warning seriously enough, however, to set up a task force to consider the policy problems involved. Made up of local and federal agency representatives and members of two large associations of home builders, the task force issued its report in May, 1965.

Prominent in its recommendations was the adoption by all local agencies of new procedures for subdivision approval, under which builders, private and public, would be induced to consult on and carry out measures for preventing soil erosion during construction work. This broad Sediment Control Program was the first of its kind in the nation to be applied to an area subject to rapid urbanization. Accepted as policy by all agencies in June, 1965 (the deadline after which federal funds would be withdrawn), it details specific techniques that builders could apply in order to cut down erosion and silt runaway during construction. Subdivision regulations provide that such measures can be required in development plans. The Suburban Maryland Builders' Association has given the program its full support. If the controls work as part of the subdivision regulations, contractors can hope to avoid a sediment-control ordinance.

Some of the suggestions of the pilot program include a "practical combination" of the following:

(1) The smallest practical area of land should be exposed at any one time during development.

(2) When land is exposed during development, the exposure should be kept to the shortest practical period of time.

(3) Temporary vegetation and/or mulching should be used to protect critical areas exposed during development.

(4) Sediment basins should be installed and maintained to remove sediment from runoff waters from land undergoing development.

(5) Provisions should be made to accommodate effectively the increased runoff caused by changed soil and surface conditions during and after development.

(6) The permanent final vegetation and structures should be installed as soon as practical in the development.

(7) The development plan should be fitted to the topography and soils so as to create the least erosion potential.

(8) Wherever feasible, natural vegetation should be retained and protected.

Other jurisdictions are watching this Sediment Control Program with the thought of possibly adopting it in their own suburban areas.

The task-force report also asked that the County Council "consider the impact of proposed rezoning on the watershed project and incorporate the State Conservationist's comments in the record of the application hearings."

While the recommendations were valid, some civic groups were concerned that major emphasis had been put on mechanical techniques for controlling erosion rather than on controlling the intensity of land development. When the report was sent to the County Planning Board, for example, members approved it with one breath, but recommended with the next that 43 acres in the watershed be changed to light industrial zoning. Only staff members seemed to see the relationship between the zoning case and the policy report just adopted.

Some interests in the County are slow to recognize that controlling erosion, vital as it is, is not by itself a total solution and that maintenance of a controlled land-use pattern is also part of the key to success of the flood-control work plan. They tend to cling to the notion that if enough mechanical measures are used to control erosion, land-use controls will not be necessary. They forget that runoff patterns change when porous ground cover is replaced by impervious material, and that the dams will still be subject to damage if land use is not controlled. Engineers have been quick to encourage structural measures. Land speculators argue that if enough structures are used, full development of the entire watershed should be permitted. Conservationists and some citizen groups insist that both erosion control *and* land-use control are essential.

Disheartening Regression

But present prospects for limiting development are not bright. Already, in the Olney and Gaithersburg areas, new proposals for more intensive land use would cut into the Rock Creek Watershed. Most of the rural-agricultural zoning in the western half of the basin has already been rezoned away. Pressures for further rezoning are in the wind. If a trunk sewer is permitted—against both the 1962 (proposed) and the 1964 (adopted) General Plan—to service the rezoned 43 acres mentioned, further rezoning demands will follow, and many other changes to denser land uses are likely to take place. Already a group of zoning applications has been filed for the area just north of the 43-acre tract, totaling over 800 acres and requesting uses ranging from developments on one-quarter-acre lots to apartments and light commercial uses. The outcome of requests like these will indicate whether or not the County Council is fulfilling the intent of the whole "rurban" watershed project.

The Montgomery County LWV has, in a sense, adopted this watershed. It has testified repeatedly, held meetings, kept track of zoning changes, talked with technical people, visited the dam sites, written letters to elected officials. Indignant at the recent swing away from the original land-use control plan, it held an open meeting in November, 1965, to explain again to its general membership why the Rock Creek Project was needed in the first place and what the result of changes in land use can mean. Representatives from both the USDA Soil Conservation Service and the Montgomery Soil Conservation District spoke and answered questions.

The LWV also issued a call to action, urging its members to attend a hearing and speak up for a Planning Board proposal that would reduce land-use densities on about 8,500 acres in the watershed to counterbalance the acreage already rezoned upward.

Also, in November, it testified against a request to rezone to higher density a tract of land next to the Upper Rock Creek Project. Its spokesman pointed out that drainage from the land would dump directly into the permanent recreation pool at the first dam. This time the County Council denied the rezoning and the case has been appealed to the Circuit Court.

Stronger Group Action Needed

In looking back over the past 10 years, League members conclude that it is at this present stage of a project's fulfillment that citizen group efforts are needed more than ever. Helping to get the initial project through seems easy now, by comparison. To stimulate broad public interest in safeguarding water quality through proper control of land use in an area subject to extreme urbanizing pressures is a continuing battle.

Some observers in Montgomery County suggest that no amount of zoning regulations will actually preserve the area from the bulldozer, that the regulations will inevitably give way to commercial interests. The alternative, they say, is public ownership of the land, the only sure solution. Politically, however, this is seldom feasible. Financial incentives to farmers to encourage them to hold onto their land and adopt sound land-conservation practices are being tried, but this technique is also being abused in some areas.

Meanwhile, those who care about what happens to the land and to the water in the Upper Rock Creek Watershed are working through existing channels to see to it that the County Council includes upstream control of land use along with its new sediment-control program.

GOING THROUGH PROPER CHANNELS

(ALBUQUERQUE, NEW MEXICO)

In Albuquerque, about once a year, 15 to 25 thousand cubic feet of water per second roars down the slopes of the nearby Sandia Mountains, whips through the city, and empties into the Rio Grande. The force of this water cuts deep ditches into the plain, washes away banks of dirt, breaks up pavement, clogs storm sewers, cuts through yards, damages houses, endangers life, stops traffic, and costs thousands of dollars for clean-up and property repair.

Duration of the flood is short, however, and between times citizens tend to forget the danger and the loss and waste. In a land where the average yearly rainfall is only eight inches (compared with the national average of 30 inches), residents are more interested in finding new sources of water or in planning irrigation projects to spread what water they have.

Officials in the area have known for years that something could and should be done to curtail this needless' invasion from the mountains. On November 7, 1952, as a result of petitions by the City of Albuquerque and the County of Bernalillo, the Sandia Conservancy District was established by court order to provide and maintain local arroyo drainage control and flood protection as well as other improvements for public health, safety, convenience, and welfare. A board of directors was appointed (later to be elected) to administer the District.

The Sandia Conservancy Plan, approved by the District Court on March 13, 1956, entailed cooperation with the U.S. Army Corps of Engineers to construct two diversion channels, one north and one south of the city, which would carry flood waters from the mountains directly to the Rio Grande, thus bypassing the developed city area. At this time, 1956, the Corps of Engineers already had authorization to build the twin-ditch project, at an estimated cost to the federal government of $12.5 million. The Sandia Conservancy District, for its part, was to provide all lands, easements, and rights-of-way. The District was also responsible for making any alterations to existing improvements required because of the new construction, for maintenance and operation of the works after completion, for enlargement of existing waterways, and for taking steps to protect the area through zoning regulations. The court order also required the Conservancy District to prepare a report outlining a method of appraising the land within the District so that property could be assessed to pay for the acquisition of land for the ditches.

The League of Women Voters of Albuquerque, after studying the plan, decided that the most useful role it could serve would be to publicize all the facts, pro and con, to help citizens to make up their minds on an informed basis. During 1956 and 1957, it took every opportunity to show colored maps to citizen groups interested in just how the twin-ditch project would look when completed. It held meetings to discuss the method of assessing property owners. Several League members acted as observers at meetings of the Sandia Conservancy District to keep themselves and the community up to date on developments.

Public Opposition

When the Conservancy District's assessment report was presented to the public in September, 1957, however, property owners were strongly opposed to it. So aroused were they, in fact, that they elected members of their own protest group to replace the board of directors. Their objections centered on the fact that the board had set "benefit percentages" on different properties in the District. It also had decided—arbitrarily, as far as citizens could determine—

that the District would be on the east side of the river only. There were also involved payment provisions that property owners thought were unfair, and many citizens felt that the board was permitted altogether too much autonomy. Civic leaders wanted more specifics on just what the vote meant, what their obligation was, and when it would terminate.

Meantime, the Corps of Engineers had specified that after November 21, 1963, it could not participate with the District in constructing the proposed ditches. Its authorization would no longer be valid. Nonetheless, the controversy continued, with little or no action taken to solve the flood problem. In March, 1962, the court stepped in and dissolved the Sandia Conservancy District.

A New Approach

But the need for flood control persisted, of course, and there was still time to take advantage of federal funds for construction of the project. So the State Legislature acted, in January, 1963, to create the Albuquerque Metropolitan Arroyo Flood Control Authority. Its five directors, appointed by the Governor, were particularly assigned to take the necessary legal steps for approval of the twin-ditch project, to get a bond issue voted upon, and to hold a public election for a new board of directors.

The Legislature also required, this time, that the entire and defined costs of the facilities be spread to cover both sides of the river and that the tax be fixed equally on all property in the area in proportion to its value. It also specified that the board could not continue with one project after another without a vote on each project by the taxpayers.

These specifications made a big difference. The LWV reactivated its public-information drive, attended meetings of the directors, and sponsored a public meeting in May to acquaint citizens with the powers and functions of the new Authority. Just prior to the $9.5 million bond-issue referendum and election of board members, in August, 1963, the League held a meeting at which all the candidates spoke and at which the bond issue was explained in detail. Costs to the federal government, it was learned, had gone up, because of the delay, to approximately $25 million.

As if nature herself wanted to assure passage of that bond issue,

Albuquerque in August had the biggest rainstorm it had had in two years. Considerable damage was suffered in the heights, owing to faulty bridge construction that blocked heavy flow, and the lower part of the city was clogged with water, mud, and silt. This rain emphasized the fact that flooding was still a present danger, that work should continue on the improvement and expansion of the storm sewer system, and that the twin-ditch project was a positive necessity.

On voting day, the public showed that it had been convinced. The bond issue passed, and a board of directors for the Authority was at last elected. One of them is a League member.

The Albuquerque Metropolitan Arroyo Flood Control Authority went immediately to work. It established cooperative agreements with the State Highway Department to acquire rights-of-way, and construction of the first phase was started on schedule; anticipated completion date: October, 1966. Work on the south diversion channels has begun. Construction of the north diversion channels will start in late 1966. The entire project is due to be completed by June 30, 1968. The lowland parts of the city will then be protected, and home owners in the surrounding area will no longer have to make annual flood repairs to their property.

PUTTING FLOOD PLAINS ON THE MAP

(METROPOLITAN CHICAGO)

Salt Creek, a chief tributary of Illinois' Des Plaines River, is only one of many streams in the metropolitan Chicago area that have been overflowing their banks for years. But the particular seriousness of Salt Creek's behavior was recognized during the 1950s, when several engineering studies of it were conducted. The Metropolitan Sanitary District, the city of Chicago, and the Forest Preserve District of Cook County made surveys. So did the Illinois Division of Waterways, a state agency with jurisdiction over all surface waters. By 1959, two major plans had been proposed and were competing for official and public approval.

To harness Salt Creek, the Illinois Division of Waterways proposed to straighten, widen, and dredge the channel and then confine the waters in a concrete-lined ditch, with sloping sides 10 feet high. The project would cost $1,202,000, which was the amount actually appropriated by the Illinois Legislature in 1959 for control of Salt Creek. Many local interests supported this proposal.

Officials of the Cook County Forest Preserve District, through which ·Salt Creek runs for many miles, could not accept the idea of a concrete trough's replacing the natural beauty of an untouched stream. They proposed, instead, that a 250-acre lake be constructed in the region, and that, except for the clearing of debris and fallen trees, no other tampering with the creek be permitted. This project, the Forest Preserve spokesmen maintained, would cost only about $300,000, and would accomplish just as much by way of flood control.

Experts Favor Mapping

After considerable discussion, the controversy was referred to the Technical Advisory Committee on Flood Control of the Northeastern Illinois Metropolitan Area Planning Commission (NIMAPC). This Advisory Committee (which includes experts from the University of Chicago, several engineering firms, the Metropolitan Sanitary District of Greater Chicago, the Illinois State Department of Conservation, the U.S. Corps of Engineers, and many others representing local, municipal, county, state, and federal jurisdictions) did not recommend either plan to its parent body, NIMAPC. Instead, it proposed a reservoir at the northern end of the stream. This suggestion was never implemented, however, and now the Soil Conservation Service will undertake a watershed protection program there.

Through its study, though, the Advisory Committee came to the conclusion that a flood-hazard mapping program was absolutely vital for the entire metropolitan area. Piecemeal decisions were not the answer. Once the flood plains were identified, according to Committee thinking, construction could be prevented in, or at least tailored to fit, an area known to be subject to possible flood damage. The fact that the 1959 State Legislature had granted new zoning powers to municipalities to enable them to plan to reduce flood damage‚ encouraged the Advisory Committee to assume that flood-hazard maps, once completed, would be used constructively.

Convinced that the mapping proposal was sound and would

People who live in natural flood plains learn to keep a boat handy and pay an annual toll in property damage. Flood-plain mapping can help curtail future damage by steering potential builders away from regions most likely to be inundated.

supply an important guide for future planning and construction, NIMAPC, coordinating group for the six-county area around Chicago, took on the job of determining a plan of action. Its study showed that the total cost would be $250,000. The U.S. Geological Survey would do the actual mapping and would pay half of the costs; the six counties to benefit would pay the other half.

Citizen Help Requested

Realizing that citizen support was necessary for success, NIMAPC asked the Leagues of Women Voters in the Chicago area to publicize the purpose of the flood-hazard maps and encourage county boards to finance their share of the project.

The 51 Leagues in the area had already established an ad-hoc committee in early 1959 to study metropolitan water resources. Having found flooding to be one of the major problems, members were anxious to learn more about the mapping proposal. They invited an advisor to NIMAPC, Dr. Gilbert White, of the Geography Department at the University of Chicago and a distinguished national authority on flood control, to speak to their group about the procedures and goals of the flood-hazard mapping program.

After further study and discussion, the League's ad-hoc committee met and planned its campaign. In a memorandum to League members in the six counties, the committee suggested the following techniques for publicizing the mapping program:

(1) A personal call on the village manager, mayor, or building commissioner to talk about the value of the maps as a planning tool and their possible use in that community.

(2) Publicity in local papers. This should describe the purpose of the mapping program and reasons for League support. Articles and editorials on flooding, which appear so frequently, can be followed up by a letter to the editor. Calls on local editors and writers who are known to be informed are also suggested.

(3) Calls on local banks and savings-and-loan associations. Flood-hazard maps might be of value to these groups in assessing land on which developers may want to build.

(4) Contact with other organizations, such as the Izaak Walton League, that are known to have an interest in water problems. Garden clubs and women's clubs usually have a conservation chairman who will be interested.

The Illinois State League also helped to publicize maps by issuing a one-page flyer about the program and distributing it to banks, insurance companies, savings-and-loan intsitutions, and real-estate groups. With this flyer was sent material prepared by NIMAPC, describing the first six quadrangles to be mapped, a schedule of the entire mapping program, and a map showing the quadrangles involved. At the State League office, a large map showing the 44 quadrangles superimposed on the six-county metropolitan area was mounted and made available to anyone who wished to study it.

What Does It All Mean?

Both the State League and the ad-hoc committee of the 51 local Leagues pointed out that these flood plains need not be left as useless waste areas. Towns could use them for recreational purposes, for parks, for agriculture, or for forest preserves. If a few swings or a park pavilion were damaged by floods every few years, the loss would be slight.

The Leagues also emphasized that the cost of this mapping service was minute compared to costs of expensive flood-control projects that would be demanded by property owners located in the hazard zones. However, the maps were not to be construed as a substitute for such projects. Where the low-lying lands were already built up, protection from floods would, of course, be needed. For future planning, however, such expense could be avoided if the flood plains were left more or less in their natural state.

This mapping would in no way curtail citizen decisions at the local level, the Leagues pointed out. It was to be a planning tool for counties and municipalities to use as they saw fit and as their citizens might determine. The mapping, to be completed in 1965 or 1966, would be, they emphasized, a step toward rational planning.

Six-County Agreement

Officials in five of the six counties quickly saw the advantages and appropriated the necessary funds for the mapping program. In Will County, however, an extra effort was necessary. The Joliet League again made individual contacts with members of the County Board, corresponded with the chairman, and sent letters to the editor expressing concern over the need for the mapping. Finally in January, 1962, the Will County Board approved the plan and agreed to pay its share of the cost.

Originally, 44 quads were to be mapped. That figure has now been increased to 63, and 39 are already complete and available. Twenty-seven have been published. Several corporations have asked for a complete set, and both the Veteran's Administration and the Federal Housing Authority are requiring that location in relation to the flood plain be specified in applications for mortgages. County maps in both Cook County and Lake County now include flood-plain information. The flood-hazard mapping program is proving so useful, in fact, that area planners wonder how they ever worked without it.

In those areas where the mapping is completed, League members are encouraging their zoning boards to translate what can be learned from the maps into realistic zoning ordinances for the flood plains. Highland Park, Wheeling, Harvey, Calumet City, Homewood, and Flossmoor already have such zoning ordinances, and Park Forest is developing one.

Flood-plain mapping is coming to be accepted not only in the Chicago area but in numerous localities all across the country. Officials will need civic support, however, if the maps are to be translated into actual flood-plain protection.

CHAPTER 4

The Problems of Planning

SOME TOWNS are refusing to allot money for small watershed projects because their officials and citizens fail to see the need for planning ahead. Other cities and counties give official approval to a regional plan but allow a type of zoning that grossly violates it. Citizen groups need to be vigilant and persistent in their efforts, first to secure a comprehensive long-range plan, and then to see that it is used as a basis for action and that its guidelines are enforced.

When a community tries to meet its particular water problem without benefit of a general plan for the area, solutions will be stopgap, at best. The type of planning that takes place and the efficiency with which it is administered and enforced can mean the difference between long-range success and irretrievable error. These two interrelated factors—planning and administration—are the core of effective water and land development and conservation.

Comprehensiveness Is Essential

A good plan is comprehensive, not fragmented. It is broad-based and has several aspects. One of the most important is the regional concept. Many new water projects can be more effective and more economical in the long run when planned as an integral part of a larger basin plan or regional plan. River-basin planning is examined at length in Part II of this book.

Comprehensive planning also includes coordination, within any one area, of all sectors of development. To provide water for irrigation of a crop already overproduced cannot benefit the region. To encourage new industry without demanding adequate waste treatment in new plants is folly. Coordinating all projects into a unified plan for the area can help to avoid such errors.

The making of a good plan depends on the cooperative effort of a number of agencies. Is the present governmental machinery at local, state, and federal levels adequate to the task of regional and comprehensive planning? Once a plan is adopted, will the several agencies involved cooperate with one another when implementation begins?

The inquiring citizen is usually surprised to find that within the federal government alone there are more than 40 different departments, offices, and commissions with varying degrees of responsibility within the water-resources field. (See Appendix A.) Happily, the trend is now toward a more reasonable distribution of responsibility and a closer coordination among federal agencies through the Water Resources Council, created in 1965.

At the state and local level, there are hundreds of other agencies, some clinging to outmoded habits, others ineffectual through no fault of their own. Overlapping or conflicting programs, inadequately staffed and financed agencies, and weak enforcement authority hamper efforts of even the most dedicated officials to accomplish the jobs for which they have responsibility. As a result, water resources are often wasted, the citizens' needs are not met, and their taxes fail to buy what they expect. If legislation aimed at improving coordination sounds dull or unimportant, its objectives are not.

Many urban and suburban communities have undertaken some form of planning. Future water supply, sewers, sewage-treatment facilities, and flood-control projects are now being considered—along with streets, lot sizes, and school sites—as part of most local plans. The press of population growth and its high concentration in metropolitan areas are forcing officials to take long-range planning seriously. Governing bodies can be encouraged to consider the best long-range use of whatever land may still be available, giving as much attention to stream protection, waterfront renewal, and public recreational needs as to attracting new industry or shopping centers. The interrelationship between land use and water is obvious.

Providing for the recreational use of water is a necessary part of any good, long-range development program.
(U.S. DEPARTMENT OF AGRICULTURE PHOTO)

Patterns of Planning

Total metropolitan planning has as its goal the planning for all needs of an area bound by economic, social, and physical ties, even though encompassing numerous political jurisdictions. This total planning would simultaneously consider highways, mass transit, water supply, a sewerage system, treatment plants, parks, police and fire protection, hospitals and other services—all on a metropolitan basis.

Another type of planning still favored in many places is the regional handling of one service only. For example, Seattle (see Chapter 2) has been able to agree on a metropolitan basis for sewage disposal alone, although legislation permits the same kind of structure to function for transit, garbage collection, and police and fire protection. To date, the more inclusive possibilities have been felt to be politically unfeasible in Seattle.

Cooperation between towns and cities on a regional basis, whether for total planning or single-purpose planning, usually calls for new administrative machinery. President Johnson said in his State of the Union Message January 4, 1965: "The first step is to break old patterns—to begin to think and work and plan for the development of entire metropolitan areas. . . ."

Breaking old patterns is never easy and not always wise, but citizen groups that study the feasibility of metropolitan planning, look into its ramifications, publicize the pros and cons, and suggest alternative choices to be considered by officials and the public fill a vital role in the governmental process. To stimulate regional thinking takes long and continuing effort, but encouraging different local jurisdictions to come together and face regional problems openly is a valuable first step.

The following case history shows this mechanism at work to meet communal problems along the Huron River.

WATERSHED ROUNDUP

(ANN ARBOR, MICHIGAN)

The Huron River is relatively small, flowing for 125 miles through 40 political jurisdictions on the western and southern outskirts of metropolitan Detroit on its way to Lake Erie.

In 1956, when Ypsilanti, Ypsilanti Township, and Belleville submitted separate requests to build greatly expanded sewage-treatment facilities that would discharge into the lower Huron, the State Health Department denied them permits. The river could carry absolutely no more sewage effluent, even if treated, and still remain usable for water supply and recreation. Hit-or-miss development was not the answer. Until localities got together and presented an area-wide, orderly plan for the river, Health Department authorities would be obliged to veto all individual projects, they declared. "The essential problem," the Department pointed out, "is to bring about the most appropriate and compatible intercommunity uses of the river." Construction of sewers for new homes and industry would have to be postponed until the region could agree upon a joint, comprehensive plan for river use.

This mandate for regional cooperation came just as the Ann Arbor League of Women Voters had started its study of national water problems. Members were already aware of the importance—in theory, at least—of watershed planning. The possible application of that theory right at their own doorstep stimulated them to learn all they could about both water-resources planning in general and the need for specific planning on the Huron.

Cooperation on a Broad Basis

After two years of broad study, the League welcomed the formation of the Huron River Watershed Intergovernmental Committee (HRWIC), in 1958. This committee, made up of representatives from 32 counties, townships, cities, and villages in the watershed, had no authority for operational or management functions. It could only study and advise, but it has, nevertheless, been instrumental in developing a workable policy for cooperation.

First, the HRWIC set about to collect the facts. It helped to finance a ground-water study by the Geology Department of the University of Michigan. It also asked the U.S. Soil Conservation Service to assist in making a survey of the relative future importance of agriculture to the basin's economy, including needs for irrigation. These studies supplemented the basic data contained in a report on the Huron River Basin issued by the Water Resources Commission of Michigan in 1957.

To handle the specific crisis of waste disposal in the lower Huron, members of HRWIC who represented the 10 cities and townships from Ann Arbor to Flatrock formed a Lower Huron Subcommittee, which hired engineering consultants to study prospective demands upon the river and alternative ways of meeting them. The engineers compared the costs of separate treatment plants for each community to the cost of building an interceptor sewer to divert municipal wastes to Lake Erie. They found the former method half as expensive, but under either alternative it was clear that more water somehow had to be added to the Huron. The engineers recommended construction of two small storage reservoirs to augment stream flow in drought years and assure enough water in the river at all times to dilute sewage effluent or, in the case of diversion, to prevent a dry streambed.

Civic Support Required

The Ann Arbor LWV has used several approaches to explain the functions of HRWIC and the need for inter-community planning throughout the watershed. It has sent a representative to every meeting of the HRWIC since the latter's inception. It conducted personal inspection trips for members to both the upper and lower watershed. It inspected the city's water-purification plant and sewage-treatment plant. Along with the Ypsilanti League, members went to Lansing for interviews with Health Department officials. The Ann Arbor League helped plan an all-day session for public-school teachers to inform them of the river's problems and potential.

When a Water Use Policy and Development Program for the Huron was proposed, civic groups studied it and then helped to publicize it. The League organized study units, held general meetings, and conducted a public tour of the upper watershed to inspect proposed reservoir sites. By asking questions of candidates for office and by writing letters to the editor, members helped to keep the importance of the plan before the public. As a corollary measure, members also strongly supported the proposed city purchase of nearby Detroit Edison properties (four dams, ponds, and adjacent lands no longer used for hydroelectric power) in order to facilitate river management and to preserve the scenic and recreational values of the river.

Provisions of the Plan

The Water Use Policy for the Huron distinguishes between suitable upstream uses (water supply and swimming) and suitable downstream uses (transport of treated wastes). It calls for management of all existing and planned impoundments for augmentation of stream flow as well as constant testing of water samples for quality control. Multiple-purpose development, including recreation, irrigation, flood control, and lake-level stabilization, is recommended wherever feasible.

When this Policy and Development Program was formally adopted by the HRWIC, in late 1960, the State Health Department agreed to grant the long-delayed permits for expansion of sewage-treatment facilities. Indirect results may be more far-reaching. For example, two decisions by Ann Arbor's City Council were no doubt influenced by the prospect of river management and low-flow augmentation. The Council voted to purchase the Detroit Edison properties and decided to depend on the Huron River for expanded water supplies rather than tap into Detroit's water system.

New Plans Necessitate New Groupings

After the plan was accepted, steps were taken to implement it administratively. The HRWIC, with the assistance of the Institute of Public Administration and the Department of Conservation of the University of Michigan, developed a proposal in November, 1962, that called for creation of two distinct but interrelated agencies, a Watershed Conservancy Council and a River Management District, each to be composed of representatives from the counties and incorporated municipalities.

To form such agencies, especially the River Management District, which would have the powers and responsibilities of a public corporation, new state enabling legislation was necessary. Several interested civic groups, including the State Board of the LWV, actively supported such an act, and in May, 1964, a bill to enable local units to cooperate in water management was signed into law. Accordingly, the Huron River Watershed Council was organized, in June, 1965. Replacing the HRWIC, it will carry on similar functions and may, if it so decides, organize a River Management District.

Some citizens are concerned that water from the two new storage reservoirs will not, in the long run, be sufficient to dilute adequately the increasing municipal wastes. Already the Corps of Engineers is studying the feasibility of a dam and large reservoir at Mill Creek, a tributary that joins the Huron 10 miles upstream from Ann Arbor. Although flood control must be its primary purpose, accompanying studies by the U.S. Public Health Service conclude that water from the proposed reservoir should be added to the Huron River during drought periods to improve water quality by increasing river flow. Provision for storage would thus be necessary.

Since the Corps cannot determine whether this Mill Creek project is economically justified until all costs are estimated, it will not present specific recommendations to local communities until the spring of 1967 or later. However, residents in the Mill Creek area have already formed a Mill Creek Research Council, after having seen a preliminary map of the proposed reservoir site.

A battle may be ahead, and civic groups in the whole watershed will need to get the facts and face alternatives objectively. Other areas in the same predicament, but without any suitable sites left for storage reservoirs, are looking into the feasibility of requiring secondary, or even tertiary, treatment by all municipal plants. New techniques of treatment are being researched at university centers and within industry that may offer some alternative to stream-flow augmentation. At any rate, the Huron River Watershed Council should serve as a useful forum for the expression of various interests within the watershed.

ARE STATE REFORMS NEEDED?

At the state level as well, citizen groups can find opportunities to work toward the joint goals of comprehensive planning and coordinated administration. More and more states are becoming interested in developing comprehensive water plans to ensure that future demands will be met.

Encouraging the states to take a more active role in water-resources planning is the objective of a number of federal programs. (See Chapter 8.) The Water Pollution Control Act, as amended in 1965, offers funds for states to plan state-wide anti-pollution programs. The Land and Water Conservation Fund Act of 1965 encourages the states to take a key role in developing a balanced outdoor recreation program. The Water Resources Research Act, signed in July, 1964, enables each state to set up water-research facilities. The Water Resources Planning Act of 1965 offers grants to assist states to develop comprehensive water and related land-resources plans.

To benefit from these federal programs, to work cooperatively with federal agencies, and to handle growing internal problems, many states need to reexamine their own administrative machinery. Can it handle its new responsibilities? Is authority for decision and enforcement clearly defined? Are water agencies adequately staffed and financed? These are questions that interested citizen groups can study and answer for themselves, and then work for the needed improvements through their state legislatures.

Leagues in Wisconsin, for example, testified in 1960 for a bill that would create a Division of Water Resources to coordinate the work of 14 different state agencies with that of various federal and local departments involved in water-use administration within Wisconsin. The proposed bill did not pass. The LWV also testified in 1963 before the State Senate Agriculture Committee for a bill to control abuse of ground water supplies. It, too, died in committee. "Special interest groups come to these hearings in Madison by the busload," remarked a League member at the time, "and we simply need more civic organizations to help us out." Considerable progress has been noted in more recent years, but a general campaign to publicize the urgency of long-range planning and coordination is still needed in Wisconsin, as in most other states. To help get basic facts to the public, the Wisconsin League has recently compiled a booklet entitled "Conservation '66."

Maryland Leaguers had an easier time of it in 1964, when they testified for four bills dealing with reorganization and planning matters in the water resources field. All four passed. Other state Leagues that have supported consolidation of state agencies are Georgia, Idaho, and Colorado.

THE FEDERAL ROLE

The problems of coordination and wise planning are enormous at the federal level of government, sometimes because of bureaucratic entanglements but usually because of the sheer size of federal projects and programs.

Federally built dams, for example, often affect several states bordering on the same river. They are huge and permanent structures which alter the face of a region for all time. For these reasons, any dam proposal generates heated discussion. Special interests, such as the steel and cement lobbies, press their own points of view. Experts talk in technical terms. Congressmen cast a calculating political eye on the plans and act accordingly. Citizen groups will be put to a severe test of objectivity in their effort to determine whether a dam's technical, economic, and social impact is compatible with hoped-for future development of the area.

Some specific questions will come immediately to mind. Who does the planning for federal dams? Are different points of view permitted in the early stages? Are alternative dam sites properly weighed? Are solutions other than dams given full consideration? Do citizens and local planning groups have a chance to present their thinking before a finished plan is presented to them on a take-it-or-leave-it basis? These questions are all legitimate, but they do add to the complications of planning for large federal dams.

A Question of Values

Some of the loudest objections to large dams have come from the numerous conservation groups in the country. They tend to object to tampering with nature's land-and-water pattern. They often don't like the idea of huge concrete structures on our rivers. They fear that wildlife areas and natural recreational zones will be lost to housing developments, factories, and highways, which, without proper planning, may be encouraged by the presence of large dams.

The continuing controversy between conservationists and water-project developers is illustrated by the opposition of such groups as the Sierra Club and the Wildlife Management Institute to the Department of the Interior's plans to build new dams on the lower Colorado River. The Interior Department claims that its proposed dam at Bridge Canyon must be built high enough to generate hydroelectric power, which, in turn, will pay for building large aqueducts and pumping facilities to bring needed water to central Arizona. Cleaner lakes, more revenues from tourism, and new funds for conservation of fish and wildlife are also promised in this huge

One of California's major reservoirs spreads through rugged country behind Mt. Shasta Dam.

Southwest water plan. However, conservationists object. Such a large dam will destroy major scenic resources, they argue, and new reservoirs will only add to the amount of water that will evaporate. They ask whether other methods of financing the Southwest diversion project have been thoroughly researched. Some are even asking why U.S. taxpayers should, in effect, subsidize agricultural expansion of an area that is unsuited, because of water shortage, for such development.

At present, Congressmen and Senators are working to obtain increasingly larger water projects for their states, chiefly to attract industry. But does this make sense from a national point of view? Conservationists are looking for alternative choices in the hope of protecting natural wilderness areas and streams that flow through them from the smog and pollution that come with high-density development.

What's Best for the Potomac?

For the past several years the U.S. Army Corps of Engineers, under authorization from Congress, has been making a comprehensive study of the Potomac River. The study has grown, like Topsy, into a proposed plan, made public in 1964. The difficulties this proposal has run into show that wise planning involves more than technical know-how.

In addition to 16 large dams, the Corps proposal includes 418 smaller upstream structures, planned by the Department of Agriculture at the invitation of the Corps. The overall proposal includes in its list of benefits: pollution abatement, flood control, water supply, and recreational uses. The plan is multi-purpose. It includes upstream as well as downstream planning, and though it is, without question, a one-agency plan, other departments of the federal government were asked to participate. The Corps held public hearings, as required by law, and gave the governors of all involved states three months to add their comments to the finished report. Nonetheless, the plan has taken many groups by surprise. Discussion of the pros and cons is lively.

Interested public and private organizations, as well as some newspaper editors, are asking if such a huge undertaking is really necessary. Are 16 dams the only answer to the many problems in the Potomac basin? They want to know about possible alternatives be-

Conservationists are frequently in conflict with developers to preserve idyllic natural areas like this.

fore backing the proposal. They ask, for example, whether the Seneca Dam, scheduled for 1977, might be omitted from the general plan without seriously limiting provision for future needs. They ask if other methods of handling pollution in the Potomac Estuary have been thoroughly studied. They wonder if flood-plain zoning might be a practical alternative to that part of the dam project devoted to flood control. Had such questions been discussed prior to announcement of the finished plan, it has been suggested, time might have been saved and bitterness avoided. Conservationists are aroused because the Seneca Dam reservoir will flood part of the historic Ohio Canal towpath and, according to these groups, will destroy the natural beauty of the Potomac and its shoreline. Residents of Loudoun County, Virginia, are not enthusiastic about giving up land for a reservoir, or about having their peaceful, rural area turned into a public recreation zone for city dwellers.

Some local planning groups are supporting the entire project. Others want to support some of the dams without having to support all of them. Still others have urged that Congressional appropriations be postponed until more studies can be made, but that the proposed sites be reserved now to prevent the inevitable rise in cost of land acquisition.

No one suggests that nothing at all be done. It is the "how it shall be done" that needs to be thrashed out among technicians, officials, and the people of the area. Informed citizens will necessarily have to carry the burden of conciliation. The hands of the clock cannot be turned backward. Some water-development programs are required. On the other hand, engineering feasibility should not be the only factor considered when a plan is finally selected.

President Johnson has taken a lively interest in future plans for the Potomac. In his Conservation Message to Congress on February 8, 1965, he asked that the Basin become a "model of scenic and recreation values for the entire country." He has also instructed the Department of the Interior to review the Corps plan to be sure that it encompasses the total needs of the people of the area. What the outcome will be cannot at this date be foreseen, but perhaps the opening up of fresh opportunities for expression of public thinking and for preparation of alternative proposals will be worth the delay. The Conservation Foundation, located in Washington, D.C., is conducting a lively series of community workshops throughout the

Potomac Basin, hoping to stimulate civic leaders to see all points of view and to express their wishes on an informed basis.

Birth of the Planning Act

With the passage of the Water Resources Planning Act of 1965, potential machinery is now available for better coordination among federal agencies and for comprehensive joint planning for water and related land resources in a river basin. States will be able to play a larger role than formerly in early planning proposals and decisions affecting their area.

Getting this Planning Act passed has taken several years of legislative effort, executive push, and civic-group support. Chief impetus toward recognition of the need for a national water policy and better coordination and regional planning came from the 1959-61 studies made by the Senate Select Committee on National Water Resources. A Resources and Conservation Act was proposed in the Senate in 1960 and again in 1961. The League gave supporting testimony each time, urging a coordination of federal efforts and establishment of priorities. This bill took an imaginative new approach to coordination and planning by proposing a Council of Natural Resource Advisors, similar to the Council of Economic Advisors. Nonetheless, the bill died in committee.

When the Kennedy Administration came into office, it proposed the Water Resources Planning Act of 1961 to implement the recommendations of the Senate Select Committee's report. The Administration gave the bill strong support, so did the AFL-CIO, the National Association of Soil Conservation Districts, and the League of Women Voters.

Several organizations testified against the proposed legislation, however, chiefly on the grounds that it might increase powers of the executive department and did not give a large enough voice to the states. Some of the groups which opposed the bill were the National Association of Manufacturers, the Chamber of Commerce of the United States, the American Farm Bureau Federation, and the National Lumber Manufacturers Association. The Water Resources Planning Act of 1961 advanced no further than the hearing.

In 1963-64 came another strong campaign for a revised planning act which would set up a Water Resources Council, provide for federal-state river basin commissions to carry out coordinated, multi-purpose planning for basin development, and offer financial aid to states for comprehensive water-resource planning.

When it became obvious that this bill was "stuck" in the Irrigation and Reclamation Subcommittee of the House Committee on Interior and Insular Affairs, Leagues all over the country put on a letter-writing drive to help get the bill released. It was finally given House Committee approval in September, 1964, but in the last flurry of Congressional activity prior to adjournment, a rule to bring the bill to the floor for a vote did not materialize.

So another water resources planning bill died. But the momentum behind it was by no means dead. Essentially the same bill was introduced in both the Senate and the House during the first week of the 89th Congress and was passed in April, 1965.

Title I sets up a Water Resources Council composed of the Secretaries of Army, Interior, HEW, and Agriculture, and the Chairman of the Federal Power Commission. These leading water-agency heads, or their substitutes, are to carry on continuing study of ways to coordinate water and related land programs and policies of the federal agencies. They are to report their recommendations to the President. To bring agencies into line, the Council is given the power, with Presidential approval, to establish principles, standards, and procedures for federal participants in comprehensive river-basin planning, and for formulation and evaluation of federal water projects.

Title II authorizes creation of river-basin commissions where one-half of the states in the basin and the Water Resources Council concur, in writing, to their formation. Each such commission for a river basin or region is to be the principal agency for coordinating federal, state, interstate, and local plans for development of water and related land resources in its territory. Each basin commission is to prepare a comprehensive, coordinated, joint plan and to recommend long-range schedules of priorities for collection of basic data, for planning, and for construction of projects. The first such commission under this new act is the New England River Basins Commission. Several others are in the planning stage.

Title III offers the individual states, through matching funds, a new opportunity to upgrade their planning for water-resource development and prepare themselves to take a more important part in planning for interstate and regional development.

PART II

Broad Strategy

CHAPTER 5

Basin Planning: Concepts

with Wide Horizons

A RIVER BASIN consists of all the territory drained by a principal stream and its network of tributaries. It almost never conforms to convenient political boundaries. The Columbia River, for example, dominates four states, as well as part of Canada. The Ohio influences the life of six states. Great rivers such as these, and many far smaller, demand some sort of regional planning by the people in their contiguous areas. In each case, the river basin itself, not state borders, determines which regions can beneficially join to use, protect, allot, and enjoy what is often their most valuable common economic asset.

River-basin planning is a matter of investigating area needs and determining how best to satisfy those needs through development of water resources and related land resources. Basin planning involves irrigation, flood control, navigation, hydroelectric power, municipal and industrial water supply, pollution control, recreation and conservation of natural areas, fish, and wildlife.

Many regions of the United States will have to make crucial plans regarding the future management of their water resources within the next 10 or 15 years. These choices will set the pattern for generations to come. Thinking and planning in terms of river basins will be new to some areas. In others, such as the densely crowded New York-New Jersey zone, sharing among adjacent river basins has already had to be adopted. There, emergency conditions have forced a service-area concept to supplant a basin concept. The ambitious Texas State Water Plan proposes interbasin transfer,

117

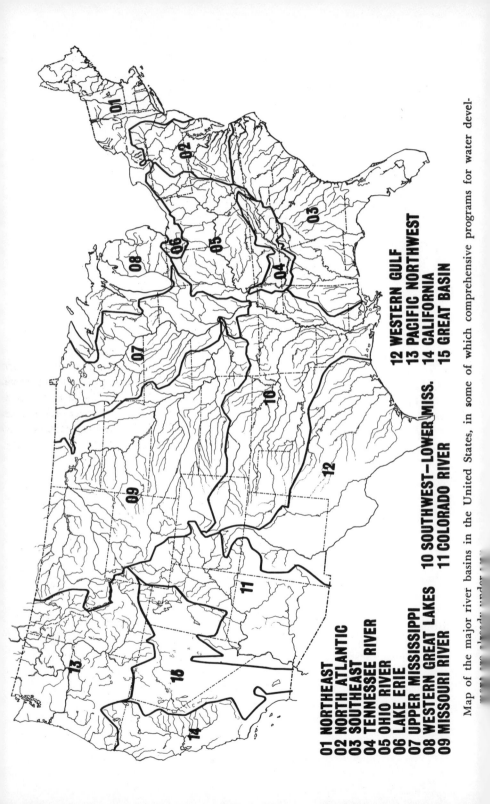

01 NORTHEAST
02 NORTH ATLANTIC
03 SOUTHEAST
04 TENNESSEE RIVER
05 OHIO RIVER
06 LAKE ERIE
07 UPPER MISSISSIPPI
08 WESTERN GREAT LAKES
09 MISSOURI RIVER

10 SOUTHWEST–LOWER MISS.
11 COLORADO RIVER

12 WESTERN GULF
13 PACIFIC NORTHWEST
14 CALIFORNIA
15 GREAT BASIN

Map of the major river basins in the United States, in some of which comprehensive programs for water devel-

through aqueducts and riverbeds, from the water-plentiful north-eastern part of the state to new storage locations in some of the drier parts of Texas. In the far western states, water diversion is in operation in some areas, hotly debated in others, championed as an inevitable trend in still others.

This does not mean that planning on a river basin basis is no longer valid. It does mean, however, that dealing with the realities of population growth and industrial expansion will henceforth require a thoughtful consideration of the full geographic potential of each river and the larger needs of all people in its general vicinity, no matter in which political jurisdiction or in which specific basin they live.

The most striking and comprehensive river-basin planning and development in the United States, if not in the world, has been done by the Tennessee Valley Authority. Created by Congress in 1933, the TVA was empowered to develop transportation, electric power, and flood control throughout the entire Tennessee River basin, an area of approximately 41,000 square miles. It includes parts of Tennessee, Alabama, Mississippi, Georgia, Kentucky, North Carolina, and Virginia. In 1933, it was largely undeveloped, though it now has a population of around 3 million persons and many important industries. The TVA has built 31 dams and reservoirs in its river basin, and created a huge electric-power capacity. It has provided a 627-mile navigation channel. In addition to dominating the area's economic life, the TVA has been active in land conservation, tree planting, and malaria control. It has helped improve fisheries, recreation facilities, wildlife, and mineral resources.

Although the Tennessee Valley Authority has become a model for underdeveloped countries around the world, this type of agency has not proved to be politically acceptable in other areas of the United States. One reason for this is that rivers like the Connecticut and the Missouri, for which valley authorities have been proposed, are already highly developed, with established administrative agencies.

Several other forms of basin organization are in use. An inter-agency basin committee was tried in the Columbia Basin. An inter-state-federal commission has been established for the Delaware. An interstate compact commission has helped to improve pollution control on the Ohio. U.S. study commissions have made comprehensive plans for rivers in the southeastern United States and in Texas. In some instances, a single federal agency, usually the U.S. Army Corps of Engineers, has been authorized to make a comprehensive basin plan with the cooperation of other federal agencies and the states involved. Federal-state commissions, under the Water Resources Planning Act, 1965, are the latest type of organization for planning in the major river basins. The organizational structure and responsibilities of these agencies differ to fit the specific needs and political attitudes of each area, but the principle of basin planning is common to all of them.

Regional organization and planning alone are not enough, important as they are. Even the best plans must still revert for final decision to the traditional governing bodies—Congress, state legislatures, and local councils. Pressures of political expediency and private interest will inevitably be exerted, so the key to transferring broad-based plans into action is the work of informed citizens. If civic groups have been in on the planning from the beginning, have understood the problems, the possible alternatives, the necessary compromises, and the recommendations of the regional planning agency, they will be better able to help in securing the voter's necessary approval.

To promote river-basin planning and development, citizen groups will find that they, too, can be more effective if they set up regional contacts within their own organizations and with interested citizens outside those organizations. Cooperation along the same river-basin or service-area lines on which governmental agencies are coordinated will strengthen the citizen's ability to help shape the important choices that must be made.

The League of Women Voters found that it could not make even an intelligent start on studying a river without first creating inter-League working committees, for Leagues were ineffective when limited to local or state boundaries. Working through committees created for the purpose, with members from other communities and often from other states, with people of different interests and with conflicting demands on a common water resource—working together to study the needs of a whole basin proved most enlightening and laid the foundation for informed regional action.

To assist local Leagues and inter-League committees in this nationwide research project, the national League office in 1958 pub-

Fontana Dam, 480 feet, is the highest dam in the TVA system. (TENNESSEE VALLEY AUTHORITY PHOTO)

lished a small pamphlet, "Know Your River Basin." It asked such questions as: What are the characteristics of your river basin? What are the water-use and control programs? What is the administrative organization in your river basin? What are the major conflicts among uses? What are the major problems of allocating benefits, responsibilities, and costs? What is the future of your basin? A companion piece, "How to Do a 'Know Your River Basin' Study," was also offered, indicating how to set up a committee for the purpose and where to find the answers to pertinent questions.

Subsequent League studies resulted in scores of valuable river-basin surveys. One of the most interesting, thought it covers only a very small geographical area, is largely reprinted as Chapter 6 of this book. Other notable studies include those made by League members throughout California, in the Delaware Basin, the Ohio River Basin, the Lake Erie Basin, and the Columbia Basin.

In California, no single river basin but plans of unprecedented scope and cost for developing the entire state's water resources became the target of coordinated research by the 56 California Leagues, beginning in 1958. As a starter, in order to minimize regional differences, northern and southern Leagues of comparable size and in similar communities paired up and proceeded to exchange clippings from local newspapers relating to water problems and proposed solutions. This technique was surprisingly effective in developing a state-wide impartial approach.

League members also drew facts and formulated opinions from studying official reports of the California Department of Water Resources, critical evaluations by the Water Resource Center at Berkeley and by the Stanford Research Institute, and the records of Legislative and Congressional hearings. The League's State Water Committee organized interviews for local Leagues with 24 water experts throughout the state. At League meetings, members thrashed out such complicated considerations as acreage limitation, sale of power, type of agency to handle planning and construction, state regulation of underground pumping, financial methods, and political climate.

In 1959, the California Legislature at last agreed on a master water plan for the state, and the Leagues published an attractive 25-page booklet, called "Water Lines," to help inform the state's voters of details of the plan and the reasons for it. At issue was the

"Lake Erie: Requiem or Reprieve?" asks the Inter-League Basin Committee in its recently published survey.

fate of a $1.75 billion bond issue needed to finance the vast project, which included creating a "manmade river" to carry surplus water hundreds of miles from northern parts of California to its semi-arid southern regions. The bond issue was to be voted on in the election of November, 1960.

"Water Lines" was hailed by authorities as having been carefully researched and for approaching the issues "in a broad, factual, and unbiased manner." It helped importantly to prepare voters to make informed judgments. In November, 1960, the huge bond issue easily passed, and California's master plan for developing its water resources is now well on the way to fruition.

Another influential League document, which helped to forge an effective instrument for intelligent, cooperative control of water resources in a heavily populated four-state region of the East, was "Man and the River." This 54-page booklet, describing both the urgent water problems of the Delaware River Basin and the earnest search for their solutions, was also produced in 1959. It was the work of an Inter-League Council set up by the Delaware, New Jersey, New York, and Pennsylvania LWVs. Its publication, reinforced by members' public speeches, letters, and phone calls, was helpful in bringing about the creation of the Delaware River Basin Commission, two years later. This unique arrangement makes the Federal Government an equal partner with the four states concerned and insures that all major water-resources activities within the basin will henceforth be under control of one overall authority.

As the Leagues of four Eastern states joined forces in 1959 to produce an informative study of common water problems and potential solutions to them, so did the Leagues of Idaho, Montana, Oregon, and Washington. They, too, formed an Inter-League Committee to do the job. The result, published in November, 1959, was a 32-page brochure titled "The Great River of the West." It pertained to the Columbia River Basin. While no grand design for handling the complicated decisions of water-resources development in the Pacific Northwest has yet emerged, many encouraging cooperative actions, including enhanced effectiveness of the Columbia Basin Inter-Agency Committee, have taken place since "The Great River of the West" was issued. The booklet has been credited with providing "a critical and highly competent overview of the major programs and issues involved in managing and developing the region's most important resources."

A comparable effort, by the Inter-League Survey Committee of the Leagues of New York, Pennsylvania, West Virginia, Ohio, Kentucky, and Indiana, resulted in the publication in 1964 of a handsome and impressive 52-page study of "The Ohio River Basin." Though it commends the anti-pollution accomplishments of the eight-state Ohio River Valley Water Sanitation Compact, signed in 1948, the booklet points out that those accomplishments "do not leave room for complacency." It concludes with this cogent reminder:

"With increasing urgency, citizens within the Basin will face many choices of programs and legislation offering solutions to their water-resource problems. Each choice will require looking beyond one's local area or state. We must consider the goals to be achieved and the best way to resolve conflicts of interest. The citizen will have to realize that solutions will depend on his efforts as well as those of government agencies."

CHAPTER 6

On the Edge of a Big City

THE SUDBURY, Assabet, Concord (SuAsCo) River Basin, in eastern Massachusetts, is a small one—charming but full of problems. It lies just west of State Route 128, the circumferential highway around Boston, on the edge of crowded suburbs. Many of the towns in the basin have doubled in population during the last 10 years, and continue to mushroom at the same rate. Major highways and industrial growth have added to the pressures on these communities. Their problems are typical of those that occur on the frontal edge of any expanding metropolitan region.

The area has great natural beauty, due in large measure to its three small rivers, its ponds, and related wetlands. In a few of the 36 communities in the Basin, strong leadership has developed for preserving these natural assets.

A significant conservation program is now under way in the SuAsCo Basin. It is a particularly interesting example of coordinated efforts in a rapidly growing suburban and rural area to preserve sections of natural beauty and conservation significance.

This program did not develop without great effort, however, including hard work by the Basin's 14 Leagues of Women Voters. One of their most effective contributions to the program consisted of producing and distributing the following "Sudbury-Assabet-Concord River Basin Study." It was published in December, 1963, by the LWV Education Fund, under a grant from Carling Brewing Company, a local industry. The study is reproduced here substantially as it originally appeared.

INTRODUCTION

This study seeks to increase public knowledge and understanding about one of our most vital resources—water. It deals with water resources problems and possibilities within the SuAsCo River Basin. This Basin, or drainage area, of the Sudbury, Assabet and Concord Rivers forms a logical planning unit for the orderly use of water and related land resources.

Usually when we think of a river basin, such rivers as the Columbia, the Tennessee, the Missouri, and the Colorado come to mind— mighty, roaring rivers on which many regions and states depend for their economic health. The rivers of the SuAsCo region are peaceful and whispering by comparison, and yet in many ways they wind in and out of our lives with equal importance.

The values of our rivers and related lands for water supply, conservation of natural resources, recreation, fish and wildlife habitat, nature education, and aesthetic purposes may be hard to assess in terms of dollars and cents, but they are enormous. And the losses that have come from high and low flows, inadequate pollution control, and poor land treatment provide an equally pressing reason for the wise management of these rivers.

The natural scenic beauty of the SuAsCo River Basin makes it a highly desirable residential area. Much of this beauty can be retained in spite of the fact that the rural aspects of the region are disappearing with changing economic conditions and spreading urbanization.

The region is near the urban centers of Boston, Worcester, and Lowell. Many of the 36 municipalities that are wholly or partly within the Basin are facing new problems due to a growing population and expanding industries and highways. Some of the old problems have become more complex.

The water-related problems that will be reviewed in this study are water supply, water pollution, flood control and land treatment, wetlands preservation, recreation and fish and wildlife programs, and open-space planning. These problems are interrelated. They involve water, land, and people. They are regional problems. No panaceas are offered, but useful tools and guidelines may be found.

This river-basin study is not an exhaustive analysis. It seeks to avoid duplicating any special studies that are readily available,

but, rather, tries to bring together in one place as much basic material as possible.

The SuAsCo River Basin Group of the League of Women Voters has prepared this booklet as an outgrowth of its study of water problems in this region from 1961-1963. This Group is composed of 14 Leagues in the region: Acton, Bedford, Billerica, Concord, Chelmsford, Framingham, Harvard, Lincoln, Lowell, Natick, Sudbury, Tewksbury, Wayland, and Weston.

The solution to many of the outstanding problems in our Basin will require the combined efforts of citizens and officials at all levels. It is the hope of the SuAsCo River Basin Group that this publication will be useful to the general public interested in knowing more about the resources of the area in which they live; schools and libraries which want to study or disseminate local conservation information; local officials and bodies, both public and private, concerned with conservation planning and action; and other government officials representing state, federal, and regional agencies working on specific projects in this Basin.

GENERAL BACKGROUND

The SuAsCo River Basin, or SuAsCo Watershed, includes a total of 405 square miles, within which lie all or part of 34 towns and two cities in Middlesex and Worcester Counties, in the northeast portion of central Massachusetts. It has an overall length of approximately 36 land miles. The watershed is a sub-basin of the larger Merrimack River Basin, which is part of the New England River Basins, one of 22 such major basins in the United States.

The Sudbury River, 36 miles in length, with a drainage area of 165 square miles, rises in Cedar Swamp in Westborough. It flows easterly, then northerly, to Concord, passing through the towns of Southborough, Hopkinton, Ashland, Framingham, Wayland, Sudbury, Lincoln, and Concord. There are 20 branches and eight upstream reservoirs, all of which are part of its system.

The Assabet River has its headwaters in a swamp east of the Grafton State Hospital, also in Westborough. It has a total watershed area of 176 square miles, and its length is 31½ miles, with 14 branches. Flowing in a northerly and northeasterly direction, it cuts through Berlin, Northborough, Marlborough, Hudson, Stow, Acton, Maynard, and Concord.

At the confluence of the Sudbury and Assabet Rivers in Concord, the Concord River is formed. This continues the northerly route for 16 miles through Bedford, Carlisle, Billerica, Chelmsford, and Lowell, where it joins the Merrimack River. The Concord River and its 13 branches have a total drainage area of 64 square miles.

Glacial Carvings

The rivers and their valleys owe their present appearance to glacial activity. The landscape was carved by a large glacier at the end of the Ice Age, 10,000 to 15,000 years ago. The ice advanced and retreated in this part of the world for about one million years before that time. There was a general withdrawal of the ice sheet from south to north, with zones of stagnation. The retreating ice left ledges and obstructions to free flow, causing the winding paths of our rivers.

Several extinct glacial lakes were present in our Basin, the largest of which, Glacial Lake, Sudbury, extended from Concord to Framingham, connecting at one time with the Charles River Basin. Another glacial lake in the vicinity of Billerica caused the formation of the Fordway Bar, which, along with ice blocks, has created the wide flood plains of the Sudbury and Concord Rivers.

Our rivers are considered mature in river characteristics, which applies to their shape, valley profile, and other physical features. Because of the effect of glacial debris and poor drainage, they appear much older than their geologic age. A postglacial tilt caused a gradual flattening of the gradient of the rivers. They probably always flowed north to the preglacial Merrimack in essentially their present form, but the junction may have been formerly Billerica instead of Lowell.

The Basin abounds in unconsolidated glacial deposits. This accumulation of debris can be seen in the drumlins and ground moraine, kames and kamefields, eskers, kame terraces, and kame and outwash plains.

Among the developed and undeveloped mineral resources in the Basin are sand and gravel deposits, crushed stone, granite, marble, flagstone, and peat.

Regional Topography

The region is mainly low and level, with hills sloping only 5 to 10 percent generally. Over 40 lakes and ponds, numerous streams, rounded hills, and sandy knolls are present. The topography differs from east to west (e.g., from Concord and Sudbury to Harvard, Bolton, and Berlin). There is a gradual change from subdued forms to steeper slopes and ridges with more relief and a rise in altitude. The difference between the elevation at the origin of the rivers (Sudbury River, 480 feet; Assabet River 420 feet) and at the confluence of the Concord and Merrimack Rivers (50 feet) is around 400 feet.

The major part of the watershed is primarily a flat valley. While the normal drop in a river bed is five feet per mile, from the Sudbury River in Saxonville to the Concord River at North Billerica, there is a drop of only two feet in 23 river miles. The flood plain is almost three miles wide in Wayland. The Assabet River lacks broad wetlands and in comparison has a steeper gradient (seven feet per mile) and more rapid runoff. The soils and the slope of the land are fairly good for water storage.

Soils of the Area

The upland areas, which comprise 70 percent of the watershed, are loam to sandy loam in texture and are moderately permeable. The remainder, of moderate to rapid permeability, are outwash or terrace soils. Mucks and peats are predominant in the swampy areas. The Concord and Sudbury soils are similar in type, resulting from alluvial deposits. The Assabet soils contain a greater amount of stone and sand.

The swampy areas, or wetlands, are characterized by the prevalence of organic materials and slow drainage, which allow water insoak. One reason the migrating birds, ducks, and waterfowl are so abundant in the SuAsCo Basin is the richness of what is called edge. This edge, or border, where two or more types of habitat merge (i.e., river with wetlands, wetlands with wooded or grassy uplands), is ideally suited for meeting the changing needs of a wide variety of organisms.

Water Supply

The hydrologic cycle—water from clouds down to land and ocean, then back to the sky through evaporation and transpiration (evapotranspiration)—is the way in which our water supply is constantly renewed. Precipitation represents our entire fresh-water supply

THE HYDROLOGIC CYCLE

source. The national average is about 30 inches annually. Our Basin average is above this, with a generous 45 inches. Distribution is fairly uniform. Heavy rainfalls may occur in any month of the year.

Our climate has been termed equable. The Basin's annual normal temperature is approximately 49 degrees, but we occasionally have prolonged cold or hot spells, which affect the water supply. The drought of summer and fall, 1963, temporarily lowered the water levels. Some of the drastic results were forest-fire and crop disasters, as well as water-supply emergencies.

As precipitation falls to the surface of the earth, some immediately becomes surface water, as in streams, lakes, and ponds, but most of it directly enters the ground where it falls. Some of this is used as soil moisture to feed our vegetation, and the remainder travels along the down gradient as ground water until it comes to the surface again in a stream. Ground water is the water that saturates the pores and cracks in soil or rocks below the land surface. This surface beneath the ground where water moves steadily is where our ground-water reservoirs are found.

The upper limit of that part of the ground saturated with water is called the water table. In Massachusetts the water table is more of a local than a state-wide phenomenon, as ground-water reservoirs tend to be shallow, owing to climate and geology. The water generally comes from ground above bedrock. Although we do not have a large amount of underground storage, our ground-water reservoirs refill virtually each year.

Half of our precipitation returns to the atmosphere as evapo-transpiration, and almost half flows to the sea as stream flow, or runoff of surface and underground water in a stream. About 65 percent of the annual flow of our streams comes from ground water. In our Basin, the average annual runoff of the Assabet River is 49 percent of precipitation and the Concord River is 47 percent.

Our present supply is a relatively small percent of the total precipitation. How this supply is used differs from location to location and depends upon variability, distribution, quality, and quantity.

The supply-demand ratio average in our Basin is favorable, but, because of variability, it may be unfavorable at particular times of year or for periods of time. In the summer months, during dry periods, there may be shortages. Unfortunately the demands made on the water supply for recreation, irrigation, public supply, and other uses are usually greatest during the time when there is the least water available.

In time of need, stored water can be released to help solve the variability problem. Assistance in withdrawing the water from underground reservoirs that is free to move by gravity can come through pumping; for example, through manmade wells. There must be adequate replenishing of the ground-water supply over a period of time through precipitation, or else mining results. This causes the water table to fall and increases the cost of pumping.

Release from surface reservoirs is another means of assisting nature in times of low flow. In our Basin very little water of the reservoirs of the Sudbury system is available for low-flow regulation, because their primary functions are water supply and recreation. However, they are regulated to a certain point to store water for flood control. In the Assabet at least one of the planned flood-control reservoirs is expected to have a permanent pool for low-flow regulation.

When supply and demand are different geographically, a distribution problem occurs. Aqueducts, or water conduits, may be needed to transfer water from one town to another, or from one basin to another, as in the case of the MDC system, which receives its supply from the Swift, Ware, Nashua, and Sudbury River Basins.

The quality of the water also affects its use. While its quality may be adversely affected by its natural properties, the term pollution here is considered to mean any deterioration in the quality of the water through human activities, by the addition of industrial, domestic, and agricultural wastes. The pollution problem is how to handle these wastes so as not to interfere with legitimate water uses. Nature assists in this process through dilution, oxidation, reduction, and bacterial action. However, treatment of the wastes at the source, rather than dependence on dilution, is the answer to the wastes problem. In the SuAsCo River Basin, inadequate treatment of wastes threatens many water uses.

Too much quantity, or excess stream flow, leads to floods. The flood plain, or land subject to periodic flooding, is the area where most flood losses are suffered. In a Basin such as ours, with undeveloped or little-developed flood plains, flood hazards can be greatly reduced by flood-plain zoning, which restricts uses that would in any way endanger life and property. When the flood plain is not regulated, unplanned encroachment can offset gains made by engineering projects.

To protect the flood-control measures under way in our watershed, stream-encroachment lines, or streamwide flood-plain zoning, are now being established by the state for the Assabet River. Sound engineering principles are applied to determine the limits within which encroachments would hamper the flood-carrying capacity of the stream. Local flood-plain zoning is considered a necessary measure to safeguard these lines.

The SuAsCo Watershed Work Plan for flood control emphasizes conservation treatment of watershed lands, supplemented by small upstream dams where necessary. About two-thirds of the region is in woodland at the present time. The Watershed Work Plan has land treatment measures under way to encourage better forestry management and improved soils and vegetative cover to preserve essential resources.

Water Management

Also affecting water uses in the SuAsCo River Basin is another complication—the question of who shall use the water and for what purpose. Someone who desires the preservation of wetlands may have a different view from the abutters on the rivers and streams, who, according to Massachusetts common law, are entitled to riparian rights, or the reasonable use of their adjacent waters. There may be other differences in points of view between the farmer, who wants water for irrigation in dry spells, and the outdoor-recreation enthusiast, who wants the flow for boating or swimming. Such conflicts of interest are in evidence as pressures for the water and related land uses increase, owing to population growth and industrial development.

Our Basin has complex water interests and varied water usage, which raises the question of the need for water management or the assignment of priorities to water use. This could involve river-basin planning or the investigation of the needs of such a region and the opportunities for development of water and related land resources to help meet those needs.

River-basin development can involve single-purpose water-development projects (flood control, irrigation, public power, recreation, fish and wildlife conservation, or municipal and industrial water supply) or multi-purpose projects, whereby several water uses are satisfied by the same project. The SuAsCo Watershed Work Plan was originally designed as a single-purpose flood-control project, but it is likely to become a multi-purpose development before it is completed.

If a single government agency is responsible for the planning and management within a river basin, it may be an interstate authority, such as the TVA, or a river-basin commission, a water-resources commission, or a similar body. There may also be a non-governmental watershed association to provide local support and participation. In our watershed, no one agency is concerned solely with river-basin problems, but rather there are many agencies that deal with special projects.

HISTORY

The exact date of the earliest human settlements in the region is unknown. Some aborigines were in this vicinity at least as early as 2000 B.C., but we don't know much about them.

The Indian tribes with which we are familiar, the Algonquins, lived here for many years before the white colonists arrived. They named the rivers the Musketaquid, which means "grass-ground river" and "dead water." Both descriptions are equally valid today. The Algonquins used the rivers for drinking water, food, and as an avenue for transportation. The level plains proved good for crops. The fishing was excellent. There appears to have been a large settlement of these Indians, but diseases cut their numbers at the time of the arrival of the first white settlers.

In 1635 a small group of Puritan farmers, anxious to use this open land for cultivation and pasture, paid the few remaining Indians for it and formed the first inland settlement in Massachusetts, at Concord. Meadowland for cattle was the basis for the division of land and for the assessment of taxes.

The problem of flooded land immediately beset these farmers, and in 1636 they presented a petition to the General Court on the need to abate the rocky "Falls." By 1638 a second inland town, Sudbury, had been established, farther south in the valley. It included what are now Wayland, Sudbury, and parts of Maynard and Stow.

Petitions from both Sudbury and Concord for the relief of flowage continued from this time on. In 1644 a commission was appointed by the General Court to provide for the draining of the meadows of the "Concord River," but there is no evidence that any major changes were brought about then or by succeeding commissions.

The Assabet region was not as important in early colonial history as the Sudbury and Concord regions, probably because its river was more sheltered, amid tall trees and narrow valleys, and it had less meadowland desirable for grazing. The village of Marlborough was founded in 1656, which included the present communities of Marlborough, Southborough, Westborough, and Hudson. Another inland village was established in Stow in 1683.

Danger from the Indians was a concern until after King Philip's War. The "embattled farmers" withstood yet another challenge when they defended their villages and their independence a century later in the Revolutionary War.

Following the Revolutionary War the rivers and tributaries were increasingly used to power grist mills and saw mills. The damming gave the farmers more cause to complain than ever, for the flood problems increased. The ledges of the Fordway Bar and the Falls at North Billerica were still the greatest troublemakers. As each new dam was built at the Falls, the water level of the river became higher, with the greatest change brought about by the Middlesex Canal.

The Middlesex Canal, opened in 1803, extended 27½ miles from Lowell to Medford. It passed through Chelmsford and Billerica and was supplied by water from the Concord River at the North Billerica site. In 1828 the Canal company erected a new dam at this location, and traffic on the Concord River considerably increased. Iron ore and firewood were shipped via this River and the Canal. Despite the woes of the farmers, others in the region benefitted economically.

The Canal, however, could not meet the competition of the railroads. In 1851 the company sold its water rights in Billerica to the Talbot family, which established a woolen mill. A secondary water right was purchased by the North Billerica Company, for another mill. The Roxbury Carpet Company was established in Saxonville, on the Sudbury River, in 1859. Long flat stretches prohibited much further major water-power use on the Sudbury and Concord Rivers.

It was the Assabet River that was most suited to mill development, and it assumed a prominent place in the rapid expansion of the textile industry in Massachusetts. In 1821 the use of the river for mill power began, and several new towns were born. During the second half of the nineteenth century such towns as Maynard and Hudson, which profited from natural falls in the river bed, became well-known centers for the manufacture of textile spindles and woolen products.

The mills flourished for almost a century. And, again, along with economic betterment for many, came problems for others, this time due to the pollution of the rivers with domestic and industrial wastes.

Farming and the mill industry made use of both the land and the water to give the region its early identity. Later, the extension of the railroad system also had much to do with determining the development of the valleys. Where the railroad came to the river industries, the towns involved grew and prospered. One example is Ashland, incorporated in 1846, but founded long before. In other instances the railroad brought new economic shifts, and such a town as Framingham mushroomed with new industries and enlarged population. The towns that were bypassed then remained rural by comparison.

Between 1848 and 1895, more and more of the water in the upper watershed of the Sudbury River was used for the Metropolitan Boston water supply. Until 1872 a large amount of this supply came from Lake Cochituate. Thereafter the newly established Metropolitan Water District created several artificial reservoirs on the south branch of the Sudbury River, drawing on 93.8 square miles of the Sudbury watershed for this purpose. A marked reduction in the flow of the river resulted, causing problems to many water users, including the upstream mills. From 1920 on there was less reliance on these reservoirs for water supply. In 1947 four of them, including Lake Cochituate, were released for recreational use. The four remaining reservoirs are kept by the Metropolitan Water District as standby supply sources. Water from 27.7 square miles of the Sudbury watershed is now diverted for this supply.

Our rivers have also provided inspiration for some of the best-known contributors to American life and thought. Thoreau chose the rivers as his highway and found his "natural rights least infringed on" where his range was widest. The light shed by the literary figures of the Transcendental movement, in the middle of the 19th Century, reflected on the whole of New England. Emerson, Hawthorne, Alcott, Channing, and others chose the background of Concord woods, meadow, and water to enlarge their vistas.

Today the rivers are no longer as important for daily survival as they were to the Indians and early settlers. They no longer provide the power they once did when the mill industries were in their prime. Nor do as many farmers cultivate their meadows. But these rivers continue to be used and abused for municipal, industrial, and private purposes, causing, as always, both pleasure and problems for the growing number of people who live in their valleys. Although threatened, the scenic natural beauty does still remain. Whether history will record the preservation of the assets and the solution of the problems is the current question.

THE LAND AND THE PEOPLE

The SuAsCo Basin presents a diversified picture of land use, which reflects the location and different zoning patterns of each community. In general the area is considered fairly "open," with only 20 percent of the land developed, according to the land-use study of the Greater Boston Economic Study Committee. Over half of the developed land is in residential use. Industry, business, and commercial activity represent a small total percentage, but such land use is steadily growing. Recreation areas, institutions, and utilities account for the remaining developed land. Water areas are not included.

Of the 80 percent undeveloped land, more than 25 percent is now in agricultural use or under forest or wildlife management. Another 25 percent is not suitable because of wetness and slope. At least 5 percent may be needed for public utilities and roads. This leaves an average of 25 percent that is open and suitable for development. In some of the communities with heavy population concentrations, such as Lowell, Framingham, Natick, and Maynard, the percentage is much less. These built-up communities show a greater tendency toward multi-family land use. In the suburbs most distant from Boston, with more vacant land still available, only a very small amount of land is zoned for this higher-density residential use.

According to Department of Agriculture figures, the land use of the Basin is divided as follows: approximately 66 percent in wood-lands; 18 percent in grassland; 2 percent in cropland; 3½ percent in lakes, reservoirs, and streams; and 10½ percent in urban use (cities, towns, roads, sub-divisions etc., but not accounting for low-density residential development). These are 1958 figures, which have already changed, for the bulldozer has advanced and the farms and trees have receded. Although exact statistics on these changes could not be obtained for the Basin itself, a projection to 1975 of esti-mated land use and conservation needs for both Middlesex and Worcester Counties, within which the Basin lies, shows an antici-pated decline in all major land uses except one—urban development.

Land Ownership

Ownership of land is predominantly private. Figures for 1958 showed that 92 percent of the land was privately owned, with the remaining 8 percent divided among the Commonwealth, 5 percent; the federal government, 1.5 percent; and municipal governments, 1.5 percent. Again, no complete, up-to-date figures are available, but the trend is toward increasing public ownership. Examples of recent changes in this direction are wetlands preservation, local con-servation acquisition programs, expanded transportation networks, local and state-water supply programs, and flood-control projects.

The major public-land ownership on the state and federal level is in holdings of the Metropolitan District Commission, the Massa-chusetts Division of Fisheries and Game, state transportation agen-cies, the Massachusetts Department of Natural Resources, the U.S. Fish and Wildlife Service, and U.S. Government military installa-tions and surplus property.

At present local holdings are generally for public-service pur-poses; i.e., for water, cemetery, school, fire and police departments. It has only been recently that municipal ownership of land for recreation and conservation use has been increasing, heretofore such activity being privately sponsored. Local efforts to acquire open land have been encouraged by enabling legislation as well as by financial self-help programs.

Private ownership of land is a longstanding tradition in the Basin. This ownership has been essentially in small holdings, but with a few large estates and some extensive farms. More and more of the open private land has changed hands, owing to the pressures of residential use and industry seeking new locations for expansion, and in some cases because of rising tax assessments.

Flood problems and loss of natural resources have resulted from some of the unplanned or poorly planned expansion. Because the public interest has been jeopardized by encroachments in the flood plain of the rivers and other conservation areas, there has been an adjustment in thinking toward ownership of land. The work of acquiring certain valuable resource areas by private and semi-public groups, such as the Sudbury Valley Trustees, has served to protect the public interest without governmental action. For any large-scale, comprehensive program to take place, however, the role of government as a landowner will have to increase. It is in this direction that the adjustment in thinking and awareness continues to take place.

Land-Use Controls and Land Values

Conservation easements and land acquisition of key resource areas cannot properly proceed without the support of zoning and planning within a region. How does the SuAsCo Basin stand in this regard? The 1950 Sudbury Valley Commission Report listed only 19 of the 36 municipalities in the Basin as having any zoning regulations whatsoever. Moreover, this report showed a great difference between the eastern and western portions of the region. In most of the western, or Assabet, region, no restrictions were placed on the location of commerce and industry, and there was also no protection for the basic water-resource areas. For the entire watershed no flood-plain zoning was yet in existence, although some local bylaws were adopted to achieve the same effect.

In the last 13 years, the increased pressures of urbanization have brought local action to close up serious gaps in zoning and planning of land use. In many cases the action was more a result of afterthought than forethought, but some of the towns have pioneered in conservation planning. Numerous problems remain to be solved, but the chart on pages 146-147 shows just how substantial the progress has been. Some types of zoning now exist in every town but one in the Basin; all towns have planning boards; most of them have conservation commissions; master plans are on the increase; flood-plain zoning and wetlands or conservation districts exist in five of the towns along the rivers, with others considering such measures.

The Sudbury Valley Commission Report says: "The general pattern is for values to be concentrated in the villages, in the areas occupied by estates and other residential types, and in the tracts devoted to intensive farming. The meadows themselves are in some towns deemed to be practically worthless." This was in 1950. By 1958 the meadows were already being used for housing and industrial development. Speculative real-estate values rose appreciably in those communities most conveniently located, because of proximity to urban centers or major highways.

Total assessed valuation in the watershed in 1949 was estimated to be in excess of 243 million dollars. By 1962 it had risen to just under 500 million dollars.

Population Pressures

The chart on pages 146-147 shows a population growth, steadily increasing from 1950-1960, in every community except Lowell. There is also an anticipated increase for every community but Lowell for the period 1960-1970. Lowell has followed the pattern of other central cities with a decline in population and established industries.

According to the Greater Boston Economic Study Committee, the estimated rates of population increase from 1950-1970 on a comparative basis are as follows: United States, 35.2 percent; New England, 20.9 percent; Massachusetts, 17.5 percent; Greater Boston, 19.5 percent; but for our watershed, approximately 72 percent. For an earlier period, 1940-1955, the Massachusetts Water Resources Commission reports that the Commonwealth gained 11.5 percent in population, while the SuAsCo area showed an increase of 38.8 percent.

These increases do not mean that our Basin is approaching the saturation point in terms of population density. According to the 1955 census the only municipality with a density of more than 2000 per square mile is Lowell: Maynard, Natick, Framingham, and parts of Ashland and Clinton reported between 1000 and 2000 persons per square mile. The remainder of the towns were under this figure, with some even below the 100-persons density. This leads one to believe that there is still room for growth to continue at a rapid rate beyond 1970.

Transportation

With the decline of central-city manufacturing and the rise of electronics and other specialized industries, the transportation pattern has changed to encourage dispersion to the suburbs. Route 128 provided a choice location for new industries seeking large sites with motor-vehicle access. No longer reliant on Boston and public transportation for employment, the industrial firm and the suburban homeowner made use of the expanding highway network and encouraged more highway construction and suburbanization.

In the early days of our region's history, it was primarily the water system that influenced its development. Then the railroad and street railway had their impact. Now development is being strongly influenced by the emphasis on highways.

The main roads in present use are the Massachusetts Turnpike and Routes 2, 2A, 3, 4, 9, 20, 25, 27, 30, 62, 85, 110, 117, 126, 129, 140, and sections of the interstate highway, 495, under construction. The Boston & Maine is the only railroad company providing full service in the area. The Boston & Albany is in limited operation.

The so-called "Outer Belt Highway," Interstate 495, will cut through many of the communities in the SuAsCo Watershed. The completed route in Massachusetts will extend from Interstate 95 at Mansfield, at the south, to Interstate 95 at Salisbury, at the north. Already open and in use is a stretch from Lowell to Littleton at Route 2.

This highway promises to make the outward movement from Boston more pronounced than ever. Interstate 495 is expected to be completed in 1967, and the projected 1970 population statistics do not fully take into consideration its probable impact. The Greater Boston Economic Study Committee, in a study of industrial land-use needs, has stated that the area from Route 128 to I-495 will experience marked economic growth in the coming years.

In the SuAsCo area, it is anticipated that the heaviest initial impact will be on the sections that are along the arteries connecting with I-495. Even though many of the towns affected by this transportation network still have much vacant land, the areas along the rivers already have comparatively heavy settlement, and difficult problems may arise with new growth.

The Boston Regional Planning Project has recently been established to develop a comprehensive plan for regional and transportation development. This type of planning may help to prevent the Interstate 495 area from experiencing such problems as those the towns in the proximity of Route 128 found facing them in the postwar years.

Economics of the Region

In the SuAsCo region many communities have opened their doors to industry in the hope of establishing a favorable tax base.

Twenty-three of the 36 communities in the SuAsCo Watershed are actively seeking to promote and develop industry through industrial development groups. Another type of organization, an area industrial-development council, has also attracted some of the towns. The North Middlesex Industrial Development Council, organized in 1962, has tentatively 10 members, seven of which are SuAsCo communities: Lowell, Acton, Westford, Billerica, Tewksbury, Chelmsford, and Littleton. This group hopes to expedite the completion of Interstate 495 in the area. A similar group, called the Outerbelt Industrial Commission, was formed in 1962 to encourage the completion of the central section of I-495.

All along Interstate 495, land is being zoned for industry, and in general the industrial zoning in the watershed follows the transportation network—the railroad, highways, and the rivers. The Greater Boston Economic Study Committee report on industrial land needs shows that more suitable land is presently zoned for industry than the future projected demand requires. In spite of this, the trend is toward more industrial zoning, not less. However, as a result of zoning measures at the state and local level, industrial growth in the flood-plain areas of the rivers will be considerably limited.

Only a few plants are still in operation that depend on the river water for processing or power. The Talbot, North Billerica, and Faulkner Woolen mills on the Concord River, the Hudson Combing Company along the Assabet, and the Roxbury Carpet Company on the Sudbury are about the only remnants from a very profitable mill era of the past. Several newer industries also use the rivers and tributaries for waste-carrying and processing, and the Carling Brewing Company uses Lake Cochituate for cooling. Some of the towns and cities with vacant mills along the river have been trying to attract new industries to the old sites. In some cases, notably Hudson, Maynard, and Marlborough, they have been very successful.

What is the expected impact of I-495 on the industrial growth of the region? Some predict that the highway will bring a $50 million investment to the area in the near future, and already several industrial parks and shopping centers have been built. Construction of one center is finished in Marlborough, another was finished in 1963 in Westford, and the planning is completed for one in Littleton. Several industrial organizations have also indicated they will build plants in these areas. Two large realty companies have purchased sizeable tracts of land for complexes in Littleton and Westford. At the Marlborough and Berlin-Hudson I-495 interchange areas, active land negotiations are going on, and real-estate values are already rising.

Industrial Employment

Some of the towns are so-called "bedroom communities," with a majority of their householders commuting to work outside the Basin to Boston or Worcester or Route 128. However, several large industrial concerns have located in our communities, with a majority of the employees residing locally. For example, Raytheon, Inc., has four plants in Bedford, Sudbury, Wayland, and southern Lowell, which each employ more than 1000 persons.

There were approximately 200 industrial organizations located in our Basin as of 1962. At least 50 of these employ over 100 persons each. The number of employees per industrial acre in 1960 was just over 20, which is an increase over 1950 figures.

Business and Commercial Activity

Local business and commercial activity continues to grow with the population, and shopping centers are well scattered throughout the Basin. Reliance on Boston (or Worcester or Lowell) for major shopping is no longer a price to pay for living in the suburbs. Several

TOWNS AND CITIES OF THE SuAsCo RIVER BASIN

Name	Watershed/ County	Highway Routes	Population 1950	Population 1960	Projected 1970	Esti- mated 60-70%	Organ- izations	Zoning Along Rivers/Tribs
1. Acton *	A/M	2, 27, 111	3,510	7,238	11,500	59%	C, LWV, G, ID, T	I&R/R*
2. Ashland*	S/M	126, 139	3,500	7,779	13,500	74%	C, ID	no restriction
3. Bedford	C/M	4, 62, 225	5,234	10,969	18,000	63%	C, LWV, G, Gr, F	R/R
4. Berlin*	A/W	62, 495	1,349	1,742	2,200	26%	C, ID, Gr, F	R&C/R
5. Billerica	C/M	85, 117	11,101	17,867	29,000	62%	C, LWV, ID, Gr, F	R&B&I/*
6. Bolton*	A/W	85, 117 495	956	1,264	1,500	19%	F	/R
7. Boxborough	A/M	2, 111, 495	439	744	1,200	71%	C, G, F, Gr	/R
8. Boylston	A/W	140, 70	1,700	2,475	3,000*	21%	ID, C, F	/R
9. Carlisle*	CA/M	25, 126	876	1,488	2,100	40%	T, Gr, F	R/R
10. Chelmsford*	C/M	3, 4, 110, 27 129, 495	9,407	15,130	19,000	26%	C, LWV, G, F, ID, T, Gr	R/R*
11. Clinton	A/W	62	12,287	12,848	13,000*	1%	F, C	no zoning
12. Concord*	SAC/M	2, 62, 126	8,623	12,517	15,500	24%	C, LWV, F, ID, T, G, Gr	FP&CD/R
13. Framingham*	S/M	9, 30, 126, MT	28,086	44,526	62,000	39%	C, LWV, F, ID, Gr, G	I&B/R*
14. Grafton	A/W	140, 122, 122A 30, MT	8,281	10,627	12,000*	13%	C, ID, G, F	/R
15. Harvard	A/W	111, 495	1,315	1,840	2,400	30%	C, LWV, G, Gr, F	/R*
16. Holliston	S/M	16, 126	3,753	6,222	8,500	37%	C, ID, F, G	no restrictio
17. Hopkinton*	S/M	85, 135, MT, 495	3,486	4,932	6,500	32%	C, ID, Gr, G	R/R
18. Hudson*	A/M	62,495	8,211	9,666	11,000	14%	C, ID, Gr, F	no restrictio
19. Lincoln	S/M	2, 126, 117	2,427	5,613	8,000	43%	C, LWV, T, G, Gr, F	R/R
20. Littleton	A/M	2, 110 495	2,349	5,109	8,000	57%	C, ID, T, G, F, Gr	in process
21. LOWELL	C/M	3, 113, 495, 3A 38, 110, 133	97,249	92,107	89,000	-13%	LWV, ID, Gr	C&I&R/I&
22. MARLBOROUGH*	AS/M	20, 85	15,756	18,819	22,000	22%	ID, C, Gr, F	R/R
23. Maynard*	A/M	27, 62, 117	6,978	7,695	8,000	4%	ID, Gr, F	R&B&I/R&
24. Natick	S/M	9, 27, 30 135, MT	19,838	28,831	36,000	32%	C, LWV, ID, Gr, G	/R
25. Northborough*	A/W	20, 135 495	3,122	6,687	10,000	50%	ID, F	R/R&C
26. Sherborn	S/M	16, 27, 115	1,245	1,806	2,500	38%	C, Gr, F	/R
27. Shrewsbury	A/W	9, 20	10,594	16,622	22,000*	14%	C, ID, Gr, F	/R
28. Southborough*	S/W	9, 30, 85 MT, 495	2,760	3,996	5,500	39%	C, ID, G, Gr, F	R/R
29. Stow*	A/M	62, 117	1,700	2,573	4,000	40%	C, ID, G, Gr, F	/R
30. Sudbury*	SA/M	20, 27, 117	2,596	7,447	12,000	67%	C, LWV, ID, G, F, Gr	FP&R/R
31. Tewksbury	C/M	38, 93, 495	7,505	15,902	24,000	59%	C, LWV, ID, F	/I&R
32. Upton	S/W	140	2,656	3,127	3,500	12%	F, C	/R
33. Wayland*	S/M	20, 30 27, 126	4,407	10,444	17,000	63%	C, LWV, G, T, F	FP/R
34. Westborough*	SA/W	9, 30, MT 135, 495	7,378	9,599	12,000	25%	ID, G, F	R/I *
35. Westford	A/M	25, 110, 495	4,262	6,261	8,500	36%	C, ID, Gr, F, G	/R&
36. Weston	S/M	30, MT, 20, 117	5,026	8,261	10,500	27%	C, LWV, G, T, F	/R

Column 1.* means community is wholly or largely in the Basin 2. Watershed: A-Assabet, C-Concord, S-Sudbury. Cou M-Middlesex, W-Worcester. 3. MT-Massachusetts Turnpike. 4-5. Population Figures, 1950-1960, U.S. Census. 6-7. Proje 1970 Figures-Greater Boston Economic Study Committee. * means not in GBESC study area. Information from commun Harvard figures exclude Fort Devens population. Towns of Hudson, Sudbury and Westborough report higher anticipated increase; Lincoln, lower. 8. Organizations: C-Conservation Commission, LWV-League of Women Voters, G-Garden Club, T-T Trust, ID-Industrial Development Commission, F-4H Club, Gr-Grange. 9. Zoning: I-Industry, B-Business, R-Resider C-Commercial, FP-Flood Plain, CD-Conservancy District * means considering flood plain zoning or districts.

TOWNS AND CITIES OF THE SuAsCo RIVER BASIN

Dump/Fill Along Water	Master Plan	Subdivision Control	Town Forest	Conservation Land	Municipal Water Supply	Present Source	Future Source	Municipal Sewerage	Industrial Waste Disposal	
no/no	yes	yes	yes	yes	yes	local wells	wells, lake?	no	yes	1.
no/yes	yes	yes	yes	yes	yes	local wells	same	in process	yes	2.
no/no	yes	yes	yes	yes	yes	local wells	MDC?	MDC	yes	3.
no/	no	yes	no	no	no	private wells	wells	no	no	4.
no/	yes	yes	yes	no	yes	Concord River	River, wells	yes	yes	5.
no/no restrictions	no	no	no	yes	no	private wells	wells	no	yes	6.
restrictions	no	yes	no	no	no	private wells	wells	no	no	7.
	no	yes	no	no	yes	local wells	wells	no	no	8.
restrictions	yes	yes	yes	yes	no	private wells	wells	no	no	9.
no/yes	in process	yes	yes	yes	yes	local wells	local	no	yes	10.
restrictions	no	no	no	no	yes	MDC-local	same	yes	yes	11.
no/yes for n-residence	yes	yes	yes	yes	yes	wells, ponds	wells, River?	yes	yes	12.
no/yes	yes	yes	no	yes	yes	MDC, wells	MDC	MDC	yes	13.
no/no restrictions	in process	yes	yes	yes	yes	local wells	same	no	no	14.
restrictions	no	yes	yes		yes	local wells	local	no	no	15.
yes/no	yes	yes	yes		yes	local wells	local	no	no	16.
no/no	yes	yes	yes	yes	yes	local wells	same	no	no	17.
restrictions	yes	yes	yes		yes	pond, wells	local wells	yes	yes	18.
no/no	in process	yes	no	yes	yes	pond	local wells	no	no	19.
no/	yes	yes	yes	in process	yes	local wells	wells	no	yes	20.
no/no	preliminary plan	yes	no		yes	Merrimack River, wells	same	yes	yes	21.
restrictions	yes	yes	yes	yes	yes	MDC and 2 reservoirs	same	yes	yes	22.
no/	yes	yes	no	yes	yes	pond	local wells	yes	?	23.
no/	general plan	yes	yes	in process	yes	local wells	local	MDC	yes	24.
no/	yes	yes	yes	yes	yes	wells, MDC reservoir	wells	no	no	25.
no/no	yes	yes	yes	yes	no	private wells	wells	no	no	26.
/no	yes	yes	no	no	yes	wells	same	yes	yes	27.
no/no strictions	yes	yes	no	no	yes	MDC reservoir	same	no	yes	28.
/no	in process	yes	no	no	no	private wells	local	no	no	29.
no/no	yes	yes	no	yes	yes	local wells	local	no	yes	30.
no/no	yes	yes	no	no	yes	local wells	local	no	no	31.
	no	yes	yes	no	yes	local wells	same	yes	no	32.
no/no enerally	yes	yes	no	yes	yes	local wells	same	no	yes	33.
no/	no	yes	yes	yes	yes	pond, wells	MDC?	yes	?	34.
no/	no	yes	yes	yes	yes	local wells	local	no	no	35.
no/	in process	yes	yes	yes	yes	local wells	MDC, wells	no	no	36.

an 10. Information on Dumping, Filling and Zoning from the communities. 11-12 Information on Master Plan, Subdivision ol from the communities; verified by the state Department of Commerce, Division of Planning. 13-14. Information from ommunities. Town forests verified by Massachusetts Association of Forests and Parks. 15-19. Water Supply and Sewerage m information from communities, verified by state Department of Public Health, Division of Sanitary Engineering.

Information to Fall, 1963.

large department stores have branched out in our area. Retail activity does not yet employ large numbers of the residents of the watershed, however, and generally these shopping centers or individual stores have aimed at local patronage only. The main exception is along Route 9.

Agriculture

Although the most important commercial land use is still farming, its role is diminishing. The farmer has been faced with problems and temptations. Some of his problems have been flood conditions, irrigation difficulties in dry spells, and high taxes in relation to many competing rural areas. Added to this has been the temptation to sell farm land for development, at a good profit. Nevertheless, 25 percent of the land in the SuAsCo Basin is still in farm use, with more than 700 individual farms in operation. Truck farming, dairying, and orchards are the most profitable. The trend is to specialized farming, more and more on a part-time basis (25 percent and rising), with less reliance on the farm for entire income.

Some of the decrease in the number of farms has been offset by the increased acreage of others through consolidation of land holdings. Farmers are now being encouraged through government programs to develop compatible supplementary uses of their lands, such as recreation, to augment their incomes. Also, local recognition of the need for tax agreements to keep this type of land open may further encourage the farmer to stay in business.

ADMINISTRATION AND LAWS

1. Planning and Coordination

The difference between natural and political boundaries is one of the problems of regional planning. River basins do not usually make handy administrative units. By the same token, political units that ignore the drainage-basin boundaries for natural-resource planning do so at their own peril. If the units are different, there must at least be cooperation between them.

No single authority is responsible for the planning and management of water resources in the SuAsCo River Basin. There are numerous existing agencies that can plan for particular programs within the Basin, and there are also many possibilities for the development of general regional planning, including water resources.

On the local level, primary responsibility for general community planning rests with the planning board, which has special powers granted in the General Laws to create a master plan, prepare an official map, and exercise subdivision control. It can also initiate zoning proposals and can meet with other planning boards of interested communities in an area to consider a regional planning district.

Other local bodies have specific powers related to water and conservation, such as the conservation commissions, park and recreation departments, boards of health, and water departments. The selectmen and town meeting or the city council may still decide how particular programs are translated into action in each community.

In the SuAsCo region, not all the communities are yet regional-minded. Some of them are not sure what region they do or should belong to. In others the general tradition of local autonomy makes any long-term regional commitment hard to accept. Even many of the local bodies are independent in nature and are not involved in joint planning at the local level. This may be due to a lack of personnel and time rather than a lack of willingness to cooperate. Most of the towns need full-time professional people who can be concerned with long-range planning problems and inter-agency cooperation.

One of the possibilities for regional groupings within our Basin is the Department of Commerce Planning Division's suggested areas for regional planning in the state, based on urban centers. Our river-basin towns and cities would be aligned in sub-regions, with Boston, Lowell, Ayer, Framingham, Clinton, and Worcester as the urban centers. None of these suggested areas has been organized in our Basin.

However, after many years of unsuccessful attempts, there is now being established a Boston Metropolitan Area Planning Council. Municipalities of the metropolitan sewerage, parks, and water districts will be members, and possibly contiguous communities, including some of the SuAsCo towns.

Any group of towns and cities can vote to be recognized as a region, under Chapter 40B of the General Laws. Informal organization is also possible to achieve a particular short-term purpose. For example, communities in the Lowell area have organized into a Greater Lowell Planning Board, and there is a Framingham Area Planning Board Association as well. An informal organization of conservation commissions or planning boards in the entire Basin could bring about many desired results.

The Soil Conservation Districts and counties can also provide a regional approach, using existing administrative boundaries that differ from the areas outlined by the state. The Soil Conservation Districts are political subdivisions of state created to administer soil and water conservation work within their boundaries. They are autonomous units and self-governed, but they have worked closely in the past with the state Soil Conservation Service. Under recent legislation, these districts will be supervised by a State Committee on Soil, Water, and Related Resources, and a new Conservation Services Division in the Department of Natural Resources will be able to provide information and assistance. This legislation will also enable the Districts to accept federal aid. With more funds they could provide a basis for cooperative efforts within river basins. Our Basin is included in two districts, the Middlesex County and the Northeastern Worcester County, which are the sponsoring organizations for the SuAsCo flood-control program.

The Division of Planning of the state Department of Commerce is the general planning agency of the Commonwealth. It has power to "initiate, encourage, and carry on regional and metropolitan planning, and advise and assist local planning boards and other municipal agencies in cooperative efforts intended for the mutual benefits of the municipalities constituting such regional or metropolitan areas." This agency feels that any regional planning program must be based on local initiative. It acts primarily in response to requests from the local planning bodies. For example, many of our towns have taken advantage of federal aid under the so-called "701" provisions of the Housing Act for professional planning assistance, a program which the Division of Planning supervises.

In addition to the Division of Planning, there are other state agencies with authority over certain water and land uses within our Basin. The Department of Public Health works closely with the communities on water supply and sewerage matters, but it is not yet involved in any comprehensive planning programs.

The Massachusetts Water Resources Commission has been co-ordinating governmental activity related to the SuAsCo flood program and flood projects elsewhere in the state. It is a promising agency for coordinating many other water activities such as river-basin water-resources development.

The Department of Natural Resources must also be singled out as a state agency that can direct conservation planning and action in our region and others.

On the federal level, no overall planning agencies exist, but through legislation the federal government has recently included planning provisions in the water resources, land management, urban redevelopment, conservation, and general regional-planning areas. There is also proposed legislation that aims at better planning and coordination of natural-resources programs.

Under the Highway Act as amended in 1962 federal money for roads is available only after evidence of a long-range plan and cooperation between the state and the communities. This insistence has resulted in the Boston Regional Planning Project, which will be a three-year study of 152 cities and towns in the Greater Boston area, including almost every SuAsCo community. The project is being undertaken by the Massachusetts Transportation Commission and the State Department of Public Works, in cooperation with the federal Housing and Home Finance Agency and the Bureau of Public Roads. The emphasis will be on highways, railroads, and other transportation needs, but its work groups also cover land use and physical facilities, including water and sewage works.

The role of the federal government in water management is generally to encourage state and local action through grants-in-aid and technical assistance. There may be direct federal participation on interstate streams, but not until recently have intrastate streams been the object of attention, either with the consent of the governor, as in the case of water-pollution control, or with state or local sponsorship, as in the case of the watershed flood-control programs.

Another example of federal direction is the development of comprehensive plans in water quality-control programs under the federal Water Pollution Control Act. After initial study of river-basin areas a program coordinating efforts of local, state, and federal agencies would be implemented. The necessary funds for a comprehensive study of the New England Basins have not yet been appropriated.

The new concern with urban problems has brought legislation

encouraging comprehensive planning for urban renewal, open-space acquisition, and parks. Federal aid made available through the Housing Act of 1961 is administered by the Housing and Home Financing Agency, which has as one duty, "to encourage cooperation in preparation and carrying out plans among all interested agencies and other parties in order to achieve coordinated development of entire areas."

It may be some time before comprehensive regional planning units become established and workable. It can be seen that present machinery exists that could undertake general planning, and additional machinery has been proposed. Whether or not this machinery will be used effectively to provide for the needs of the future will depend largely on an informed and motivated public.

2. State Water Rights Doctrine

Just as hydrology is not an exact science, neither is our water law an exact law. A full discussion of existing doctrines and their interpretations would require more detail than this brief summary allows.

There are two basic approaches to water law—the riparian doctrine and the appropriation doctrine, with wide variations or combinations of these two.

The appropriation doctrine applies the principle of priority in time of use of water rather than contiguity to the water. Beneficial use is the basis of rights, and the earliest beneficial use has preference over later use. This doctrine was based first on custom, and many western states have enacted detailed statutes to codify these rules.

The riparian doctrine relates to proprietary interests through landownership. Based on common law, it is composed almost entirely of judicial decisions. Its adoption by the English courts made it part of the law of many jurisdictions, particularly in eastern states.

In Massachusetts the riparian system prevails. An owner of land abutting a watercourse acquires rights to make reasonable use of its water, these rights being real property and belonging with the land. The rights can be enlarged or diminished by grant or prescription. The term "reasonable use" is usually construed to mean that the riparian owner can make any lawful, beneficial use that does not damage other legitimate users. At least three limitations to these rights can be listed: the rights pertain only to the watershed of the stream in which they are asserted; the state has a paramount interest in the water of navigable streams and riparian owners may not interfere with these overriding rights; and prescriptive rights, or rights earned by usage, are recognized if the appropriation continues for at least 20 years without interruption.

A different approach applies to ground water. In Massachusetts there is absolute ownership of the ground water rather than reasonable use. Common law does not impose limitations on the landowner's right to obtain underground water from his own property, unless this use affects a public water-supply source.

Common law may recognize many legal classifications of water, and the same rights may not apply in each case, as differences among surface watercourses, diffused surface water, and ground water, either as a definite underground stream, underflow of surface stream, or percolating water. New study and analysis are in order to determine which distinctions are physically artificial and which are necessary in terms of water rights.

Our riparian doctrine of reasonable use also involves the court's ability to analyze many problems to decide just what in a particular case may be deemed reasonable. Criteria for determining reasonable use could be set forth by the legislature.

Because litigation has been the means by which conflicts have been resolved, the rules of the game are not simple and clear. It is sometimes necessary to review a wide range of cases before something approaching a generalization can be made. Most individuals are not aware of past judgments and do not usually resort to litigation, a lengthy and expensive process, unless damage has already been done.

The uncertainty of water rights and the difficulty in establishing clear distinctions through litigation have raised the question of a new approach to water law. As an alternative, the appropriation doctrine, with its tighter controls, would be accepted only as a last resort. The tradition of respect for private property has gone hand in hand with an ample water supply to make the riparian doctrine well suited to this state. Since the water supply is no longer so ample, some changes may be necessary.

Although controls in general have been avoided, there are some precedents in this state concerning legislative action. In the middle of the 19th Century several statutes were enacted, known as the

Mill Acts, that authorized the erection of mill dams under certain rules and set up special procedures for the assessment of damages. These Acts provide one example of legislative measures to update the riparian doctrine to meet a social and economic challenge. Another earlier instance where the General Court legislated on public water rights is the Great Pond Ordinance, which dates back to early colonial times.

If new legislative revisions occur they will not be drastic: a realistic goal may be clarification of the present system with some compromise with the appropriation doctrine to meet special problems. Before this happens, a thorough study of water rights, including an appraisal of scientific data on the amount and source of available water supply and present and anticipated demands, will be necessary. Careful attention will also have to be given to balancing the public good with respect for individual water rights.

Such a thorough study has been greatly aided by the groundwork laid in a report of the Legislative Research Council. When it presented its report to the General Court, in 1957, it pointed out the paucity of material on the whole subject of the state's water resources and the legal rights to their use. This Council did not draw conclusions on legislative proposals but hoped they would come in time through the newly established Massachusetts Water Resources Commission.

The Water Resources Commission has been hampered by a lack of funds and staff, but it has been helping to shape basic water policies through specific legislation dealing with certain areas. In 1958 the Commission expressed the feeling that a written state water code would be rigid, whereas the common law stems from customs and usage and can be more flexible.

The riparian doctrine is often criticized because it does not encourage maximum use or equitable distribution. The contention is that its limitatons on the place of use of water usually reserve the water for the use of adjacent owners on riparian land, making efficient development unlikely. Does our common-law doctrine actually present obstacles in the way of orderly development of water resources? Is it too complicated? Is it outdated or is it misunderstood? These questions need prompt consideration.

PROBLEMS AND PROGRAMS
IN THE SUASCO RIVER BASIN

1. Water Supply

The not-too-distant future is already here. The excessive heat and dry spell of the summer and fall of 1963 brought water-supply emergencies and a strong reminder to almost every community in the SuAsCo Basin. Temporary measures were undertaken: bans were instituted for outside use; standby pumping equipment was used or readied for use on lowered surface supplies; additional water-works equipment was acquired or borrowed; and new sources of supply were actively sought. For many of the local citizens used to wasting water, it was a surprise and shock to discover that our supplies are not inexhaustible.

We have been particularly blessed in our section of the country with a plenteous supply of water, and we have come to take for granted that resource on which all life depends. Our common-law doctrine of riparian rights and reasonable use has proven practical in many ways, but it has encouraged waste and lack of management of water uses. With greatly increased demands, the supply is no longer endless and the balance no longer so favorable.

While we normally have about 45 inches of precipitation annually, half of this runs off to sea and much is lost in evapotranspiration. The rate of loss by runoff will increase if absorbent land cover continues to disappear; that is, if woodlands are cut beyond a desirable point, if too many grasslands are replaced with hard top or cement, and if wetlands and swamps are destroyed. Uneven distribution is also a problem in our Basin, with some of the communities facing a constant water-supply problem. Still, our Basin-wide supply is not insufficient, and with wise planning and efficient management of our water resources we should have enough to meet all our needs for the foreseeable future.

The water-supply needs of our Basin include domestic supply, industrial use, and agriculture. Domestic-supply demands doubled in the years 1940-1955, and the anticipated rate of increase is almost as great. Approximately 20 MGD (million gallons daily) is currently consumed for domestic supply, and 45 MGD is the estimated use by the year 2000.

In the state, industry uses twice as much water as domestic supply, with agriculture third, but the exact amount for these two categories in our Basin is not available. Agriculture is generally highly consumptive in water use, while industry is not, since it uses water for processing, power or cooling and most of it can be returned after use to the streams. The quality of the water, however, may be affected by pollution.

In the past the question of a local water supply was largely one of individual concern. Until recently not many public water-supply systems existed in this area, inhabitants depending chiefly upon private wells. These private wells still dot the landscape, but the number of communities making a public supply available to at least a portion of their citizens, including the Metropolitan District Commission supply, has increased to 30 of the Basin's 36.

Over half of the community water supplies come from underground sources, the remainder from surface sources or a combination of the two. Five of the localities receive at least part of their supply from aqueducts of the Metropolitan District Commission system: Clinton, Framingham, Marlborough, Northborough, and Southborough. Weston has recently been included in the Metropolitan Water District. Of the other towns with a public supply, only one, Billerica, takes water from the river, and only one other, Concord, has considered deriving a portion of its supply from the river to meet future needs. Lowell has returned to the Merrimack River, which, after filtration and purification, is the city's major source of supply. Acton, Bedford, Billerica, Bolton, Chelmsford, Concord, Harvard, Holliston, Lincoln, Natick, Northborough, Shrewsbury, Tewksbury, Westford, and Westborough all indicate shortages for the future, and there may be others. Hudson and Maynard are actively looking for additional sources of supply. Where will the water come from?

The rivers do not hold out much promise as an additional source of domestic supply for many of the communities, because the quality makes expensive treatment procedures necessary. The quantity of the rivers is also a limiting factor, since the low flow during the dry season would not permit much greater use than at present without additional works to catch and reserve the water during high flow. Not many towns can look to the MDC in the future because of distance and expense.

Reducing pollution and increasing storage capacity through reservoirs could make useful certain sources not presently available, as could new treatment procedures for removing iron or other undesirable minerals from marginal underground water. Research is also revealing new ways of reusing the same water, which might be a practical answer to the growing demands of industry and agriculture. Desalinization is not as yet economically feasible.

In general, underground sources offer the most hopeful possibility and will undoubtedly be tapped to a greater extent from now on. Basic ground-water studies for the entire area are needed.

The primary responsibility for solving the water-supply problems rests with the towns and cities, which have the power to purchase rights to a water supply, to acquire land for the protection of the supply, to take steps to insure its purity, and to restrain its use when necessary. The community may receive this supply through a water district or water department which has been authorized by the legislature. State assistance comes through the Department of Public Health and the Water Resources Commission.

The state Department of Public Health is charged with the responsibility of supervising the sources of water supply and their development for municipalities, water supply for fire districts or public institutions, or for any water company in the Commonwealth. This Department is a member of the Water Resources Commission and cooperates with that agency in connection with the development of water-supply sources and related matters.

The Water Resources Commission assists communities that are searching for a supply or are establishing a new system. Rainfall-measuring stations are maintained in Concord, Berlin, and Marlborough, and stream-gauging stations are maintained in cooperation with the U.S. Geological Survey to measure stream flow for the Assabet River at Maynard, the Concord River near Lowell, the Sudbury River at Framingham, and at the outlet of Lake Cochituate.

The Water Division of the Metropolitan District Commission supplies 30 cities and towns in the Greater Boston area with water, and it will soon be supplying its 31st member, Weston. Five communities in our Basin that are not part of the Metropolitan Water District are hooked up with the MDC system.

From its beginning, its source of supply was largely the reservoir system it established in the Sudbury drainage area, but water impurity and other factors made it turn to a new and larger water supply from the hills of central Massachusetts. An extensive network of aqueducts travels to the Boston area, the Weston, Sudbury, and High Pressure aqueducts traversing our Basin. Construction in our region is currently taking place parallel to the Wachusett Aqueduct. A new tunnel connecting the Wachusett Reservoir with the Hultman Aqueduct at Marlborough is expected to be completed in 1964.

One of the MDC's three laboratories for sampling water quality is located in Framingham. Rainfall-measuring stations are maintained in conjunction with its present or former water-supply reservoirs at Framingham, Ashland, Lake Cochituate, and Southborough.

Of the eight reservoirs in the Sudbury drainage area, two have been retained by the MDC as active sources of supply (Framingham Reservoir #3 and Sudbury Reservoir), with over 27 miles of the Sudbury watershed currently diverted for this supply. They enter the Commission's Metropolitan distribution system through the Weston and Sudbury aqueducts. Two other reservoirs, Framingham #1 and #2, are primarily standby sources, but they could be used in an emergency after heavy chlorination.

The four remaining reservoirs have been turned over to the Department of Natural Resources—Cochituate, Whitehall, Ashland, and Hopkinton. At one time the MDC considered expanding its system in the Cedar Swamp headwaters area of the Sudbury River, but because of many reasons, including new developments in the Quabbin area and deterioration of waters in the South Sudbury branch, it lost interest in this project. It still owns a fair amount of land in this area and in general is a large landowner in our Basin because of its water-supply interests.

For the most part the federal government has limited its activity in the water-supply field to basic research. In our Basin, the U.S. Geological Survey is now involved in ground-water surveys in the Assabet Valley and has completed surveys for the Lowell area. This agency is responsible for research and investigations relating to hydrology, geology, and surface and underground water.

The U.S. Weather Bureau maintains climatological records and presents summaries of temperature and precipitation over a period of years. There are no round-the-clock U.S. weather observatories in our Basin. However, field data from Hanscom Field in Bedford, just outside the watershed, is on file and available from National Weather Records Center, Asheville, North Carolina. Cooperative stations at Framingham, Lake Cochituate, and Bedford record daily temperature and precipitation, and Ashland records daily precipitation.

The U.S. Public Health Service conducts research on water-quality standards, water-treatment methods, and waste-water treatment.

The effect of wetlands on water supply has been a question of particular interest in our Basin. The water-retaining qualities of our wetlands are well known, but how much of the water stored finds its way to ground-water and surface supplies has not been established. The State Climatologist of the U.S. Weather Bureau states that the average evaporation from wetlands is greater than average Basin evaporation, and concludes:

"It is seen that an increase in lake area or of wetlands will not increase but rather decrease net water yield of a basin, though there may be many other desirable hydrological or wildlife conservational effects."

The U.S. Geological Survey, Ground Water Branch, has been engaged in a study of the water resources of the Ipswich River. Their observations to date are as follows:

"Among the many types of geologic materials existing in the river valleys of eastern Massachusetts, swamp deposits exert a predominant influence on hydrology far out of proportion to their relative volume. . . . Although large amounts of water are lost to further use by evapotranspiration each year, large amounts are also made available for the recharging of ground-water bodies and for addition to streamflow. Water which has been stored in swamp deposits during periods of high runoff in the spring is often available during much of the summer when streamflow and ground-water recharge decline to their lowest annual levels. Recent studies by the U.S. Geological Survey in a typical drainage basin of eastern Massachusetts have shown that runoff from swamps in a drainage basin of about 124 square miles is capable of adding more than 50 million gallons per day to streamflow during the early part of the summer period of low flows."

Although specific questions remain to be answered, important first steps are being taken in the water-supply field. Recent water shortages have brought some awareness of the need for long-range planning to meet the water-supply problem. Some provision for assistance to the communities is already available; however, more money and more Basin-wide planning are generally required. A determination of potential underground sources, more knowledge of the relationship of wetlands to our sources of supply, and a basic hydrologic study of our Basin would contribute to our present understanding and make future planning more simple.

2. Water Pollution

In the SuAsCo Basin the once refreshing and sparkling waters have been filled with an increasing amount of domestic and industrial waste. At the end of the 19th Century the mill activity had created such intolerable pollution that the rivers were considered a health hazard. A 1901 comprehensive report of the State Board of Health recommended immediate action to remove pollutants from these rivers. Little action was taken, but the decline of mill operations somewhat improved the rivers temporarily. At the time the Sudbury Valley Commission was appointed, in 1949, pollution resulting from domestic and industrial waste was again considered in need of immediate attention. Some beneficial changes have been made since that time, but the picture is still not bright.

Two sources that created a nuisance factor on the Sudbury River have been eliminated. Since the diversion of Framingham and Natick sewage to the Metropolitan District Commission system was completed, in 1957, considerable improvement has been noted in the area below the former sewage-treatment plants in these towns. When Ashland hooks up with the MDC sewage system, there should be further improvement in the Sudbury River.

In the headwaters area of the Assabet River, where flow is at a minimum, two municipal sewage systems are now located, and two more are in the planning stages. The pollution resulting in both the Assabet and Concord Rivers may become slightly reduced through the augmentation of low flow as a consequence of the SuAsCo flood-control project. The regulation of levels for flood-control purposes in the Sudbury system will also continue to be a little helpful to pollution abatement in the Sudbury and Concord Rivers. But complete treatment of wastes at the source is needed before any major changes will occur.

There are at present eight municipal sewage systems, 16 industries, and two institutions that dispose of wastes within the SuAsCo Basin. The pollution in our rivers is due primarily to lack of treatment or inadequate treatment of some of these wastes. Additional pollution sources may arise from dumping, spraying, seepage, and other private waste-disposal problems.

There is also some natural pollution in the rivers, which cannot be removed. The pollution caused by human activities can be treated. One of the more common municipal treatment procedures involves removing settleable solids (sludge) and treatment of the liquid that flows from the settling tanks (effluent). Significant bacteria may be present if this effluent is not properly chlorinated. Complete treatment of wastes is expensive, and certain pollutants such as synthetic detergents, radioactive wastes, and insecticides as yet defy simple treatment methods. Treatment plants have a designed lifetime of about 25-30 years, and are subject to periodic rehabilitation and surveillance.

Bedford, Billerica, Clinton, Concord, Framingham, Hudson, Lowell, Maynard, Marlborough, Natick, Shrewsbury, Upton, and Westborough have a public sewage system for at least a portion of the community. Bedford, Natick, and Framingham divert their wastes via the MDC system. Clinton is served by a treatment plant owned, operated, and maintained by the Water Division of the MDC, with the effluent discharged into the Nashua River. Upton uses the Blackstone River for waste-carrying purposes. The remainder of the communities with a municipal system utilize our rivers for treatment-plant effluent disposal.

Ashland has negotiated a tie-up with Framingham to use the MDC sewage system. Billerica is working on a new plant, to be completed in 1965. The towns of Grafton, Hopkinton, Littleton, Chelmsford, and Southborough also have need for new systems, and a new system for Northborough is in the planning stages. Maynard, Framingham, Marlborough, and Westborough are planning for an expanded system in the near future. Concord has recently improved its system, and Hudson has installed new treatment works. Many of the towns without a system indicate sewage disposal is on private premises, and there are no immediate plans for a town system.

There are approximately 16 industrial concerns having liquid wastes, and all but four of these have treatment plants. Those without systems include two woolen manufacturers and a rendering company along the Concord River in Billerica. Engineering reports have been made to have the wastes enter public sewerage for treatment after the completion of a Billerica municipal system. A vinegar company that uses an Assabet tributary for processing does not treat its wastes. Of the industries with treatment plants, one in Ashland creates a local pollution problem and several others present pollution problems intermittently, but most of them have satisfactory treatment. There has been progress in the industrial waste-disposal area. In the past few years quite a few new treatment plants have been built.

There are two institutions—the Billerica House of Correction on the Concord River and the Concord Reformatory on the Assabet River—that have sewage effluent that is treated satisfactorily.

Waste-carrying is a beneficial water use when it does not interfere with other legitimate water uses. What are the multiple-use possibilities of our rivers and tributaries, and what should their water-quality standards be? There are no state pollution-control laws to provide for the classifications of inland waters. However, tentative classifications of our streams have been given by the state Department of Public Health based on classifications of the New England Interstate Water Pollution Control Commission for interstate streams. According to these:

A. means suitable for any water use, character uniformly excellent.

B. means suitable for bathing and recreation, irrigation and agricultural uses; good fish habitat; good aesthetic value. Acceptable for public water supply with filtration and disinfection.

C. means suitable for recreational boating; irrigation of crops not used for consumption without cooking; habitat for wildlife and common food and game fishes indigenous to the region; industrial cooling and most industrial-process uses.

D. means suitable for transportation of sewage and industrial wastes without nuisance; for power, navigation, and certain industrial uses.

(These standards do not apply to conditions brought about by "natural causes.")

The Sudbury River is classified as A at the North Branch, where the MDC reservoirs for public water supply exist. The South Branch above Framingham is classified as B, as is the river from the junction of the two branches to its confluence with the Assabet, and these classifications are not expected to change. Although in Class B, the river probably is not subject to all of the uses listed under this category. Its opaque quality, due to natural causes, makes it unlikely that it will be made suitable for bathing.

The Assabet is D throughout, and its highest future use classification is expected to be C, with the headwater areas remaining D, unless the flow is augmented and the discharge of sewage effluent and industrial wastes is more effectively treated.

The Concord River above Billerica is C, but the requirements of Billerica for its water supply brings its portion up to Class B. Below this treatment plant to the Merrimack the condition is D, because of discharged wastes, and with considerable additional treatment this could be raised to C.

These tentative classifications were reported by the Water Resources Commission in a 1960 study. They are subject to change and could be raised if new conditions arose and additional need for cleaner water could be demonstrated.

The local agencies most active in working on the water-pollution problem are the Boards of Health, Selectmen, or City Councils, and in some cases the water departments. The Board of Health has as one responsibility the enforcement of the state sanitary code within each community. The job of detecting local temporary pollution sources and doing something quickly about them can best be done at the local level, with assistance from state sanitary-engineering experts. Likewise, for any progress on major pollution sources, local initiative and cooperation, as well as tax dollars, are essential first steps.

The Division of Sanitary Engineering of the Department of Public Health is the state agency responsible for dealing with water pollution. This Division cooperates with the Boards of Health and other local officials in the establishment of sewage systems, and can require that a city or town or water company make necessary improvements to bring treatment systems up to standards for safeguarding public health. Most of its work is done through suggestion and consultation. Enforcement procedures are conservatively used.

The Division of Sanitary Engineering bases its water-pollution-control work on programs for individual river basins. The Division feels that progress in our Basin has been satisfactory.

There seems to be effective cooperation with the federal government on water-pollution research and programs. Through the Sanitary Engineering Division, the state acts as a broker in terms of the federal funds available for municipal treatment plants.

The state does not provide financial aid to the communities for construction of sewage works. The Water Resources Commission was authorized by the General Court in 1961 to make an investigation and study of the need for state aid to the communities for this purpose, but legislation subsequently introduced to provide additional help in the form of grants-in-aid and long-term borrowing credit did not pass.

Another state agency with authority in the pollution-control field is the Sewerage Division of the Metropolitan District Commission, which operates its own sewage network through the Greater Boston area, with the effluent entering Boston Harbor. Its waste-water system serves two million people and 40 communities, three of which are in the SuAsCo Basin. The South Metropolitan area treatment plant is located on Nut Island, and the new treatment works for the North Metropolitan area will be at Deer Island. Two underground tunnels to Deer Island are already completed, one seven miles long and the other four and a half miles long. The plant should be ready to use in 1965.

The Charles River clean-up will be part of this improvement program. Its summer odors are well known to Boston area residents. The MDC has found it necessary during certain drought periods to pump millions of gallons of water into this River from the Sudbury system, first from the Cochituate Aqueduct and since 1962 from the Sudbury aqueduct.

The federal program that offers the greatest constructive help to meet the pollution problem is under P.L. 84-660, the Water Pollution Control Act, administered by the U.S. Public Health Service.

As amended in 1961, it strengthens the measures by which it provides interstate cooperation, research and investigation, training, grants for water-pollution-control programs, enforcement measures against pollution of interstate waters, cooperative comprehensive planning for water-quality control, and grants for construction of treatment works. In our Basin recent federal grants have been made to Hudson, the Billerica House of Correction, and Shrewsbury.

The development of a comprehensive water-pollution-control program for river-basin areas is possible under the revised Water Pollution Control Act. A comprehensive water-quality study of the New England Basins is awaiting funds. The Basin under which the SuAsCo area would be considered is the Merrimack River Basin.

The Merrimack River is an interstate river, and its pollution control will involve scores of communities as well as the federal, state, and interstate authorities. This river, which is said to account for 70 percent of the state's pollution, will require intensified efforts and large sums of money before it can be accepted as clean. Such industrial areas as Haverhill, Lawrence, and Lowell are involved. Included in the Lowell area are portions of Billerica, Tewksbury, and Chelmsford at the lower end of the Concord River, which also contributes to the pollution of the Merrimack.

Several bills passed by the 1962 and 1963 sessions of the state legislature prepare the way for a solution to the Merrimack problem, including the establishment of a Merrimack River Valley Pollution Abatement District. Under the authority of the Water Pollution Control Act, Governor Peabody has requested a conference in February, 1964, to consider pollution problems of the Merrimack interstate streams and the related intrastate streams in the Massachusetts portion of the Merrimack River Basin, with the SuAsCo Basin in this latter category. Technical discussions have been held by the government agencies concerned in preparation for the conference.

Other facets to the pollution problem will require more than money and effort. Eliminating detergents from water through treatment has been a difficulty since these products first appeared on the market. Today they represent 80 percent of the household cleaners sold. These foaming synthetics do not break down in soil or water and become food for bacteria as regular animal-fat soaps do. Experiments have been conducted to discover more effective treatment procedures. New products are also being readied for the housewife, so some solution may be in sight. The actual threat of detergents to health is not yet determined. The aesthetic aspect has brought alarm, however. In our Basin we see evidence of detergents in some of our streams containing sewage effluent, making mockery of the lovely countryside. [Ed. note: It is only fair to point out that though this alarming situation was widespread when the study was published, it has been greatly alleviated since. By July 1, 1965, producers of 90 percent of all detergents in the U.S. had changed formulas in a voluntary effort to put an end to the blight just described.]

Contamination of the environment by pesticides is another phase to the pollution problem that raises more questions than there are available answers. While some health and conservation experts have been warning for years of the hazards that spraying chemicals in the atmosphere can have on living organisms, it was not until the publication of Rachel Carson's book *Silent Spring,* in late 1962, that widespread public reaction followed such warnings. President Kennedy appointed a panel of his Science Advisory Committee to make a study and recommendations on the use of pesticides.

Pesticides are here to stay, all the experts seem to agree, but their proper use needs to be insured so that their benefits can clearly outweigh the harm they are causing.

The U.S. Public Health Service, the University of Massachusetts, the state Department of Public Health, and the Massachusetts Pesticide Board recently held a conference on mosquito control and the safe use of pesticides. The Pesticide Board, established in 1962, is now preparing a licensing procedure for pesticide application to insure proper regulation. The U.S. Public Health Service is supporting research by other agencies, universities, and industries on the effect of insecticides on land and water organisms. A study is now going on in the Sudbury Valley, which will provide facts to evaluate intelligently the present spraying programs.

The state Division of Fisheries and Game is attempting in this study to find out whether there is a residual buildup of DDT in fish and wildlife after repeated sprayings. Starting in summer 1962, an initial grant of $12,000 was provided for a three-year study, with additional funds granted for fiscal year 1964. A progress report for the first year includes this summary from the Division:

"During the first segment of this project, 32 sampling stations were established and fish and soils collected to determine present

DDT levels in the watershed. To date, tissues from 565 fishes have been analyzed. Forty-three percent, or 242 fish, from this sample contained an average DDT residue constituting 35.4 ppm of their dry weight. (Fish from) surface water supplies showed as high concentrations of pesticide residues as (those from) recreation areas. Greatest concentration of the residues within the fish are located in the wall of the digestive tract and the brain, or that portion generally not consumed by the public.

"Laboratory fishes are presently being exposed to sublethal doses of DDT and their residue storage capacity being measured in the hope of providing a yardstick for decisions concerning necessary recovery time between sprayings in any given watershed."

A federal Water Pollution Control Laboratory for the northeast area is slated to be built in Jamaica Plain, as one of seven regional field stations and research centers in the country selected and administered by the Department of Health, Education, and Welfare through the Public Health Service. The present headquarters for federal water-quality research is the Robert A. Taft Sanitary Engineering Center in Cincinnati. A salt-water quality-standards laboratory is being built at Kingston, Rhode Island, and a similar one for fresh water at Duluth, Minnesota.

The research programs planned or now going on may provide some of the answers lacking with regard to treatment of detergents, the effect of certain vegetation, pesticides, and radiation on water quality, and other present imponderables. The contribution of town dumps to air and water pollution and the consideration of clean substitutes also need to be explored.

In the SuAsCo Basin a regional approach would be advantageous, since pollution does not recognize town boundaries. An ounce of prevention could save costly damage from occurring in such areas as the I-495, or Outer Belt, area where changes will occur with population and industrial expansion. With the Assabet River already heavily used for waste-carrying purposes, the question of how much additional use it can safely take should be analyzed now, before it is too late. If necessary, provision for using another watershed for some of this waste should be planned in advance. The Boston Regional Planning Project is concerned with planning for the future highway needs of this area, but waste disposal will not be emphasized in their regional study. The Division of Sanitary Engineering will consult with industries, industrial parks, and localities to determine the treatment needs before development begins. But the kind of thorough and long-range planning needed is not yet evident.

The need for overall planning to meet properly the water pollution problem has become increasingly evident throughout the country. Stop-gap measures merely prevent the situation from further deteriorating and do not bring about the Basin-wide improvements needed. The Wildlife Management Institute recently reported that in spite of the fact that one-third more municipal sewage plants were constructed in the country in 1961 than in any previous year, the number of communities with inadequate or no sewage treatment facilities continued to mount in the same year. Apparently it is a matter of running just to stand still. To win the uphill battle, all-out efforts at all levels will be required.

Some of the basic needs for effective pollution control in our Basin bear repeating. These are: wider public understanding of the importance of clean water to meet growing demands; more planning to bring the localities, industries, and agencies into closer cooperation and to bring the problem into sharper focus; more public willingness to use tax money for its solution and more assistance to the communities to stimulate immediate action; more research on the treatment of wastes and water contaminants; and more enforcement of existing sanitary provisions to prevent pollution and punish violators.

3. Flood Control

Flood control is one water problem that has plagued our watershed since the early settlers farmed along its meadows. Commissions dating back to 1644 have studied the subject, and proposals have been made for the drainage of wetlands and removal of flow obstacles. None of the plans met with success, because of lack of funds or because of lack of agreement on procedures and priorities, although temporary measures have been undertaken in particular locations.

The most extensive plan put forth was that of the Department of Public Works, prepared by Howard M. Turner in 1951, which would have called for the removal of the Fordway Bar and the addition of a movable crest gate on the Talbot Dam, as well as thorough dredging in that area of the Concord River. The cost was considered too high in relation to anticipated benefits.

Usually flowage was viewed in terms of early spring flooding, which annually gave the farmer headaches but did not cause general concern. However, several tropical storms in recent years focussed dramatic attention on the flood-control problems in the area. The most disastrous of these, Hurricane Diane, in 1955, caused an estimated damage to industrial property, roads, bridges, residences, and agricultural land of nearly two million dollars in the SuAsCo Basin alone. Reaction followed and then further study, which finally resulted in an acceptable watershed work plan that should contribute at least significantly to the solution of the area's flood problems.

The SuAsCo Watershed Work Plan was established in 1959 under the authority of Public Law 566, the Watershed Protection and Flood Prevention Act, which gives the Soil Conservation Service responsibility for assisting local organizations in carrying out approved small watershed programs when requested. Under this Act, the maximum acreage for a small watershed is listed as 250,000 acres. With the elimination of one brook in Chelmsford from the study area, the SuAsCo Watershed includes 241,617 acres for flood-control purposes.

The Work Plan with a suggested revision includes these principal features: (1) the installation of six to 10 small flood-control reservoirs on the Assabet River and its tributaries, with the possibility of regulating two for multi-purpose activity; (2) provision for flood storage in six of the existing reservoirs on the Sudbury River controlled by the Metropolitan District Commission and the Department of Natural Resources; and (3) use of land-treatment measures and good soil-conservation practices for watershed protection. Wetlands drainage and downstream measures were not deemed feasible flood-control features for this watershed, though they had been in earlier plans.

As of November, 1963, the location of six flood-control structures was definite, and four more were being investigated. One of the additional four structures being investigated would be multi-purpose, providing permanent water for recreation and stored water to supplement low flows. The three other structures would provide flood storage only. Development of these additional four structures will necessitate a revision to the Work Plan and supplementary funds from the Legislature.

The U.S. Soil Conservation Service has provided financial and technical assistance, surveys, preparation of the Work Plan, and supervision of project construction. In the land-treatment program, assistance has been given by the U.S. Forest Service, including woodland management, tree planting, improvement and harvest cutting, and other technical services. The U.S. Fish and Wildlife Service has made studies concerning possible effects of the program on fish and wildlife. Suggestions have been made for the inclusion of improvements at flood-control sites to provide for coordinated multi-purpose activity.

The Army Corps of Engineers has been engaged to undertake engineering surveys on the Assabet in relation to the establishment of stream-encroachment lines. The data from this study will be used by the Water Resources Commission to establish a reserved flood-way. In addition, the local communities will be encouraged to adopt flood-plain zoning by-laws.

In a flood-control project considered to be separate but not in conflict with the Soil Conservation Service Work Plan, the Corps of Engineers has completed a study of the Roxbury Carpet Dam in Saxonville (Framingham), and has determined that a local protection project consisting of dikes and walls could be justified. The Corps of Engineers recommended further detailed studies provided the town of Framingham would agree to participate in those items of local cooperation as required by law. In March, 1963, Framingham voted to pay for its share of landtaking and maintenance costs, and requested that the Federal Government proceed with detailed studies. The project will provide protection to approximately 22 acres of industrial, commercial, and residential land on the left bank of the Sudbury River. Project costs are estimated at $940,000, of which $90,000 will represent a local cost.

A private engineering firm, Anderson-Nichols & Company, was engaged by the Soil Conservation Service to make studies of the upper Sudbury River above the Sudbury marshes. This same firm also made a study concerning the drawdown of the reservoirs of the Sudbury River as part of the watershed plan.

Several agencies are active at the state level. The Water Resources Commission coordinates all activity connected with the SuAsCo

Work Plan and arranges the necessary hearings and negotiations for landtaking as well as administering the contracts for construction. The Commission has initiated most of the legislation by which the state participates in this program. Through such legislation the General Court has approved the establishment of stream encroachment lines for the Assabet; authorization for the change in number and location of the reservoirs when necessary; provision for study of low flow in the rivers; and a ground-water study for the Assabet. The local sponsoring organizations submitted the legislation approving state financial assistance for the costs of the project (state share $300,000; federal share $1 million). Any special studies or projects not included in the original Work Plan have required additional legislation. While the bills have generally passed, they have not all been accompanied by the necessary appropriations.

The Water Resources Commission has also provided the supervision for the informal operating agreement reached with the Metropolitan District Commission and the Department of Natural Resources, which makes available additional flood-storage capacity in six of the existing reservoirs on the tributaries of the Sudbury River under their jurisdiction. During the three summer months 1,500 million gallons and during the rest of the year 2,600 million gallons of flood-storage capacity is available. This arrangement has been on a trial basis, and so far has proven satisfactory. It is expected to continue in the future.

The work of the Department of Natural Resources in preparing a study of the wetlands provided a framework for the passage of legislation authorizing their purchase by appropriate agencies. The flood-storage capacity of these wet areas was stressed as a necessary part of a flood-control program for the Basin.

Other state agencies whose work has related to flood-control activity are the Department of Public Works, which has been concerned with the improvement of the Sudbury channel above and below the Saxonville Dam; the Fisheries and Game Division, which may participate in multi-use programs at some of the reservoir sites; and the Division of Forests and Parks, which has been cooperating with the U.S. Forest Service in providing technical assistance to landowners installing forestry-related land-treatment measures.

The communities have provided support of the Watershed Work Plan through the sponsoring organizations, the Middlesex and

Northeastern Worcester County Soil Conservation Districts, with the early assistance of a private group, the SuAsCo Watershed Association. They are interested in soil-conservation practices such as land-improvement measures. Over 50 percent of the farm lands above each proposed retention structure are under conservation agreement with the districts. The landowners are receiving technical assistance through the districts to carry out a recommended program of land stabilization, including such activity as crop rotation, contour farming, cover cropping, etc.

The SuAsCo Watershed Association was a private organization instrumental in causing this watershed to be the first in New England accepted for study under Public Law 566 and also gave support to the formation of the Massachusetts Water Resources Commission. Though the latter is no longer functioning, many feel that it or some other regional organization is still needed to provide local leadership and improved communication between the agencies and the communities concerned.

Flood-plain zoning on the local level is an important way in which the communities can act to help prevent flood damage. Enabling legislation came from the state in 1954. In 1958, Wayland was the only town in the Basin which had enacted such zoning, and encroachment had already begun to have serious effects, especially because of upstream urban development.

Recently Concord and Sudbury have passed flood-plain zoning laws, and at least Westborough, Harvard, Bolton, and Acton were considering it, as of spring 1963. Billerica recently voted down flood-plain districts. Framingham has approved the establishment of wetlands districts. Lincoln has open-space zoning, with voluntary conservation districts that protect the flood-plain areas. The wetlands acquisition programs will result in additional protection in certain areas along the Sudbury and Concord Rivers. The Sudbury headwaters areas remain without flood-plain zoning.

In 1962, legislation submitted by the Water Resources Commission was passed by the General Court to provide a reserved floodway for the Assabet River, where residential and industrial encroachment in the flood plain threatened to interfere with the success of the flood-control program. In 1963, a Sudbury town committee introduced similar legislation to provide stream-encroachment lines for the Sudbury and Concord Rivers, which was passed.

Once such engineering lines are established, it is still important that local efforts safeguard these lines and supplement them where necessary locally.

One particular area that has been developed residentially and that has received heavy flood damage is in the Baiting Brook Watershed, wholly within the town of Framingham. This brook is a tributary to the Sudbury River and part of the SuAsCo Watershed, but because of the nature of its flood problems, a separate work plan for it was developed by the Middlesex Soil Conservation District, assisted by the Soil Conservation Service. As yet the necessary local support for its implementation has not been forthcoming. Some changes are being made in the plan, which may make a local flood-protection plan acceptable in the near future.

The localities can also participate in the watershed flood-control program through multi-purpose development of the flood-retention sites. For recreation, fish and wildlife, and water-supply purposes, the localities can request expanded works from any federal agency engaged in water resources. In our Basin, the Soil Conservation Service is the agency directly involved in such multi-purpose activity. Until 1962, only the fish and wildlife features could receive federal support for a portion of the costs, but a recent amendment to P.L. 566 has added recreation to the cost-sharing provisions. Loans for municipal water-supply purposes are also available.

So far the communities affected have been reluctant to participate because of financial problems, although numerous meetings have been held to discuss such action. Although there will not be as much multi-purpose activity as was considered possible and suitable, some of this potential will be realized. Provisions for regulating low flow will be incorporated in at least one reservoir plan, and recreation features will be included in an additional site. Recent state legislation granting long-term borrowing credit to the towns and cities for multi-use projects at the flood-control sites should prove helpful, along with the increased federal funds now available.

The communities are already pledged through legislation to participate in the watershed flood-control program to the extent that some assessments will be made on certain towns in relation to benefits received. For example, the tax losses incurred by one town may result in improvements to other towns only, and therefore those other towns benefitting will pay back proportionately on this amount to the town with losses. This procedure is being worked out through the Water Resources Commission.

Since the Watershed Work Plan was first approved and published, many changes have been necessary, and further modifications will result from the studies and surveys completed or under way. All of the changes take time, and they must finally be approved by the sponsoring organizations, the soil-conservation districts. When the revised work plan is completed, many of the existing questions concerning possible new construction works, multi-purpose possibilities, and local cooperation may be cleared up. In spite of these questions, this flood-control program is proceeding with good results both in the planning and action stages and in terms of inter-governmental cooperation.

4. Wetlands Preservation

The average citizen's reaction to the sacrifice of wet areas for housing developments, highways, industries, and shopping centers in an age of urban expansion has been one of indifference. Little thought was apparently given to the danger to health and property and to the loss of irretrievable assets that have resulted from the exploitation of wetlands. In recent years, however, there has been a growing awareness of the need to preserve the wetlands for flood control, water resources, recreation, wildlife habitat, nature education, and open-space planning.

This awareness helped to bring about the passage of enabling legislation, in 1961, involving government acquisition of the Sudbury-Concord wetlands. The law was permissive in nature, with no appropriations. Authority was granted in the so-called "Wetlands Bill" for the federal government to acquire 4,500 acres along the two rivers, the state Division of Fisheries and Game to acquire 500 acres contiguous to its Pantry Brook Management tract in Sudbury, and the state Department of Natural Resources to acquire 1,000 acres in the towns of Concord and Lincoln. Approximately 1,750 acres in the Cedar Swamp area, or headwaters of the Sudbury River, were assigned for acquisition by the Division of Fisheries and Game, but this section was deleted from the Bill as signed into law.

With the successful enactment of the Wetlands Bill, the federal Bureau of Sport Fisheries and Wildlife, of the Fish and Wildlife

Service, made the necessary biological and engineering studies and thereafter approved the sponsorship of a Sudbury National Wildlife Refuge. The required final approval of the Migratory Bird Conservation Commission came in May, 1963, making provision for the purchase of 3,879 acres at an estimated cost of 1.2 million dollars. Land negotiations are now actively under way, and it is expected that by 1965 most of the acreage will have been acquired. Eminent-domain proceedings will not be resorted to unless all efforts at direct negotiation fail. By June 30, 1963, 16 purchase agreements covering more than 800 acres had already been signed. Funds are available for any options negotiated during the next fiscal year. Money for the Refuge will not involve general tax funds but will come from the sale of Duck Stamps.

The Sudbury National Wildlife Refuge will include a Sudbury River unit of 2,489 acres within the following towns: Wayland, 1,593 acres; Sudbury, 805 acres; Concord, 73 acres; and Lincoln, 18 acres. This unit will extend from Heard's Pond, south of Route 20 in Wayland, northward along the Sudbury River as far as Route 117, which runs parallel to the most northern reaches of Farrar Pond in Lincoln. The Concord unit of 1,390 acres adjoins the Great Meadows National Wildlife Refuge and extends north along the Concord River, including 244 acres in Concord, 326 in Carlisle, 87 in Billerica, and 733 in Bedford.

According to the federal Bureau of Sport Fisheries and Wildlife, the areas will be preserved as nesting, resting, and feeding grounds for migratory waterfowl, and the landscape will remain essentially the same. Management will be directed toward the preservation of habitat, control of vegetation, and the maintenance of water levels favorable to waterfowl and wildlife, through a system of man-made low dikes, which will be "topped" during period of high flow.

On the state level, the Department of Natural Resources has been concerned more with the planning for wetlands preservation than in outright acquisition. In late 1960 this agency met with numerous town officials and private groups, as well as other state and federal agencies, to explore the possibilities of a regional wetlands program. With the special assistance of the Massachusetts Wetlands Committee, a private group, the necessary gathering and evaluation of data proceeded rapidly, and a report dated January, 1961, was introduced in the General Court. This report was instrumental in mustering the required support for the subsequent passage of the Wetlands Bill.

Of the 1,000 acres of wetlands in Concord and Lincoln that the Department of Natural Resources was granted power to acquire, these towns were given a flexible period of time to preserve them on their own, prior to any state action. The two towns report success in acquiring or otherwise restricting the use of 90 percent of this land, and the Department is now free to acquire the rest if it so desires. The other state agency included in the authority of the Wetlands Bill, the Division of Fisheries and Game, has no funds earmarked for the additional 500 acres of Pantry Brook wetlands it is permitted to acquire.

One important recommendation made in the January, 1961, report of the Department of Natural Resources, but not included in the text of the bill, related to the role of the communities in the wetlands program. It was suggested that the towns in the region preserve approximately 3,000 acres of marsh and swamp in the Sudbury-Concord valley, most of which were in lots too small or isolated to warrant federal or state acquisition. Most of this acreage is not along the rivers but on headwaters of tributary streams, or related to town water-supply systems, or in some way considered important to the continuity of a wetlands program. Of the 620 acres remaining of the originally proposed 4,500 to be federally acquired, presumably the local governments and land trusts will have to assume the burden of responsibility for their preservation.

Much of the local acquisition may come through the recently authorized conservation commissions, which can acquire land for conservation purposes. The self-help program of the state, initiated in 1960, provided great incentive with a portion of an annual million-dollar fund for the general expansion of parks, available to the towns toward reimbursement of up to 50 percent of the cost of projects approved by the Department of Natural Resources.

There are conservation commissions in all but six of the SuAsCo communities at the present time, and land trusts in at least seven of them. The towns particularly affected by the provisions of the wetlands bill all have conservation commissions. Perhaps these commissions can become eligible to qualify for funds under the Housing Act as part of an overall regional plan. The federal Bureau of Sport Fisheries and Wildlife has already consulted with some of the towns within the project and will work more closely with the conservation commissions when greater progress has been made, so that correlation of efforts is possible.

There are many other local groups concerned with wetlands preservation that will exert a strong influence on the outcome of the acquisition program. Special mention should be made of the role of the Sudbury Valley Trustees, which, as early as 1953, recognized the need to alert the residents of the valley to the need to start acquiring conservation land for the future, and much of the land they have secured (more than 400 acres) is marshland near the Sudbury River. They have also aided in the valuable public-education program needed to get any large-scale acquisition efforts launched, as has another private organization, the Massachusetts Audubon Society.

Garden clubs, sportsmen's groups, recreation agencies, granges, and similar groups are also actively engaged in the struggle to promote conservation interests. One outstanding example of the accomplishments of such groups is the Educational Marsh Management Area (EMMA), which is a reclaimed swamp covering approximately 40 acres on the Millbrook tract of the Sudbury Valley Trustees in Wayland. After EMMA is completed in late 1963, "she" will serve as an outdoor classroom demonstrating such types of water management as fish and wildlife propagation, flood control, recreation values, and experimental mosquito-breeding control through water-level control, rather than drainage or pesticide spraying. Sponsored by the Massachusetts Wetlands Committee, this project has involved technical and financial contributions from many public and private agencies, including supervision from the Massachusetts Audubon Society and funds from the Carling Conservation Club. Another imaginative wetlands project is the Wayland Garden Club's wild-life sanctuary and wetlands arboretum, on town land in front of the junior high school. Nearing completion, it will prove that a water area can be reclaimed with both artistic and practical results. Its plantings were chosen for year-round color and as a source of food and shelter for wildlife.

The job of wetlands preservation involves all groups, private and governmental, and a progress report at this time is largely optimistic. Some definite action has been accomplished. A good deal of work still remains to implement fully the provisions of the Wetlands Bill and to extend this program of wetlands protection.

5. Recreation, Fish and Wildlife

Public outdoor-recreation facilities are generally underdeveloped in the SuAsCo area, but there are plans to supplement the present programs with future state parks and greater access to existing ponds, lakes, and rivers suitable for recreation. Our rivers do not figure prominently in current plans because of the poor conditions of the water and perhaps also because of local reluctance to open protected areas to development. Even without further development, the rivers and related lands promise to remain highly valuable to canoers, fishermen, bird-watchers, nature lovers, and other participants in quiet outdoor recreation.

A good deal of the present recreational activity in our Basin is municipally or privately sponsored and limited in its availability. There appears to be a strong tradition of private action in this field, and recreation programs have been harder to justify in terms of tax money than some other more "tangible" needs. The need for additional recreation areas has become more pressing. Private facilities are no longer adequate.

Not until recently have many communities had an active park and/or recreation program. The local desire for privacy has continued, however, and usually programs have developed locally for the benefit of residents only. The numerous great ponds in our region that by law are public are generally without access and have not been developed by the towns for recreation purposes, either because of finances, the impurity of the water, or the fear of attracting crowds from the cities.

In 1957, a report on Public Outdoor Recreation submitted by the Department of Natural Resources gave an inventory of existing facilities and resources and proposed new state programs. Both a lack of money and a lack of public support may be reasons for inadequate progress on the proposals.

The machinery and the plans do exist, but it will take time for the plans to be translated into action. For example, 1959 plans for a $2.5 million Hopkinton State Park are only beginning to become definite. Already at least half of the classified land in this seven-year-old inventory is no longer available. There is some feeling that with the absence of regional planning and strong state confidence the communities will continue to work on a protective basis, desiring state public-recreation facilities in other communities but not in their own.

Of the four Metropolitan District Commission reservoirs turned over to the Department of Natural Resources for recreational use in our Basin, only one, Lake Cochituate, is considered highly developed. Of the others, Ashland, Whitehall, and Hopkinton Reservoirs, Hopkinton alone is slated for extensive development, although fishing and limited access already exist on all of them. If other standby water-supply reservoirs are released in the future, they could provide excellent recreation sites. Another future recreation possibility is the Milham Reservoir in Marlborough, near the Assabet River. Walden Pond State Reservation at present offers several types of recreation facilities and is also a site of historic and cultural interest.

In the 1963 session of the General Court, the Massachusetts Association of Conservation Commissions introduced a bill calling for an investigation and study relative to promoting and developing the natural resources in the cities and towns in the Metropolitan Parks District. A similar type of bill, sponsored by Representative James De Normandie of Lincoln, calls for a study and investigation of facilities in certain state forests and recreational needs outside the Metropolitan Parks District.

Perhaps new studies of this type will spur further action before the race for available space is lost. This race is going on throughout the country, but nowhere with the same urgency as in the northeast section, where the demand for additional outdoor-recreation facilities rises as much as 10 percent a year.

Direct federal activity in the recreation field is very minimal in our Basin, although funds are offered under several programs, and a considerable amount of research is being carried on. An ad-hoc Presidential Commission on Outdoor Recreation Resources Review (ORRRC) has published numerous reports covering every conceivable phase of related recreation activity. Included in the final report of this Commission was the recommendation that a Bureau of Outdoor Recreation be created. Such a Bureau was established by Executive Order in 1962, within the Department of the Interior, to coordinate outdoor recreation programs of 20 federal agencies and to work with the states to gain more outdoor-recreation space.

Interest-free loans for parks and recreation facilities are made by the Community Facilities Administration of the Housing and Home Finance Agency. The Urban Renewal Administration of this same agency provides grants for the acquisition of open-space land in urban areas for recreation and conservation purposes.

Federal financial assistance for recreational multi-purpose activity related to flood-control programs can be administered by both the Army Corps of Engineers and the U.S. Soil Conservation Service. One of the proposed flood-control reservoirs along an Assabet River tributary is expected to be developed for recreational use through the Soil Conservation Service Watershed Work Plan.

In addition to assistance to the community, there is aid to the individual farmer through a new program to boost his income, combining recreation enterprises with regular farm operations. For example, a portion of the farm land might be used for camping, public access for fishing, and so on.

Plans are already under way for the National Park Service of the Department of the Interior to establish a Minute Man National Historical Park in the Lexington-Concord area. They are authorized by Congress to acquire up to 750 acres of land to conserve the battle route of the opening day of the Revolutionary War. As of June, 1963, the Park Service has title to about 165 acres in 55 parcels, some of which is along the Concord River. On July 1 it began to operate the North Bridge Battleground in Concord.

Another site of historic interest is located in Sudbury, where Longfellow's Wayside Inn and grist mill are open to the public through private sponsorship.

Billerica, Carlisle, Marlborough, Sudbury, and Hopkinton are the only SuAsCo communities in which state forests exist. Both the Upton State Forest, which is located in Hopkinton, Northbridge, and Upton, and a State Nursery in Clinton lie just outside our Basin. A bill has recently been signed by the President by which additional funds will be available to states for forest-management programs.

While the state forests are not numerous in our area, local action to preserve wooded areas has been reassuring. There are 21 communities in the SuAsCo Basin listed by the Massachusetts Forest and Park Association as having town forests, with a total area of 4,177 acres. Still more towns are considering this type of acquisition for watershed purposes, recreation benefits, and even for monetary reasons. Only three of the town forests, in Bedford, Billerica, and Marlborough, are also town watershed lands. Some of the SuAsCo communities have watershed reservation land that could be used for outdoor-recreation purposes. The potential for multiple use of forests or watershed lands is great. When requested, the Forest and Park Association, the state Forest and Park Division of the Department of Natural Resources, and the U.S. Forest Service cooperate with the localities in developing forestry programs.

The towns are also showing initiative in acquiring other lands as part of town conservation programs, through local conservation commissions and private groups. There appears to be sentiment in favor of keeping conservation land undeveloped or for limited recreational activity.

In terms of fish and wildlife programs, the SuAsCo River Basin is recognized as one of the finest areas for such activity, and resulting income to the Commonwealth is substantial. The role of the wetlands in protecting a valuable segment of fish and wildlife habitat cannot be overstressed.

The U.S. Fish and Wildlife Service, which already manages the Great Meadows Wildlife Sanctuary along the Concord River, will be responsible for a sizeable new program along both the Sudbury and Concord Rivers as a result of the wetlands-acquisition program. Management as seen at Great Meadows aims to preserve habitat for nesting and migrating waterfowl by maintaining favorable water levels to increase production of waterfowl food plants. Under federal Refuge Laws, controlled public hunting is permissible on up to 40 percent of a refuge if conditions warrant.

Additional wildlife management and fishing facilities may be possible at certain of the Assabet reservoir sites and partial cost benefits are available through P.L. 566, the Watershed Act. The U.S. Fish and Wildlife Service may work with the state Division of Fisheries and Game on management and development.

The state Division of Fisheries and Game has two wildlife management areas in our region. The Pantry Brook Wildlife Management Area in Sudbury could be greatly expanded as a result of the Wetlands Bill, but this is not imminent. Without such expansion, its use will remain limited to hunting. The Division also maintains a Wildlife Management Area in Westborough, which, in addition to hunting and fishing, has dog field trials.

These two Areas are the only public hunting grounds in our Basin, but hunting is permitted in many of the communities, subject to state and federal hunting laws. In Natick, however, hunting is prohibited. Bedford, Boxborough, Carlisle, Concord, Framingham, Lincoln, Sherborn, Sudbury, Wayland, and Weston have ordinances requiring hunters to obtain written permission of landowners or town authorities before hunting can take place. Billerica requires permission of property owner to fire a rifle within town limits. Several rod-and-gun clubs have purchased property, especially along the Sudbury and Concord Rivers, in order to provide private hunting grounds.

The fish-and-game program in the state has been hampered by a lack of funds, but there are indications that the situation is improving. Money from a motorboat gasoline tax is expected to allow greater development of facilities for fishing and other forms of recreation. A Public Access Board has been established in the Department of Natural Resources to approve and purchase access rights where necessary.

The Division of Fisheries and Game already leases six miles of shoreline in Marlborough, Berlin, and Northborough for fishing along the Assabet River. The Metropolitan District Commission permits residents of Marlborough and Southborough to fish from a limited portion of the Sudbury Reservoir shoreline under special permits issued by its Water Division.

While pollution in the SuAsCo rivers has been a particular problem for fishermen in the past, this has been corrected to the point where the Sudbury River and portions of the Concord are again considered excellent and produce more fish than the anglers harvest. However, there is a concern that present spraying operations are adversely affecting fish and wildlife in our Basin. The state Fish and Game Division is now studying this problem.

Again the role of private groups is very important. To mention a few: the Massachusetts Audubon Society, rod-and-gun clubs, Carling's Conservation Club, and private town conservation trusts have provided funds and leadership in our Basin to a high degree. The programs and tours of Drumlin Farm Wildlife Sanctuary and Nature Center in South Lincoln at present serve about 20,000 children a year.

The Marlborough Fish and Game Association sponsors a junior

conservation camp for youngsters in its area. The Middlesex County League of Sportsmen's Clubs has begun a public land-acquisition program that will attempt to preserve areas for multiple-use public outdoor recreation, to be eventually turned over to the Division of Fisheries and Game to develop and manage. The newly established Fund for the Preservation of Natural Areas and Wildlife is another outstanding example of private initiative.

As valuable as the private activity will continue to be in the outdoor-recreation, fish-and-wildlife areas, public leadership will be necessary for large-scale programs to meet the growing demands of an expanding population. The Department of Natural Resources will have to assume increased responsibility for coordinating efforts toward this end if the resources of the Commonwealth are to be effectively used.

6. Open Space Planning

The saving of open land has become an urgent problem. Urbanization has been generally accompanied by an unconfined scattering of development that has been eating up the countryside. Proper planning is needed to see that this development does not take place at the expense of using land more suitable for public-benefit purposes such as water supply, flood storage, watershed protection, parks and recreation, aesthetic needs, and the orderly channeling of urban growth.

The more urbanized an area becomes, the more essential it is that a certain amount of land be saved to provide citizens with an outlet for their leisure time. Yet the pattern that is true throughout our country is that the more people there are in an area, the less open land there is reserved for their enjoyment. The National Park Service reports that in the crowded northeast, with one-fourth of the country's population, only one seventy-fifth of the publicly owned land exists.

According to the Greater Boston Economic Study Committee's land-use study, the amount of open space in its study area that has been permanently reserved is very small. There is a total of 92,330 acres within 153 cities and towns that is reserved either as recreation, forest, and wildlife-management areas or as undeveloped town land. About 60 percent of the total is held locally or privately. The shortage of permanent open space is, of course, much worse in the core than in the outer band of the study area where many of our communities exist. In our Basin the amount of vacant land is actually plentiful in total acreage, but it is not permanently reserved. The outward movement is rapidly increasing. Unplanned growth in some of the suburbs has already robbed the area of some of its natural resources and has produced major headaches to local government.

The GBESC states that 65 percent of the population of Massachusetts resides in the Greater Boston area, with tremendous recent growth in the suburbs and more predicted. It stands to reason that the remaining open areas of the outer towns will be subject to heavy pressures in the years ahead to provide open space for the entire Greater Boston region. If the right land is to be preserved by local conservation groups, and supplemented by any regional and state programs, it is necessary for open-space planning to proceed now, before the bulldozers, highways, and power lines chew up the remaining areas.

In our Basin, much of the land that must be high on any conservation priority list is wetland or areas related to water supply or land in one way or another connected with a water problem. It has been pointed out by a leader in open-space action, William H. Whyte, that water can be the unifying factor to bring groups into a cooperative effort. A regional or river-basin approach to open-space planning could further coordinate study and action, but in the absence of this, any efforts, whether private or public, must be considered as contributing toward the desired end. In Mr. Whyte's words: "Though communities can take first steps, there can be no large-scale open-space program unless there is a cooperative regional effort. And this means that the role of the state government is critical." In the initial stages both local agencies and private groups such as land trusts can play an important role.

Local conservation commissions offer a vital means for acquiring open space on a town-wide basis. Since the state enabling legislation of 1957, 30 out of 36 communities in our Basin have established conservation commissions, most of them within the past three years. Their aims are to promote and develop the natural resources, protect the watershed resources, and acquire open spaces within the community. Projects can be financed in several ways:

1. *Community tax money*—one-twentieth of one percent of the total

assessed valuation of the community may be appropriated each year (total not exceeding $15,000 in any year) and can be accumulated from year to year in a Conservation Fund.

2. *Self-help conservation program*—offered through the state Department of Natural Resources, by which up to 50 percent of the costs of an approved project can be reimbursed.

3. *Open-space land program*—offered by the federal Housing and Home Finance Agency; funds made available by the Housing Act of 1961 for urban recreation and open-space acquisition. Localities may be reimbursed for 20 percent of costs of a project, and if the body requesting the funds exercises responsibility for an urban area as a whole, 30 percent. Project must be part of a comprehensive plan for a community or region.

The tools available to a community for preserving open space, through the conservation commission, planning board, and other local bodies, include acquisition of land, acquisition of rights in land, zoning and planning, and a corollary tax-abatement or tax-deferral program.

There are at least the following possibilities for acquisition of land and land rights:

1. *Fee simple or outright purchase.* This is a highly desirable way to preserve open space, but lack of adequate funds and a deadline may make another approach practical.

2. *Gifts by grant or devise* (will) of either money or land help solve the financial problems, and the donor can receive federal income-tax deductions for his gift.

3. *Sale and leaseback* is a feasible arrangement in some instances, when, for example, the land purchased could be put to beneficial farm use or recreation use, with income from rent received by the community.

4. *Life Estate.* The owner who gives or sells land can retain use and occupancy of land for life through legal agreement.

5. *Rights in land.* A conservation easement or other restrictive agreement can limit the use of land. Owner can confer these rights free or be compensated for the loss of his development rights, this compensation usually costing less than outright purchase.

The conservation easement is a relatively new device for keeping land open which offers many advantages, especially when used in conjunction with other tools such as tax abatement and zoning.

Zoning, subject to community approval, is a tool of local bodies such as the planning board, which regulates land use through the use of the police power. It is a negative tool and does not involve compensation for loss of rights. Any extension of this power is usually open to legal tests, and must therefore be exerted with great caution. However, when properly used, the following approaches can direct conservation planning within a community:

1. *Flood-plain zoning* restricts building in the flood plain to prevent damage to life and property on areas subject to periodic flooding.

2. *Conservancy-district zoning* is usually tied to flood control. Prevents building on and filling in of land to be kept open for public health, water supply, and other conservation purposes. New concept not yet tested legally.

3. *Minimum-lot zoning* is often the means of encouraging large-lot land use and discouraging small-acreage housing development.

4. *Cluster zoning* represents a different approach to saving open space. The house lots are fairly small, but a correspondingly larger area remains open for recreation, aesthetic, and conservation purposes.

5. *Agricultural zoning* makes it possible for vital farmland areas to be greenbelted. This is more of a western phenomenon.

6. *Campus-type industry* is another new concept, combining open-space planning with industrial zoning. The industrial plant occupies a small percentage of the land purchased, and restrictions are placed locally on the use of the remaining open land.

7. *Master Plan—or Official Map.* Both of these planning tools can set guidelines for community development.

8. *Subdivision control* goes hand in hand with zoning. The planning board has power to require many specifications to be met before development plans are approved.

The tax approach is beginning to gain ground as a measure to accompany other programs; for example, a conservation easement. Some towns have encouraged their farms, golf clubs, and other open areas to remain undeveloped through taxing them on their open value only, not on their highest development value. This is considered preferential assessment, and it can be accompanied by an easement or legal agreement that development will not take place. Or in the absence of such an agreement it can be part of a tax-deferral system that would discourage or at least hold off premature development, and make back taxes available to the community when the land is sold for development.

In Connecticut the first open-space assessment act was enacted in 1963. It provides for assessment of classified open land based on undeveloped value rather, than full market value. In Massachusetts a proposal for tax deferral by Charles W. Eliot was first put forward in the 1961 session of the General Court, without subsequent action. In the 1963 session the bill was again considered "to preserve open space in private ownership through the postponement of part of the real property taxes on classified open land until the restrictions on such land are changed or relaxed." When the bill emerged from committee it was part of a one-year investigation and study by the State Tax Commission relative to certain tax laws.

The above listing of tools available to the communities for open-space planning is by no means final. This is an area subject to constant revision and updating. Many of the precedents now being established, especially in river basins, will have much to do with the patterns set for the future. Through the careful and justified use of these tools, singly or in combination, the communities can help solve the problem of wasted natural resources and unplanned urban sprawl.

These approaches have been mentioned in terms of local action because in our Basin the local agencies are in the best position to take advantage of them at this time. Some of the approaches would apply to any recognized regional group, and the MDC has been using the acquisition tools for some time.

However, on the state level, action is usually more indirect. Aid is given the communities to allow their action, either in the form of financial or technical assistance or through enabling legislation. The Department of Natural Resources has given guidance in this regard. The self-help program and Regional Advisory Teams are offered through this Department. It is the logical agency to provide leadership for a cooperative open-space program. The Department of Natural Resources has not yet embarked on a full-scale program

of direct action for the acquisition of open space. The Public Outdoor Recreation Report of 1957 listed areas in the state in their
order of priority for acquisition and development, but there has
been little action to date. The legislature authorized the Department to carry out a long-range acquisition program, but the appropriations have not been sufficient.

The progress in some of the big urban states has shown that large
programs are catching on and that public support is behind them.
In the past year or two New York citizens voted three to one on a
$75 million bond issue, and New Jersey's request for $60 million
passed in the legislature without difficulty. In Wisconsin $50 million
was allocated after a statewide campaign. California has proposed a
$150 million plan, and Pennsylvania a $70 million program for
open-space acquisition.

On the basis of a $10-per-capita program, similar to those above,
whereby direct state acquisition plus local grants-in-aid would be
possible, Massachusetts would have to allocate $50 million.

Aside from such a possible large-scale program by the state, there
is existing legislation that authorizes acquisition for conservation
purposes. For example, both the Division of Fisheries and Game
and the Department of Natural Resources can acquire land as part
of the wetlands regional preservation plan, but no funds were included in the authority. Another regional program of concern to
our Basin is the Massachusetts Bay Circuit, or Green Belt, program, but again the General Court has made no appropriations to
accomplish the aims of the legislation.

Pressure for a Bay Circuit program dates back to the beginning
of the century, but it was not until 1956 that basic legislation
passed by which the Department of Natural Resources could acquire or otherwise preserve a wide strip around Boston. Cutting
through the SuAsCo region, this strip would include parks, scenic
and historic sites, waterways, and pleasurable roadside areas. No
widespread governmental cooperative effort to carry out the program has been attempted. Property values have been increasing,
some of the desired land is already gone, and the chances of governmental action before it is definitely too late are dim.

A Harvard Law student in a thesis on open-space laws in Massachusetts suggested that the project might be eligible for Housing
Act funds as a regional plan if proper sponsorship could get under
way soon. Perhaps a combined local, private, state, and federal pro-

gram might make positive results possible. A great deal of public enthusiasm will be needed to prove that the program is still worthy of government money and action.

The federal government has recently authorized grants for open-space purposes through the Housing Act of 1961. Its encouragement of preliminary and comprehensive planning has added a new dimension to the program, and such federal requirements promise to give some needed guidelines. The funds available through the Housing and Home Finance Agency could be augmented, and other acquisition programs related to parks and land conservation could be accelerated in the next few years.

Technical assistance can be received from a number of federal agencies, including the Soil Conservation Service, which can make an acre-by-acre inventory of the town's resources, providing scientific soil and water information that can facilitate local planning for the best land use.

Public education to bring the community into support of a conservation program is essential. Here private groups can be the most helpful. The Trustees of Reservations and the Massachusetts Audubon Society have already shown leadership in this respect. Land trusts or corporations and forest-and-trail associations are among those groups active in acquiring land for conservation use and promoting conservation education. The Massachusetts Association of Conservation Commissions has sponsored meetings and made other efforts to coordinate conservation activity, especially among conservation commissions.

There are some present healthy signs that local, state, and federal action is beginning to stem the tide of urban sprawl, and public awareness of the need to set aside open areas is growing.

QUESTIONS REMAINING

The six major water-resource problem areas singled out for study in the preceding chapter are not the region's only water-related problems.

Some problems, like unattended and unrepaired dams, present dangers from time to time. Other questions, such as pesticide control, are beginning to assume greater importance in the light of new research and analysis. Already many of the towns are reappraising their spraying programs. The same can be said of the question of rubbish disposal, which is proving more vexing daily as many of the communities must search out new locations or find corrective measures to remove the danger of water and air pollution. Nuisance vegetation such as duck weed, resulting from sewage pollution, has caused alarm in the past; the vegetation encouraged by detergents may require special attention in the future.

Another problem is also a question and a challenge. In a day of space-age wonders, are we letting our children pause long enough to study and understand the natural wonders in their own backyard? Science classes could make more use of our unique conservation laboratory. It is encouraging, however, that in 1962 a state advisory committee on conservation education was appointed, and some of the communities are already taking the lead in encouraging nature study.

Still other problems have been touched upon only slightly in this study, but they may well be on the priority list for the future. For example, the regulation of the low flow of the rivers could be as crucial to the region as flood control. Land-management methods are herein described only as they relate to the flood-control program. They also could be examined in much greater detail, because sound land management is essential to the well-being of the entire watershed.

Finally, as we view the land, water, and people as part of the complex water picture of this Basin, new types of problems relating to conflicts of interest must be studied.

In our Basin conflicts of interest in water use do not fall into neat categories such as private vs. public, upstream vs. downstream, or big dams vs. little dams. Some of these elements do exist, but more often than not it is a case of different groups requiring different uses at different times, with conflicts shifting in relation to the pressures for use.

There are obvious conflicts between the users who are polluting the water and those who need clean water for bathing, water supply, irrigation, etc. But the question of conflict becomes more difficult when tax dollars may be needed to clear up the pollution source, or when an industry on which many depend for jobs, or a town desires for tax purposes, threatens to leave the area rather than initiate expensive treatment procedures. When water is needed by the municipalities and industries to carry off certain discharges, it is considered a beneficial water use if the river system can contain them. The question then becomes one of properly treating the wastes, and new conflicts arise over disagreement on what is clean.

The quantity of the water also plays a vital role in determining use. The greatest demands are usually placed on water at the same time, during the low-flow or dry periods of the year when recreation, water supply, irrigation, and other uses may be in competition. Needless to say, all interests are agreed that flood control is necessary, but different groups favor different methods that will aid their own water-use functions.

The farmer is interested in cultivating the maximum amount of his meadowland without having to provide his own drainage facilities, so he is more interested in dry land for planting than in preserving the wetlands for flood-control purposes. These same wetlands are attractive to development contractors looking for inexpensive land with few obstructions. Some industries have also found it economical to build in marsh or river areas, especially when the water is needed for wastes, power purposes, or cooling systems. Some towns have felt it in their best interest to zone for industry and allow filling for large developments along the rivers. Proponents of the preservation of the wetlands or flood-plain zoning may be in conflict with some or all of these uses. Bird-lovers and sportsmen may disagree over some issues, but in the matter of preserving wetlands for wildlife habitat, they are united in effort.

Outdoor recreation raises an equal number of questions, because it means many things to many people—a Sunday drive as a sightseer, a quiet day of contemplation in nature's lap, or active participation in outdoor sports. All interests may be agreed on keeping the waters clean and available, but they confront each other on the question of the size and speed of boats, the types of access and facilities needed, and the kind of management desirable.

Riparian owners may be in conflict with each other over whose "reasonable use" is the most reasonable, and non-abutters may object to any use by the riparians, when wetlands, for example, might be involved. Litigation has provided one means for settling certain types of conflicts in water uses. In our Basin, the Talbot Dam and the Fordway Bar in North Billerica have been notable sources of dispute over the years.

These are some of the conflicts of use that exist in the SuAsCo

Basin. It would certainly be ideal to have without cost and compromise an ample supply of clean water to satisfy all uses, but this is a luxury of the past. Today we must view our water picture realistically and aim for a reconciliation of as many beneficial uses as possible, with some uses essential for the public good, such as water supply, getting top priority.

SUMMARY

The SuAsCo River Basin is a small watershed that has many varied and complex water problems that could best be handled within a river-basin context.

Owing to the type of metropolitan and regional development that has taken place in Massachusetts, the SuAsCo River Basin is part of several regions (e.g. one larger watershed, two counties, two soil-conservation districts, and three urban centers). It is still an independent unit in terms of its particular assets and problems. Its history, geography, and common land and water-use problems have given this region unmistakable identity.

Certain economic and political questions affecting the region may arise outside its borders, making cooperation with other planning units necessary.

This Basin is a sub-basin of the larger interstate Merrimack River Basin, and water-resources planning for the smaller unit would have to be integrated with any comprehensive planning for the larger.

The Basin is located near three urban centers, Boston, Worcester, and Lowell, and its rivers are within easy reach of three million people. The pressures on the region's land and water uses have increased and will continue to do so.

There are 36 communities in the River Basin, most of which have been experiencing growing pains during the years since World War II. The communities have had to consider new types of zoning and planning to control the pace of development. New highways and industries have brought major changes. Not all the towns have felt the pressures of urbanization in the past. They all will in the near future.

Most of the growth was not anticipated and many of the communities were not prepared to cope with the problems of rapid

growth. The lack of orderly development and the misuse or inefficient use of basic conservation resources have posed serious
problems.

Water supply heads the list of these problems. The amount of
precipitation is generally ample to meet all our water-supply needs,
including domestic, industrial, and agricultural, but only if wise
planning and management are exercised. Waste and abuse of the
supply in any way affects the public good.

Pollution remains a problem that has not noticeably been met
despite many efforts dealing with water-contamination control.
These efforts will slightly improve our waters, or at least prevent
their further deterioration, but much more needs to be done to
make our rivers suitable for all uses.

Flood damages within the Basin have always been a major problem. Reaction to recent floods has produced a Watershed Work
Plan for the SuAsCo Basin. The program now underway will considerably lessen the flood hazards for the future, but many supplementary efforts will be needed to insure its success.

Wetlands preservation suffered setbacks for many years as valuable conservation land was sacrificed to "urban progress," but in
recent years a growing group of agencies and individuals has been
acting with some success to halt the exploitation of these marsh
and swamp areas. A large area of the Sudbury-Concord wetlands
will be included in a Sudbury National Wildlife Refuge, which
will preserve one of the best-known habitats for waterfowl in this
section of the country.

Recreation is a problem only to the extent that the Basin is rich
in outdoor resources but poor in facilities or access to them. The
area is unsurpassed in scenic beauty and natural recreational opportunities. Fish and wildlife values alone are recognized as being the
finest in the state.

Open-space planning to preserve land, both wet and dry, because of its present and future benefits to the public, is a new concept that is beginning to make more sense to more people, who
view with alarm the loss of land, trees, and brooks in the wake of
urban expansion. If something is not done now, the right kind of
land may not be left for conservation or for the enjoyment of our
grandchildren.

These are some of the outstanding problems in our Basin which will require time, effort, and money for their solution. Henry David Thoreau wrote, more than 100 years ago: "The town is but little conscious how much interest it has in the river, and might vote it away any day thoughtlessly." Today the solutions to our outstanding problems depend on a willingness of the citizens of the region to understand how much interest they have in the river, and to initiate, encourage, and support necessary programs. Local enthusiasm is infectious. The conservation commissions, for example, are already beginning to undertake active programs through local initiative.

The water problems do not recognize town boundaries, and protective attitudes about their solution without outside help or cooperation can lead to inefficient and unwise choices. Local and regional planning and action can go hand in hand. The water resources and conservation problems of this Basin are all interrelated and will require long-range planning and coordination of effort for the best results.

An evaluation of the type of planning and cooperation possible and desirable, as well as the kind of machinery needed to carry out the plans, must be considered now. The goals must be agreed on.

While the problems in the SuAsCo River Basin are many, so are the possibilities for their solution. Many of the elements for a sound program already exist. Many plans for the solution of individual problems also exist, as does present machinery for executing plans.

Unified efforts will be required to assure optimum development of all natural resources, including water. This Basin is very fortunate that it is richly endowed with both natural and human resources, and it is time now to call on the latter to save the former. Water can not be dismissed as a dry subject—but rather it is the resource on which we all must depend for future growth.

CHAPTER 7

Group Action Along

the SuAsCo

MANY VICTORIES have been won in the conservation battle since the SuAsCo River Basin Study was completed in the fall of 1963. In this River Basin, elsewhere in Massachusetts, in New England, and throughout the country, the tide has definitely turned in favor of the long-range view of preserving our natural resources for the future.

In the summary of the study reproduced in Chapter 6, it was stated that while the problems in the SuAsCo River Basin were many, so were the possibilities for their solution. More possibilities than ever exist today, because of new legislation, new legal tools, and new sources of financial and technical assistance. Even more importantly, a new outlook is evident.

This new outlook involves an "ecological approach," considering man inseparable from his environment, in a contract with nature. It can be seen in the increasing number of earth-science courses and nature-study areas in our schools, in the new suburban developments planned around the natural contours of the land, in the town and city beautification programs, and in the shift from single-purpose to multi-purpose projects.

The conservation movement is gaining momentum. Previously, groups such as the SuAsCo River Basin Group and other traditionally conservation-oriented organizations had to plead and work feverishly against odds to convince legislators and voters that the cause of resource planning was an urgent and just one. Now, many legislators are in the forefront of the battle, with additional forces joining the ranks. It is still very late in the day to overcome the shortsightedness and waste of the past, but recent efforts are encouraging and producing immediate results.

In view of the many changes that have been taking place in the SuAsCo River Basin in these past few years, constant updating of the Study's information on communities, legislation, and active agencies and programs would be necessary to give it maximum value. However, the Study still truthfully reflects the forces affecting the water picture within that Basin and within many similar areas throughout the country.

Rather than attempt the laborious task of updating, this chapter will merely suggest the kinds of concrete steps being taken toward solution of the SuAsCo water problems, and also provide some examples of citizen and group action at local and regional levels.

Aftermath of Publication

The SuAsCo River Basin Group of the League of Women Voters agreed that the preparation of its Study was not a goal in itself. Through disseminating its findings, the Group hoped to build a broad base of informed and interested citizens to promote constructive action.

Therefore, the Inter-League Group attempted to circulate the Study as widely as possible. Almost all of the 3,000 published copies were distributed throughout the Basin, although some were sent to river basins in other parts of the country, and individual requests came from as far as England. The price (30 cents) was held to a minimum, thanks to a grant from a public-spirited corporation. Free copies were received by libraries, schools, and town officials concerned with conservation problems in the 36 communities in the Basin.

Cooperation with the press was sought and achieved. One resulting series of articles on river improvement, by a Maynard editor, sparked the formation of CURE (Clean Up the River Effort), a small group of volunteer men who hauled truckloads of debris from the Assabet River.

To publicize its findings further, the Inter-League Group invited members of conservation commissions, garden clubs, and land trusts to tour with them the partially completed Assabet River flood-control system. Similar tours have since been arranged by the Conservation Districts, with encouraging attendances.

A file cabinet was purchased to house the numerous resource materials and maps gathered for the study. This research file is being kept up-to-date and made available to interested groups and individuals at the Conservation Education Building of the Massachusetts Audubon Society.

Other ways of spreading the word have included appearances at seminars on land and water use, assistance in the formation of new river-basin groups, and testimony at pertinent hearings. The Inter-League Group was asked by the Chief Engineer of the Massachusetts Department of Public Health to testify at an enforcement conference on the pollution of interstate waters of the Merrimack and Nashua Rivers of New Hampshire and Massachusetts.

Wetlands Support

In the SuAsCo River Basin Study, considerable attention was paid to the values of wetlands in the Basin. The task of saving a major wetlands area along the Sudbury and Concord Rivers proved to be a formidable one, requiring the combined efforts of many groups. When the Wetlands Bill was in legislative committee, early in 1961, it appeared to have little chance of passage. Pressure from the citizens of the area was mobilized through efforts spearheaded by the League of Women Voters and the Massachusetts Audubon Society. (It was in the attempt to get regional League support for the Wetlands Bill that the River Basin Group, then an ad-hoc committee, was formed.) Attendance at hearings was swelled by town officials and civic groups from the affected towns, who voiced their support. When the Bill was arbitrarily reported out as a study bill—essentially an unfavorable report—the protests mounted. Telephone squads were organized, with the result that telegrams and emergency calls saved the Bill from defeat. When the Bill was finally signed into law, in May, 1961, thanks were owed to many conservationists who became lobbyists for the first time and who learned it was worth fighting for their beliefs.

Conservationists also learned the need of being organized for future legislative battles. Through the good offices of the Massachusetts Forest and Park Association, which provides a legislative summary of all bills affecting natural resources, organizations and individuals are now able to keep track and swing into action. Other groups, such as the Massachusetts Association of Conservation Commissions, help alert and inform leaders on vital issues.

Many civic-minded groups, such as the League, have learned that the passage of legislation is only the beginning of the job. Take again the example of the Sudbury-Concord Wetlands Bill. Since this was permissive legislation, enabling several agencies to acquire the essential wetlands, it has taken time to get machinery into motion, to raise funds, and to get landowners to sign on the line. With several levels of government involved, it is not surprising that the time schedule has not kept pace with the original estimate of 1965, as reported in the River Basin Study. Such problems notwithstanding, the acquisition has been proceeding. The U.S. Fish and Wildlife Service now has over half of the 4,500 acres it was authorized to acquire, and 1967-68 is the new target date for completion of the project. A refuge manager is being trained and will soon be located in Concord or Bedford. He will seek to coordinate work on the project and communicate with the affected towns on such questions as access, trails, and other recreational features. There are still many adjacent areas that the localities should acquire for additional protection, and Leagues and conservation commissions need to see that this part of the Wetlands Bill becomes implemented.

Since the passage of the Wetlands Bill, many other conservation measures have followed. It has been suggested that the work done on this bill served to lay the foundation for the later, important Coastal Wetlands Study (1964) and Bill (1965), and the Hatch Act (1965), relating to the protection of interior wetlands. It is interesting to note the immediate reaction produced by the Hatch Act. Over 300 applications for filling wetlands areas have been reviewed by the Department of Natural Resources in less than a year, and restrictions were placed in about 40 cases.

Hunting for New Water Sources

In a water-hungry area, attention has turned to new sources to offset old shortage problems. The rivers may be tapped more and more in the future. There have been suggestions of reactivating the old Middlesex Canal to draw water from the Concord River for another thirsty river basin, the Ipswich. Billerica, the only town that now draws water from the Concord River, would not be affected because it is upstream from the canal site, but undoubtedly other towns would object to an outflow to another watershed.

Even though the Assabet is now a waste-carrying river, it is becoming increasingly attractive as a potential source of water for the water-short towns in that sub-basin. A 1965 water-resources report for the Assabet Basin provided communities with a record of wells, test-hole materials, and chemical analyses of the river that they will have to study seriously. Water shortages have been most acute in this section of the SuAsCo River Basin, and will become worse as Interstate Route 495 continues to bring new industries and development to the area.

The Growing Acceptance of Planning

While stopgap action is easily accepted in a time of crisis, it is more difficult to convince people of the need for long-range planning. Many communities bolstered the budgets of their water departments to provide for new equipment, but planning was often neglected. In the water-resources field, however, the trend is generally turning toward more planning. Ground-water studies at the state level and a study by the Soil Conservation Service for determining future sites for water impoundment throughout the state have been proposed. Coordinated planning efforts at the federal level are now possible because of the Water Resources Planning Act of 1965 (see p. 113).

One portion of Route I-495, running through the Assabet area, was completed without benefit of planning or cooperation with the communities. Now, a comprehensive planning program for most of this area is under way, as part of a prerequisite for federal road money. Another example of federal grants being contingent on evidence of planning or participation in regional planning can be seen in the formula for obtaining funds under the Housing Act's Title 7. Communities can now receive up to 50 percent reimbursement for open-space and recreation projects when those projects are within an active regional planning area officially recognized by the state. Several SuAsCo communities are now eligible under the Metropolitan Area Planning Council and Central Planning (Worcester) Districts.

The drawing of stream-encroachment lines by the state is a relatively new concept in conservation planning. In 1962, when authority was given for Assabet lines, and, in 1963, for the Sudbury and Concord Rivers, support was provided by the Inter-League Group, including the use of its overlay map. Earlier, one League member had been instrumental in submitting legislation for the Sudbury and Concord Rivers. She helped to get a resolution proposed and adopted at her town's annual meeting to establish a basin-wide committee to determine the feasibility of establishing such lines and to submit any related legislation.

Sowing the seeds for community and regional acceptance of conservation programs can be the job of individuals as well as of groups. A League member who walked the entire length of Hop Brook, a tributary of the Sudbury River in Sudbury and Marlborough, took colored slides which were later shown at public meetings. These slides helped persuade residents of Sudbury of the need to preserve their portion of the brook, facilitating the acquisition of easements from private owners along its banks by Sudbury's conservation commission.

The Struggle for Flood-Plain Zoning

Related to stream-encroachment lines are flood-plain lines, involving conservation planning at the local level. Here is an important area for citizen cooperation, but once you get involved, watch out for other jobs! One League member worked with her local planning board to draw up a town-meeting article on flood-plain zoning. She soon became the liaison between the state Water Resources Commission, the town planning board, the board of health, and the conservation commission. A fact sheet she prepared for distribution at town meeting helped produce a successful vote on the flood-plain-zoning article.

It pays to do your homework, as many citizen groups have discovered, and also to keep trying. In Billerica, flood-plain zoning failed to gain a two-thirds majority in 1963, 1964, and 1965, but in 1966 it is again before the town meeting, though its outcome is still in doubt.

In general, flood-plain-zoning progress along the Sudbury and Concord Rivers has been good, but along the Assabet fewer protective measures have been taken. Both the nature of the river itself, encouraging settlement by industries along its banks, and local reluctance to establish flood-plain zones as a corollary to state action have hampered such progress. Acton is currently considering flood-plain zoning, and other towns may follow as a result of the recently completed Corps of Engineers' flood-plain study, which makes clear the hazards of continued encroachment toward the river. With a large-scale flood-control program for the Assabet in process, local cooperation is important.

The SuAsCo Watershed Work Plan flood-control projects proceeding under P.L. 566 have changed in number and scope since the River Basin Study reported their progress. Five of the original eight dams (designed as dry dams, but with provision for adding recreation features later) are now completed. Plans for the sixth have been abandoned because of the high cost of land, and the seventh was incorporated into another project. The remaining dam has been redesigned to include flow augmentation in the headwaters area during low-flow periods to provide needed dilution of sewage effluent.

A Supplement to the Work Plan became necessary because of dramatic changes that occurred in the watershed beyond those envisaged in the original plan. Population grew 25 percent in four years. Assessed property values increased 68 percent in seven years. Economic growth within the flood plain of the Assabet River from 1956 to 1962 increased the flood-water damage potential by more than 300 percent, with the trend continually rising. In the light of these changes, greater flood protection became necessary, and new water-associated recreation and fish and wildlife features appeared desirable.

Multi-Use Projects Expand

Four additional projects have been proposed, two of which would involve multi-purpose activity. One of these, called the Delaney Complex, would include corners of Harvard, Stow, and Bolton and contain two dams, which would further fish and wildlife development. An even more ambitious multi-use project has been planned for the Nashoba site, in Westford, Littleton, and Acton. The original estimate called for combining flood control with a reservoir for recreational purposes, encompassing 600 of the planned 1,000 acres.

The plans for parking areas, picnic tables, fishermen's landings, and other facilities that would make it a model state recreational facility may shrink before local differences are reconciled. Local resistance prevented an appropriations bill for developing the Nashoba site from passing in the 1965 Legislature, but $100,000 was granted for a detailed study of the feasibility, costs, and values of such an undertaking. In the course of this study, attempts will be made to review local attitudes and objections.

Malcolm Graf, director of the Water Resources Commission, reported that the SuAsCo flood-control program, excluding the Nashoba project, is costing the federal government $2.5 million and the state $300,000. When all the flood projects are completed, he said, the reduction of flow at flood water would be six feet at Hudson. (Under the original plan, it would have amounted to only 1½ feet.)

Writing for the *Massachusetts Audubon* magazine (Winter, 1965), Barbara B. Paine commented on the SuAsCo flood and related projects as follows: "The important fact about SuAsCo . . . is not the private enterprise which started the program and has filled in many important gaps since, but the exciting accomplishments of Public Law 566 and other government acts, agencies and agents, both state and federal. Taxes, it has been said, pay for civilization. Occasionally they also pay for keeping civilization in its place and giving nature a chance—and SuAsCo is one of these lucky areas."

Anti-Pollution Outlook Less Bright

But the area is not so lucky when it comes to pollution. For every step forward, there seems to be a backward one, owing to the new pressures created by rapid urbanization. This is one problem on which groups can do plenty of work and need to do a lot more. Nevertheless, there are some advances to report. New state legislative measures to keep open dumps from creating air and water pollution and additional federal aid for sewage-treatment facilities are on the plus side.

There is also a new awareness of the effects of insecticide control on water quality. The state Division of Fisheries and Game has studied the pesticide load in the SuAsCo River system and reports a decrease of 60 percent due to declining use of DDT. The Division further emphasized, "The biologist feels that this is a result of increased awareness of the dangers of unwise use of pesticides, pointed out by concerned conservation agencies, and is reflected by the hesitancy of many municipalities to use this pesticide in the face of mounting public objection." It added the warning, though, that more DDT remains about, because of its persistence, than the decline in its use would appear to indicate. Additional review of these levels could continue as a result of approval by the new Federal Committee on Pest Control of a national program to monitor levels of pesticide residues in humans, fish, wildlife, food, feed, soil, and water.

The main problem in the Assabet is not its pesticide load but its heavy cargo of domestic sewage and industrial waste. If this river is to move out of its present Class D, so that its use for recreation, for example, could be allowed, some vigorous cleaning is in order.

Lagging Recreational Program

Not just pollution but lack of funds and lack of access have also kept outdoor-recreation programs from advancing. But the public is beginning to stir. Recreation studies, commissions, and directors are appearing here and there in the Basin. Park Departments in some towns are being enlarged to become Park and Recreation Departments. Public monies are being allocated for recreational programs in an area where private resources were relied on in the past.

Although the communities are beginning to provide more recreational opportunities, state facilities are still very weak in the SuAsCo region and in the entire Boston metropolitan area. The Nashoba site, earlier described, could help close this gap. A state park planned for the Hopkinton reservoir area would also provide outlets for recreation. Plans for the latter are moving slowly, but the Department of Natural Resources reports it is scheduled to become a $2.5 million park of 1,500 acres (including water) offering every available activity. The state Public Access Board is also moving ahead with its program to develop new access routes for recreational purposes. And, finally, outdoor-recreation planning has been given a boost by financial reimbursement offered through the Land and Water Conservation Fund Act of 1965, administered by the Bureau of Outdoor Recreation. Approximately $2 million a year is available for Massachusetts and its communities.

Success Story: Conservation Commissions

At several points activities of local conservation commissions have been mentioned. The most exciting story of all concerns their blossoming growth and impact at the grass-roots level. They have been called "the most successful action program in the country" by a speaker from Connecticut at the White House Conference on Natural Beauty in 1965. Because many of the new financial and technical tools being offered the communities can best be utilized through these conservation commissions, they have moved vigorously ahead where there has been a will. There is mounting evidence that when such commissions offer imaginative and well-thought-out programs, their communities give wholehearted support.

In the SuAsCo Basin, all but four of the communities now have conservation commissions. Excluding action that may develop at the 1966 annual town meetings, commissions have spent almost $500,000 on 47 projects for land acquisition in the Basin. This represents two-thirds of the entire amount spent in the state at the local level for this purpose, according to Bruce Gullion, of the Department of Natural Resources. Mr. Gullion heads a new Division of Conservation Services set up to assist conservation commissions and districts in the formulation of programs for the development of local resources, as well as to promote long-range resource planning at the state level.

At least one town has moved boldly ahead in acquisition proposals in 1966. Concord may soon hold the distinction of permanently preserving the greatest amount of open land within any municipality in the state. In addition to holding the Minute Man National Historic Park, the extensive wetlands of the Great Meadows and Concord National Wildlife Refuge, Walden Pond Reservation, and a Town Forest, Concord has now committed itself to acquiring a tract of 250 acres for the conservation commission. In the 1966 town meeting, Concord accepted an overall commitment to acquire the major portion of Mill Brook Valley, at an estimated cost of $184,780. A grant of $78,000 was immediately made to acquire the first negotiated parcel of 40 acres. Harvard University has also chosen Concord as the site for an outdoor laboratory. Over 300 acres have been purchased near the Carlisle line to provide an ecological study area, to be kept in its natural state. It is believed that Concord was spared from burning by the Indians in King Philip's War because it was looked on kindly by the gods, and it still appears to be in a favored position.

The problems of conservation commissions differ from one community to the next, but the commissions are proving adaptable to each situation. In Ashland, the commission has focused attention on industrial-pollution problems. Bedford's commission has worked diligently to combat pollution of its two rivers, the Shawsheen as well as the Concord. In a rapidly growing suburb with several expanding electronics industries and unprecedented demands for housing, the Bedford commission has worked to limit heedless development, particularly in marginal lands. Its members hope their public-relations and educational activities will pay off when the 1966 Town Meeting votes on flood-plain zoning.

In Stow, where little industry exists, the changes now taking place reflect the influence of new highways and accompanying development on a rural area. To keep pace with some of these changes, Stow's conservation commission and planning board have been working on an inventory of natural resources. With the help of a team of experts now being offered through conservation districts, a soil survey and self-study have been completed that will greatly aid Stow in determining its planning priorities. In that town, the four questions that authorities asked were: What are the town's best potential recreation sites? Where are crucial water-management areas? Where might town forests, trails, historic sites, and nature-study areas be developed? What areas are not suitable for building construction? Naturally, in an industrial area, other questions would have been asked.

The use of soil surveys and other mapping data is proving of enormous assistance to the communities. In Wayland, a conservation master plan is under way, using on subcommittees the specialized skills of over 50 members of the community. In addition to interpreting a soil survey, Wayland's committees have prepared overlay maps and aerial-photo markings to make recommendations. The planning consultant hired to provide technical and clerical assistance feels that this is the first time a town has presented a master plan to a planner.

There are several land trusts in the Basin, carrying on their related tasks of acquiring and preserving open spaces with dedication and zeal. In certain areas, they work side by side with conservation commissions. One striking example of cooperation concerns the purchase of Round Hill and its vicinity, in the Sudbury Valley. The Fish and Wildlife Service is acquiring the flood plain along the river. In an adjacent swamp, the state Division of Fisheries and Game now operates Pantry Brook Wildlife Management Area. An especially good view of the extensive meadow area, as well as the Sudbury River's meandering path, can be had from the top of Round Hill. When this drumlin appeared in danger of being developed, a private trust, the Sudbury Valley Trustees, set out to save it, at a cost of $55,000. If several large connecting strips around this hill could also be saved, a continuous green belt would stretch out over a significant portion of the Sudbury Valley. The Sudbury conservation commission moved ahead to protect the land surrounding the hill, with Sudbury's town meeting authorizing purchase for $40,000. Because of last-minute problems in the transaction, an additional $2,500 was immediately needed. The Sudbury Valley Trustees donated the amount of this deficit to the Sudbury commission, thus permitting the negotiations to conclude successfully.

Not all stories in the SuAsCo River Basin end on this cheering note, but significant achievements are being made. The new legislative acts at both state and federal levels are impressive and essential, but they would mean little if the will to act, to support, to initiate did not reside with the citizens. In the SuAsCo area, this spirit is spreading, and it is good news for conservation.

PART III

A Guide to Tactics

CHAPTER 8

Governmental Tools

Available

TO BE EFFECTIVE, citizen groups must learn not only the specific facts about a problem but also what tools and techniques are available to help solve it.

Clean water, adequate supply, open space, wilderness preservation, recreational parks, and attractive urban waterfronts are all high on the public's list of needs and desires. But who will pay for the planning, the technical advice, the construction, and the enforcement that may be necessary?

The demand for necessary services arises with population growth and industrial development. The need for schools, police protection, sufficient water supply, sewage systems, garbage collection, parks, roads, repairs—all are putting increased demands on local taxes. Though lack of funds is sometimes a spurious excuse in areas quite capable of raising enough money locally, other regions are truly unable to finance needed planning and improvements.

If local and state governments are financially unable to carry the entire burden, and if the private sector has not made a good record in providing these necessities for a better community environment, perhaps a new era of partnership among all levels of government and industry can provide practical solutions in time to save us from committing "mass suicide through neglect of our environment."

Federal Aid to States

Federal incentive programs, voted by the Congress, help municipalities and states get on with the job of rescuing the local environment

209

The cost of large facilities for purifying city water or treating city sewage can be enormous. Here is Chicago's $105,000,000 Central District Filtration Plant in Lake Michigan.

from destruction. These programs provide both incentive and assistance.

Such federal programs spread the tax burden and set standards of performance to bring into balance the efforts of the different states.

Numerous such programs are now available. Citizen groups can encourage local and state governments to take advantage of them.

Some federal programs help states finance long-range planning and stimulate the states to get their own houses in order. The Water Resources Planning Act of 1965, for example, offers aid as never before for state water-resource planning and for regional or river-basin planning. Previously, there had been little effective inter-state cooperation. The Act also provides for better coordination among agencies through the Water Resources Council. In its long-range, comprehensive studies in such areas as the northeast and Appalachia, for example, the Corps of Engineers is instructed to comply with the provisions of the Water Resources Planning Act for cooperation with the local, state, and other federal agencies.

The Soil Conservation Service, in the Department of Agriculture, helps communities in a watershed join forces to plan programs for land conservation and flood control, after which they can qualify for aid under the Watershed Protection and Flood Prevention Act.

Aid under the Land and Water Conservation Fund Act requires that various state agencies first submit a state-wide outdoor recreation plan.

The Water Quality Act of 1965 gives the states a chance to set their own water-quality standards by June, 1967. They have always had this authority, of course, but few have implemented it effectively. Under the new legislation, they have another chance. If they fail, the federal government is authorized to set the standards. Some say that this may be the last chance states will have to act for themselves in the matter. Others say that the outlook for independent state action is hopeless. The present Administration in Washington, however, is relying on an increased incentive program, the effects of reapportionment on state legislatures, and as yet unformulated other reforms to bring about what the President calls "creative federalism."

On a regional basis, some states already have shown the necessary coordination to pick up and use the federal programs. The New England states, for example, even before the Water Resources Planning Act of 1965 was passed, had worked together and were thus ready to be chosen as the first area under the new Act to get a River Basins Commission. New York State, through passage of its billion-dollar clean-waters bond issue in 1965 (see Chapter 9), showed that it was ready and willing to put up funds of its own as well as pre-finance monies that might later come from federal taxes. The over-whelming 4-to-1 vote for this bond issue in New York is a prime reason President Johnson has hinted that the Hudson River Basin may be selected as a pilot area in the Clean Rivers Demonstration Program.

While some governors are looking with interest at the proposed Heller Plan, which would return surplus federal tax receipts to the states, with no strings attached, the trend now is to do whatever is necessary at the state and local level to qualify for federal assistance under the new programs.

In addition to offering financial and technical aid to help states strengthen their water-pollution-control programs, the federal government, through grants, is helping states and localities to start construction or repair of needed pollution control facilities. In its first session, the 89th Congress passed monumental water legislation. This "Conservation Congress," knowing that the pollution crisis called for immediate action, voted (among other water-related measures) to increase grants-in-aid and federal insurance for loans for planning, construction, and improvement of sewers and treatment works. The Water Quality Act of 1965, the Housing and Urban Development Act, the Rural Water and Sanitation Facilities Act, the Public Works and Economic Development Act, and the Appalachian Regional Development Act all have provisions aimed at getting on with the job of cleanup. Some of these laws provide for federal financing of a part of the local share where communities have previously been unable to take advantage of federal aid programs because of inability to finance the nonfederal share. Some greater amount of financial help is available to large cities under a new provision of the Water Quality Act.

The addresses of the federal departments, commissions, and offices involved in the implementation of these and many other programs are given in Appendix A, along with an organization chart. Each publishes fact sheets and brochures describing its various programs.

State Tools for Action

The federal government is not the only source of aid to localities in meeting water-and-land-use problems and planning needs. Every state government has some sort of program. Technical advice, long-range studies of the state's water needs, planning of reservoirs, flood control programs, ground water studies, help with soil surveys and flood-plain mapping are some of the services offered in many states. Some states offer financial aid for local and regional long-range planning. State establishment and enforcement of standards of drinking water are common. States are now asked to take a more forceful role in the setting and enforcing of pollution control standards. Many states participate in interstate water pollution control agencies. A few states offer aid for treatment plant construction. Others have funds available for maintenance of such plants. Some states offer training for treatment plant operators and set standards for plant operation.

Many states now help localities acquire land for parks and recreational areas, improve shorefronts, and preserve wetlands. Some states also have the power of allocating water in time of drought or may delegate this power to a regional water-management agency, such as the Delaware River Basin Commission.

Some states are using incentive programs to get municipalities to cooperate with their neighboring jurisdictions for regional water supply and treatment plants, regional flood-control works, regional parks, and other vital aspects of metropolitan planning.

If a state is unimaginative and fails to take responsibility in these fields, it is the localities within the state that suffer. Local civic groups play a role in encouraging the election of able state officials, in seeing that adequate budgets are passed, that new ideas are forthcoming, and that good state programs are well interpreted to the public to set the stage for passage by the legislature or by referendum.

Local Tools for Alleviating Problems

Although some localities are developing their own water supply through small reservoirs or driven wells, the trend in supply—as in other water-related needs—is toward the regional approach. Several towns can share the costs as well as the water from a common

Installation of sewer pipes and interceptors often guides the direction of community development.

source, as in the case of Onondaga County, N.Y. (see Chapter 1). State and federal projects to increase supply are sure to become more prevalent.

In the field of pollution control, localities have primary responsibility. Whether to construct sewers and treatment plants is voted by the local governing body, and at least partial financing of these facilities comes from local taxes. With the national drive for water cleanup, however, pressures will increasingly be put on towns to install secondary treatment. New Jersey is even proposing tertiary treatment as an across-the-board edict, with exceptions made only on proof that such treatment is not needed. Several states have passed legislation waiving the requirement of a popular referendum before borrowing for a sewage treatment plant if the municipality has been ordered to clean up its pollution.

Citizen organizations that get their towns to construct treatment plants now are doing their communities a service. The longer construction is postponed, the costlier it becomes. Careful planning is required, of course, to assure that the new plant will be adequate for at least the next 20 years, in light of population and industrial growth projections. The possibility of a regional plant should also be considered carefully before construction begins, but not as a delaying tactic.

In localities where a treatment plant is already operating, citizen groups might check to see whether properly trained operators are running the plant at its peak of efficiency and keeping it in good repair. They might encourage state standards for operators, regular refresher courses, and the like. Texas has an outstanding program for its plant operators.

In addition to support of treatment plant construction, there are other tools available at the local level, such as zoning, land acquisition, and easements, that are useful in the development and protection of water and related land resources. (See the story of Montgomery County, Maryland, in Chapter 3). Water supply and a sewage system always affect the situation. Under building codes, some areas are now requiring that a developer install sewer pipe at the time of original construction, even if it has to be "plugged" and septic tanks used until a trunk line can be built.

Cluster zoning has also been approved in some areas. If handled correctly, its use can cut the costs of providing water supply and a sewer system and at the same time offer needed open space.

The creation of regional parks that include water for recreation is one way to start inter-community cooperation, which may be extended to more controversial water matters.

Local interest in protecting wetlands and areas for parks, scenic beauty, water recreation, and protection of fish and wildlife is increasing in many communities. (See discussion of local tools in Chapter 6.)

One of the most interesting local tools is flood-plain zoning, described in Chapter 3. It is designed to keep development off the natural flood plains or at least restrict development to such things as recreational facilities or barge landings for trucks which will not be greatly damaged by floods. For this tool to be available to a community, there must be state enabling legislation, and stream-encroachment lines must be established, either by a flood of record or by the state or by a federal agency, such as the Corps of Engineers or the U.S. Geological Survey.

Several states have passed statutes to enable their communities, with the help of a state agency, to preserve critical wetlands. Others have passed, or are considering, legislation that will help them and local communities protect lake shores from the kind of development that pollutes the water and destroys the scenic and recreational value of the lake. This is accomplished by zoning, required setback, regulation of uses, easements, or outright public purchase of land.

A land-use inventory to discover and designate the most appropriate uses for different pieces of land is another technique being used by states and local communities. To implement the findings, new tools are being devised to make it possible to hold good farmland, keep land in forest or open pasture, protect scenic assets, and keep needed development in appropriate places, through new assessment and tax policies or legislation to permit zoning for conservation or even aesthetic purposes. In many states, this will require constitutional amendment as well as changes in community attitudes, but others are able to experiment.

Perhaps the most effective new tool is the increasingly popular state enabling legislation that permits a community to combine with other towns in nearly every phase of water-resources management (see Chapter 4). An alert, concerned citizen group can sometimes initiate discussion of such metropolitan or regional groupings, start the exploratory momentum, and work along with governmental representatives from the very earliest stage of planning.

CHAPTER 9

How to be an
Effective Citizen

DECISIONS concerning water resources are made within a complicated political process, through interaction among many groups:
experts in and out of government, elected officials, political parties,
private lobbies, and citizen groups. This process of interaction goes
on at every level of government. It also travels up and down along
the many lines of communication between local, state, and federal
levels. The citizen who is willing to jump into this maze of criss-
crossing influences will find plenty of opportunities to use his political pressure effectively. It must never be forgotten that water is a
political problem.

Choices Are Seldom Black or White

Even when the need for a water-resources program is generally accepted, there may be a choice among two or more solutions, equally
feasible from an engineering point of view but offering quite different lines of future development. One plan may encourage industrial growth at the expense of vacation and recreational facilities. Another may provide water for irrigation at the expense of
industrial expansion. As simple a matter as the location of a sewage-
treatment plant or interceptor lines will affect land use far into the
future. Property values may decline near the treatment plant; they
may go sky-high along the selected path of a sewer line. Each
method of financing a project will also have a different economic
impact on the community.

During the next decade, more storage reservoirs will have to be built. When and where, for what purposes, and as part of what long-range plan are all crucial questions. Our rivers, lakes, and sea-shores will have to be cleaned up. But how, how quickly, paid for by whom, administered by whom? These are political choices, which the voter should understand and weigh carefully, because the direction in which he exerts his support and the way he casts his vote will have far-reaching economic, political, and social ramifications. By turning his back he cannot stop the decision-making process. The question is whether these important decisions will be made with or without benefit of his—the citizen's—point of view.

Decision-Making Without Citizens

In areas where civic groups are scarce or uninformed or poorly co-ordinated for effective participation, communities run the risk of having to accept decisions which are not adequately representative. For example, a special-interest group can dominate. Decisions that benefit only one particular group are seldom in the community's best interests and are hard to reverse. The profit motive is basic to our private economy and must, of necessity, dominate the thinking and actions of the business sector. Cement and steel spokesmen tend to like dam-building projects. Real-estate developers are seldom found lobbying for preservation of open space. Mining interests, farmers, paper and pulp companies, chemical industries, and multitudes of others maintain and finance active lobbies ready to press for particular interests. When water decisions are being made, the opinions of the business sector contribute a great deal, but every community should have the benefit, as well, of other points of view.

Sometimes, a local, state, or federal agency can dominate. A powerful agency often thinks it need not consider alternative solutions. Or it may be so wedded to the status quo and its own prestige that it lacks the drive to try new techniques, new forms of cooperation, new proposals for long-range planning. A local or state agency is sometimes so jealous of its power and prerogatives that it will oppose assistance from the next higher echelon of government, even when it knows it cannot handle the problem alone. Financial aid is often quite willingly accepted, but any suggestions, advice, minimum requirements, or set standards of performance that may be attached to those funds are strongly resisted.

Another stumbling block is administrative overlap and lack of coordination. Hundreds of big and small governmental jurisdictions, each clinging to its own authority despite changing demands, tend to breed confusion and delay in acquiring the services the public wants.

Occasionally decisions are made on the basis of who pays rather than on the intrinsic value of a specific project. In an effort to escape, temporarily at least, paying the bill, a community may be tempted to choose a large project, financed by the state or federal government, when a smaller, local solution would be equally if not more satisfactory. It is, after all, not unheard of for communities to vote to raise their own taxes or their own water rates once they understand that action simply cannot be postponed, once they realize that what they buy is well worth the price.

A campaign that faced up to many of these problems, and proved that citizen action can play a key role, was waged recently in New York State.

VOTING A BILLION-DOLLAR CLEANUP

(New York State)

The people of New York State, in November, 1965, voted 4 to 1 for a billion-dollar bond issue to fight water pollution. Funds will now be available for state aid to localities for building sewage-treatment plants. More than 1,000 communities will benefit.

Why did the voters rally round this basically unglamorous cause? Many factors played a role. Governor Rockefeller had proposed in January, 1965, a strong, seven-point "Pure Waters" program, including the bond issue, and gave it his unflagging support. The State Legislature approved the whole package by unanimous vote, thus cutting down partisan sniping and outright opposition. Several civic and conservation groups throughout the state had already conducted studies and knew at first hand the need for cleanup.

The U.S. Department of Health, Education, and Welfare had stated, after thorough studies, that "the entire Hudson River, from the Albany-Troy-Rensselaer area to the Narrows, can be categorically described as polluted. The pollution from the equivalent of more than 10 million persons is discharged to the river in this area. Forty-three per cent of this is discharged without any treatment; 38 per cent receives primary treatment."

All of these important factors were not, however, thought to be enough to guarantee effective results. A full-fledged, grassroots campaign would have to be launched to explain to every voter the need for the huge bond issue. Such a statewide campaign was organized, launched, and proved to be overwhelmingly successful.

As a result, in the next six years, New York State is expected to take great strides to remedy its appallingly polluted condition. The positive commitment by the people of the state at the polls last November may serve, in fact, as an inspiring example to those states that are slow to prepare effective plans of their own for fear the subject of treatment plants is not a popular one with the voters.

The Governor's "Pure Waters" program includes tax incentives for industry to clean up its wastes, stricter enforcement of control laws, curbing of pollution from state and federal installations, state funds for operating and maintaining community treatment facilities, a water-quality monitoring system, and increased research.

Key to the entire program, however, was the billion-dollar bond issue to help localities construct needed facilities. It was this part of the package that called for voter approval, and the Governor was determined to launch a broad public campaign before the November 2nd deadline.

The Call Goes Out

The Governor assigned the job to an already existing statewide organization, the State Charities Aid Association (SCAA), which had both professional staff and funds available. Although its initial concern with water pollution hinged on health aspects, the Association soon realized that it would need a much broader appeal than that to make any real impact throughout the state. So the SCAA called a meeting of interested organizations to discuss setting up a unified educational campaign. Among those that responded early were the National Audubon Society, New York State Conservation Council, the New York State Jaycees, the PTA, the Tuberculosis and Respiratory Disease Association, and the LWV of New York State.

Around this nucleus, 32 organizations and individuals came together and formed a voluntary organization, the Citizens Committee for Clean Water (CCCW). These state-level organizations each had local units, or closely involved allies, in upstate counties and in New York City, so the Committee aimed through these channels to set up a network for distribution in quantity of program guides, fact sheets, sample press releases, etc.

Committee members realized that the ballot was going to be confusing. There were to be three statewide propositions, nine amendments, and one question to be voted on, and in some instances additional local issues would be added. So, early in the summer, the Committee requested the Secretary of State to give the "Pure Waters" bond issue the number-one spot on the ballot. "Sell Proposition One" became its rallying cry.

Despite the diverse interests on the Committee (industry, recreation, university, health, and civic points of view), the urgent need for cleanup was accepted by all. This unity of purpose was probably the most effective part of the campaign. It helped members to work together and set an example throughout the state for co-operative action among organizations.

Working Out the Proper Timing

There were "wild" and "frenetic" aspects of the campaign, but they stemmed from the pressure of time. The actual campaign could not get going until late summer. The November 2nd election date could not be extended. So the Committee set itself a work schedule, as follows:

PHASE ONE: "Late July or early August should be devoted to expanding the statewide Committee and developing similar community groups. During this organizational phase, basic contacts should be made with potential allies—the press, radio-TV, service clubs, the clergy, the medical society, individual merchants and commercial groups, labor unions, restaurants, etc., etc. Newsletters should begin publicizing the campaign. An important move in Phase One is to organize a Speakers' Bureau and get on the fall speaking schedules of clubs and civic groups."

PHASE TWO: "Late August and early September is the time to compile expanded mailing lists, based on the contacts you have developed. Also order special items from the statewide Committee for both specialized and community-wide audiences. If, as is hoped, a meeting is to be staged by the local Committee for Clean Water, speakers must be selected and the necessary arrangements completed. Post-vacation issues of newsletters should feature the campaign."

PHASE THREE: "From Labor Day to mid-October, the first broad publicity push should take place; initial mailings to all members and newly-recruited allies, stimulation of news stories and features in the press, talks before community groups, placement of campaign items with supporting merchants, publicity in house organs, etc."

PHASE FOUR: "The homestretch; the last two weeks before E-Day, November 2. All publicity activities should be intensified—followup mailings, renewed editorial support in newspapers, radio-TV panel and interview shows, endorsements by *all* local candidates, window displays, possible use of floats and sound trucks, door-to-door distribution of publications if feasible, special events and tie-in events, display of ballots or model voting machines, mention in sermons, displays at supermarkets and shopping centers, radio spots ('courtesy of a local sponsor') and disc-jockey plugs, displays in libraries and museums, street banners, displays in sporting-goods stores, street-corner booths, displays in hospitals and clinics, use of available film in movie theaters, stuffers and throwaways—in short, the maximum saturation campaign the Committee is capable of mounting."

These schedules were not met in every instance, but served as workable guidelines. Some felt that too much time was spent on Phase One to broaden the statewide Committee and that more energy should have gone at this time into assuring good channels of communication with local units.

Paying the Bills

At first, the CCCW thought it would produce materials for resale at cost to local units, but several members pointed out that while their local units had know-how, energy, knowledge, and enthusiasm, they lacked money. Taking orders and keeping books would also complicate the administrative work of the Committee, so it was decided to circulate materials free of charge.

This put a heavy strain on the Committee's limited finances. While several of the member groups donated varying sums, it was realized—somewhat late in the campaign—that funds would have to be raised outside the Committee. Although contributions could not be deducted by a donor either as a charitable contribution or as a business expense (because the Committee was working for a specific "Yes" vote), several large corporations interested in clean water made contributions. Both the Associated Industries of New York State and the Commerce and Industry Association of New York were Committee members and helped with fund-raising efforts. The Committee finally collected some $74,000 from a variety of sources, but could have run the campaign for less if it had not issued such a variety of materials. About 25 percent of the total went for newspaper advertising, 12 percent for full-time Committee staffing (including office and communication expenses), and most of the balance (63 percent) for production and distribution of materials to local groups.

The Committee sent out a wide variety of aids. These included posters; a four-page folder giving facts and what to do about them; bumper stickers; envelope stuffers; envelope stickers that read "Vote 'YES' for Clean Water—Proposition #1, November 2nd;" brochures; a redesigned 16-page booklet originally produced by the Governor's office; slide films; a 26-page mimeographed fact book on the whole seven-point program; question-and-answer sheets; sample letters-to-the-editor; sample press releases; sample editorials and radio-TV spot announcements; sample speeches.

Bumper Sticker, Anyone?

Put together into attractive kits, this material was sent or given to hundreds of different outlets throughout the state, from garden-club presidents to editors of more than 500 newspapers. The cry from many local groups was "Send us more material." Bumper stickers were especially popular in upstate New York, and the Committee's clipping bureau found that the sample letters and editorials were being put to good use. Most popular of all were the handy four-page folder and a brochure describing the seven-point program, which listed the names of all CCCW member groups.

Newsletters of member organizations helped. So did the State Health Department, by using kits, movies, television productions, and newspaper-radio publicity to educate citizens on the dangers of polluted water.

Just prior to Election Day, the Associated Industries of New York State called together over 500 influential business leaders to hear the Deputy Mayor of New York City and Governor Rockefeller emphasize the importance of Proposition One.

Periodic county-by-county checks with the field indicated purposeful activity virtually everywhere in the state. Where a lack was noted, an eleventh-hour effort was made to stimulate a drive by a unit of at least one of the Committee's member organizations, more often than not the League of Women Voters. Scores of PTA groups, the Jaycees, conservation organizations, some Junior Leagues, and especially the volunteer group known as "Friends of the Hudson" put on effective local drives.

The People Vote Resoundingly

An astonishing 80.9 percent of those casting ballots on Proposition One had got the message. "Yes" votes totaled 3,037,370; "No" votes trailed 718,398. In upstate New York, the "Yes" vote was 80.3 percent, and in New York City it was 82.1 percent. Also unusual was the fact that 61.6 percent of all voters took the trouble to register a decision on Proposition One. In fact, nearly 500,000 more people voted on that proposition than on any of the other propositions and amendments. Proposition One was the only money bill approved by the voters. Proposition One was the largest borrowing ever voted in New York State.

Thus, that wild and frenetic campaign stirred the voters to register their disgust with water pollution and their willingness to help pay for cleanup. The Citizens Committee for Clean Water plans to continue its educational campaign through its local units to encourage every community, large and small, to take advantage of the new funds voted.

LET'S GET DOWN TO WORK

Effective participation by citizens in land-and-water-use decisions involves a continuing effort, particularly in the local community. It is there that many programs must be initiated and carried out. Voters usually learn how to participate in civic life by joining an organization. There they develop an interest in a problem, get much of their information, discuss it, reach a conclusion, and are ready to take action. A well-run and effective citizen group follows certain patterns of operation. Here are well-tested techniques.

Getting the Facts

• Find out who the officials are in your local and state governments who are in charge of water-pollution control, water supply, flood control, water-related recreation, and planning. Get acquainted with them. Ask about their plans and programs. These officials may well have good plans in mind, but hesitate to propose them publicly if no civic interest has been expressed.

• Be aware of the power structure in your community. This is usually not a monolithic or obvious structure. In big cities, it is more fragmented and harder to find than in small communities, but in any case the power structure is a combination of forces with different aspects, different people, and different interests coming into play as the goals of action vary. Learning which is the appropriate power to approach and on what basis is important in building community-wide interest for a particular proposal. Ask the help of professionals, the practical politicians, the political scientists, and the economists, if you need a better picture of the forces at work in your community. If members of your group are on friendly terms with newspaper editors, industrialists, and others who know the workings of the power structure, consult them on the best way to reach your goal. In summary, know the vested interests that have a stake for and against your proposal, and learn how best to deal with the situation presented.

• Seek out other organizations likely to have an interest similar to yours, talk to their leaders, find out their plans, and lay the groundwork for future cooperation.

• Learn who your friends are in strategic places. One may be a member of the city council, another an official in the county health department, another a state legislator. Once any one of them knows that you share his interest in water-resource questions, he will help you get necessary information, tip you off when hearings are called at short notice, and encourage your presence at conferences and meetings. He will probably be in a position to alert you to upcoming problems and guide you in learning who and what the opposition may be, so that you can prepare appropriate facts to bolster your point of view.

• Be objective in your fact-gathering. For example, if you think a particular factory is responsible for serious pollution in your area, have the courtesy and good sense to talk to the management, find out what its problems are and how it is proposing to cope with pollution.

• Find a basis for evaluating your facts and proposals. Perhaps a model law is available as a kind of checklist against which you can compare your present legislation and discover its weak spots. Going to other towns or states that have already found a workable solution to the same sort of situation that faces your community is another good way to test your own proposals. Talk to their officials. See if they might be willing to talk to your own officials, or address a public meeting in your area.

• Get whatever help is available from state reports and personnel.

• Keep posted on state, federal, and regional proposals, trends in planning, and types of research that are under way.

• Check which state and federal programs might be available to help your area attack its problem. Often a single community cannot afford to undertake a needed improvement. Imaginative civic groups can analyze the multitude of state and federal aid programs that might apply, and then determine what minimum local requirements must be met in order to qualify.

• Get help on gathering the facts, and at the same time develop wider interest in them, by drawing in representatives of other groups with a common interest. Also try to enlist a few from groups with an entirely different approach. Different points of view will be presented, objections can be met at the outset, and agreement may be reached on some points if not on all. A joint-study committee can often do a better job than a single organization, and it frequently turns into a joint-action committee when the facts are all in.

Choosing a Course of Action

The particular situation will indicate which of several possibilities for action might be most useful. Your study may have shown, for example, that the various local agencies in your community must, at the very least, sit down together and learn what each is doing and planning for the future. Bringing the groups responsible for economic development together with those in charge of water supply, sewage systems, land conservation, and parks and recreation is, in too many cases, still an untried action. Citizen organizations can act as a catalyst by bringing these agencies into contact with one another.

If, on the other hand, you find that a local agency or elected official already has a well-thought-out proposal to offer, your course of action will be to help develop community support for it.

Or you may decide that the best role you can play is to arouse the public to a certain critical situation in town, to awaken them to a pollution condition or to the threat to a nearby lakeshore. The more people who hear about a crisis, learn the facts, and react through letters to the editor and talk within their circle of acquaintances, the better chance you have of setting up a community-wide action committee that will be listened to by the political leaders and governmental agencies.

Perhaps your group will decide that an official study needs to be conducted, or that both sides of a current proposal have not been fully aired before the public, or that an existing program is not being enforced properly, or that a particular agency cannot do the kind of job it has authority to do because its budget is too small. Or you may choose to support local participation in a metropolitan or regional plan. There are literally hundreds of possible areas for action by an alert and well-informed civic group.

Building Public Support

Working through other organizations can be one of the most effective ways of building support for your objectives.

• Set up a well-organized speakers' bureau. Provide your speakers with colored slides, if possible. Help them with their talks. See that you have variety, so that speeches are tailored to specific audiences. Then publicize your service, and go to as many different groups as possible.

• The Go-See Tour, either by bus or by boat, is a successful technique for stimulating interest. Visit a treatment plant or a particularly abused shoreline or a potential reservoir site. Bring well-informed guides to explain the implications and answer questions. Local agency officials are usually more than glad to serve in such a capacity and are in a position to know their facts. Perhaps you will want to combine the trip with a luncheon or supper, so that personal friendships are built among the group.

• Issue fact sheets, pamphlets, flyers, answers to common objections, suggested material for each organization's bulletin, or any current legislative information that bears on your particular project.

• Initiate a joint committee to make a survey of open space, sources of pollution, points of beauty, wetlands, and other areas of conservation value. Supply your committee with adequate tools, such as briefings, a set of questions to keep in mind, a map, a chart to fill in.

• Set up workshops for community leaders, so they can learn how to bring their own organizations into a more effective role.

To reach the general public, those not in organizations, you will want to work closely with the mass media. If you are lucky enough to have a newspaper editor on your planning committee, this may not be difficult. Or if the big paper in town already agrees with your goal, just supply the facts and be content to let the editor handle the material as he sees fit. If you send in press releases to a paper, don't haggle about the treatment you do or don't get. Editors have space problems, and their judgment must usually be respected as to what should take news priority.

For a purely local project, a public meeting to which everyone in the community is invited is one way to disseminate information and involve interested individuals and groups. Such an endeavor should not be undertaken, however, until you have already achieved some support and until you are prepared to speak knowledgeably and answer questions. If you are asked questions you cannot answer, don't cover up. Say frankly that you don't know, make a note of the question, and supply the answer as soon after the meeting as you can, both to the person who asked it and to the public.

Setting up a large conference (one to three days) is another means for reaching new groups. This takes careful planning, down to the last detail, and should not be undertaken unless you have the manpower and time to do it right. The people you invite are busy people, and they have a right to expect that the program and physical arrangements will be thoroughly and carefully worked out. If planned and executed well, with a definite goal understood at the outset, large conferences with follow-up contact can be extremely effective.

Your civic group might choose to initiate a university extension course for community leaders, meeting perhaps once a week for an entire semester. This is an ambitious program, in which the university would have the larger responsibility for the course content. Your civic group might be instrumental in helping to recruit the best civic leaders to be invited to participate, those who would benefit most and stay with the course from beginning to end.

Expressing Public Support Where It Will Count

The citizen organization that shows an interest in water resources, a desire to get the facts, and willingness to do its homework not only gains respect in the community but also finds increasing opportunities to take part in decision-making. As you have been gathering information and sharing it, you will have located present and potential allies (and possible opponents) among other organizations, among administration people, within legislative bodies, and within the mass media. Capitalize on these contacts.

• Continue to feed ideas and information to local, state, or federal officials and agencies.

• Report to them the public support you find for both your ideas and theirs, and see that word of their support is expressed repeatedly to legislators.

• Show your continuing interest by attending meetings of the city council, planning board, etc., and by being present at state and federal hearings.

• Give carefully prepared statements at public hearings. Hearings at all governmental levels offer the citizen, through his group spokesman, a chance to express his needs, to suggest lines of attack, and to state his views on specific proposals. Hearings also provide government officials with a sampling of public opinion and usually stimulate additional community interest. Advance talks with friendly members of legislative committees will pave the way for a favorable reception at the hearing.

• Serve on advisory committees and study commissions when asked. These often include community leaders as well as experts, administrators, and legislators. Those who serve should be on guard, however, that the group is not being set up merely to act as a respectable rubber stamp for an already determined plan. Often this is not the case, and service on the commission can be an effective way to help shape public policy.

• Publicize the answers of political candidates as to their stand on water conflicts. This will heighten the voters' awareness of a particular problem and can elicit statements of which those candidates, if elected, can be reminded. If you plan a candidates' questionnaire or a public meeting for candidates, it is useful to supply each candidate with background information before you put him on the spot. Those who take advantage of this briefing will be grateful to you.

• Submit statements to the platform committees of national political parties. Though the worth of party platforms is often doubted, the presence of a strong water-resources plank serves notice that there is citizen demand for action in this field. It proclaims that the problems of water are so crucial as to be included in a list of major state or national concerns, recognized by the politicians, and provides—in writing—a goal for action.

• Set up a joint-action committee in certain situations, as in the case of a referendum for a bond issue to finance sewage treatment or an open-space program, or of some important piece of state legislation which needs support. Include representatives of several leading organizations in the community or state. This committee will plan the strategy and prepare the materials needed, such as fact sheets, answers to common objections, posters, and stickers. It will set up a speakers' bureau and develop a demand for its speakers among all sorts of groups in the community. It will promote maximum coverage by the mass media. And, finally, it will get the voters out to the polls, or a flood of letters to legislators, as the case demands.

In summary, these are the chief responsibilities of any civic organization promoting the wise use and development of water resources:

(1) Get the facts.

(2) Share the facts with other groups and the general public.

(3) Bring new problems to the attention of appropriate officials.

(4) Mobilize support for sound proposals, from whatever source.

(5) Press for adequate appropriations to carry out a program already authorized.

(6) Follow through. Being an effective citizen is a continuing process.

APPENDIX A

Addresses

of Federal Departments, Offices, and Commissions Most Concerned
with Water and Related Land Resources

FEDERAL DEPARTMENTS

DEPARTMENT OF
  AGRICULTURE
14th & Independence Avenue, S.W.
Washington, D.C. 20250

DEPARTMENT OF
  COMMERCE
14th & Constitution Avenue, N.W.
Washington, D.C. 20230

DEPARTMENT OF DEFENSE
Pentagon
Washington, D.C. 20301

DEPARTMENT OF HEALTH,
  EDUCATION, AND
  WELFARE
330 Independence Avenue, S.W.
Washington, D.C. 20201

DEPARTMENT OF HOUSING
  AND URBAN DEVELOPMENT
1626 K Street, N.W.
Washington, D.C. 20410

  (After December, 1967:
  7th and D Streets, S.W.
  Washington, D.C.)

DEPARTMENT OF THE
  INTERIOR
18th & C Streets, N.W.
Washington, D.C. 20240

THE EXECUTIVE OFFICE
  BUILDING
17th & Pennsylvania Avenue, N.W.
Washington, D.C. 20503

OFFICES AND COMMISSIONS

(See above for addresses of Departments)

AGRICULTURAL RESEARCH SERVICE, Department of Agriculture
AGRICULTURAL STABILIZATION AND CONSERVATION SERV-
  ICE, Department of Agriculture
BUREAU OF INDIAN AFFAIRS, Department of Interior
BUREAU OF LAND MANAGEMENT, Department of Interior
BUREAU OF OUTDOOR RECREATION, Department of Interior
BUREAU OF RECLAMATION, Department of Interior
BUREAU OF SPORT FISHERIES AND WILDLIFE, Department of
  Interior
BUREAU OF THE BUDGET, The Executive Office Building

CIVIL WORKS PROGRAM, Corps of Engineers, U.S. Army, Department of Defense

COMMITTEE ON WATER RESOURCES RESEARCH, Office of Science and Technology, The Executive Office Building

CORPS OF ENGINEERS, U.S. Army, Department of Defense

DIVISION OF ENVIRONMENTAL ENGINEERING AND FOOD PROTECTION, Public Health Service, Department of Health, Education, and Welfare

DIVISION OF WATER RESOURCES, Geological Survey, Department of Interior

ECONOMIC DEVELOPMENT ADMINISTRATION, Department of Commerce

FARMERS HOME ADMINISTRATION, Department of Agriculture

FARM RESEARCH DIVISION, Agriculture Research Service, Department of Agriculture

FEDERAL POWER COMMISSION, 441 G Street, N.W., Washington, D.C. 20426

FOREST SERVICE, Department of Agriculture

GEOLOGICAL SURVEY, Department of Interior

INTERNATIONAL BOUNDARY AND WATER COMMISSION (U.S. & Mexico), Mart Building, El Paso, Tex.

INTERNATIONAL JOINT COMMISSION (U.S. & Canada), 1711 New York Avenue, N.W., Room 208, Washington, D.C. 20440

INTERSTATE COMMERCE COMMISSION, 12th & Constitution Avenue, N.W., Washington, D.C. 20423

JOINT FEDERAL-STATE REGIONAL ECONOMIC DEVELOPMENT COMMISSIONS (Inquire from Office of Regional Economic Development, Department of Commerce.)

JOINT FEDERAL-STATE RIVER BASIN COMMISSIONS (Inquire from Water Resources Council, Suite 900, 1025 Vermont Avenue, N.W., Washington, D.C. 20005)

LAND AND FACILITIES DEVELOPMENT ADMINISTRATION, Department of Housing and Urban Development

MIGRATORY BIRD COMMISSION, Fish and Wildlife Service, Department of Interior

NATIONAL PARK SERVICE, Department of Interior

OFFICE OF EMERGENCY PLANNING, The Executive Office Building

OFFICE OF PLANNING STANDARDS AND COORDINATION, Department of Housing and Urban Development

OFFICE OF REGIONAL ECONOMIC DEVELOPMENT, Department of Commerce

OFFICE OF SALINE WATER, 1107 16th Street, N.W., Washington, D.C. 20242

Federal Departments, Offices, and Commissions Most Concerned with Water and Related Land Resources

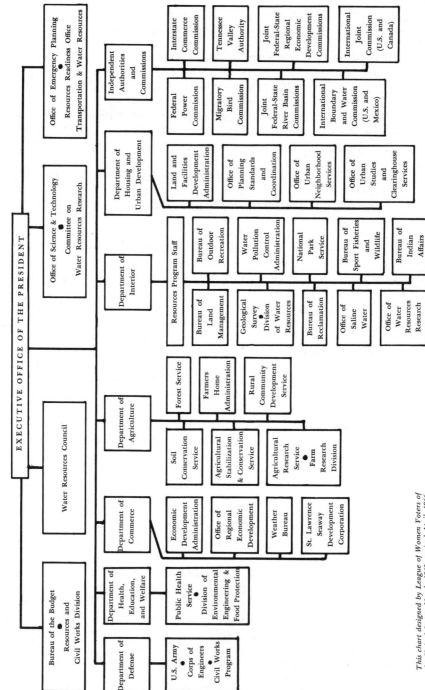

This chart designed by League of Women Voters of the United States, March, 1965—revised April, 1966.

OFFICE OF SCIENCE AND TECHNOLOGY, The Executive Office Building

OFFICE OF URBAN NEIGHBORHOOD SERVICES, Department of Housing and Urban Development

OFFICE OF URBAN STUDIES AND CLEARINGHOUSE SERVICES, Department of Housing and Urban Development

OFFICE OF WATER RESOURCES RESEARCH, Department of Interior

PUBLIC HEALTH SERVICE, Department of Health, Education, and Welfare

RESOURCES AND CIVIL WORKS DIVISION, Bureau of the Budget, The Executive Office Building

RESOURCES PROGRAM STAFF, Department of Interior

RESOURCES READINESS OFFICE, Transportation and Water Resources, Office of Emergency Planning, The Executive Office Building

RURAL COMMUNITY DEVELOPMENT SERVICE, Department of Agriculture

SOIL CONSERVATION SERVICE, Department of Agriculture

ST. LAWRENCE SEAWAY DEVELOPMENT CORPORATION, Department of Commerce

TENNESSEE VALLEY AUTHORITY, Woodward Building, Room 437, 1426 H Street, N.W., Washington, D.C. 20444

WATER POLLUTION CONTROL ADMINISTRATION, Department of Interior

WATER RESOURCES COUNCIL, Suite 900, 1025 Vermont Avenue, N.W., Washington, D.C. 20005

WEATHER BUREAU, 2400 M Street, N.W., Washington, D.C. 20235

Names and Addresses of a Few Organizations
from Which Further Information is Available

American Institute of Planners
        Room 800, 917 15th Street, N.W., Washington, D.C. 20005
Conservation Foundation
        1250 Connecticut Avenue, N.W., Washington, D.C. 20036
Izaak Walton League of America
        1326 Waukegan Road, Glenview, Illinois 60025
League of Women Voters Education Fund
        1200 17th Street, N.W., Washington, D.C. 20036
League of Women Voters of the United States
        1200 17th Street, N.W., Washington, D.C. 20036

National Academy of Sciences—National Research Council
   2101 Constitution Avenue, N.W., Washington, D.C. 20418
National Association of Counties Research Foundation
   1001 Connecticut Avenue, N.W., Washington, D.C. 20036
National Association of Soil and Water Conservation Districts
   1424 K Street, N.W., Washington, D.C. 20005
National Audubon Society
   1130 5th Avenue, New York, N.Y. 10028
National Wildlife Federation
   1412 16th Street, N.W., Washington, D.C. 20036
Resources for the Future, Inc.
   1755 Massachusetts Avenue, N.W., Washington, D.C. 20036
Soil Conservation Society of America
   7515 N.W. Ankeny Road, Ankeny, Iowa 50021
Water Pollution Control Federation
   3900 Wisconsin Avenue, N.W., Washington, D.C. 20016
Wildlife Management Institute
   709 Wire Building, Washington, D.C. 20005

APPENDIX B

Glossary of Terms

Acre-Foot—A volume of water sufficient to cover one acre to a depth of one foot. One acre-foot equals 325,851 gallons.

Alluvium—Soil, sand, gravel, or similar detrital material deposited by running water.

Appropriation Rights—The right of a landowner to adjacent or underground water for use for beneficial purposes, as given by act of prior use, law, or regulation.

Aquifer—A water-bearing bed or stratum of earth, gravel, or porous stone. Sometimes used to designate individual water-bearing beds, perhaps only a few feet thick, and sometimes to designate thick series of beds of varying permeability, where the individual beds are more or less interconnected. "Ground-water reservoir" and aquifer are often used interchangeably.

Artesian Well—A well drilled through an impervious layer, tapping an aquifer under hydrostatic pressure. Because of this pressure, many artesian wells are free-flowing.

Beneficial Use—Has been declared to be the basis, the measure, and the limit of a water right. (The question of what constitutes beneficial use of water is gradually being determined.)

Common Law—The general non-statutory law of a country or community, as developed by the courts, evolving from English common law.

Comprehensive Development—Basinwide development for optimum beneficial uses of a river system and its watershed. This means planning, construction, and management that will include all socially pertinent purposes (or uses) on an interrelated basis, and all economically relevant means of providing these purposes.

Cover Crops—Feed or food crops that protect and improve the soil.

Drainage Area or Basin—Synonymous with watershed. A watershed is the area contained within the boundary divides above a specified point on a stream. In water-supply engineering it is termed a watershed, and in river-control engineering it is termed a drainage area, drainage basin, or catchment area. For various planning or program purposes, the United States has been divided into 18 major drainage areas.

Easement—An acquired privilege or right of use or enjoyment that the owner of the easement has in the land of another.

Effluent—Something that flows out, as, for example, liquid wastes from an industry, a conduit, or wastewater-treatment plant.

Eminent Domain—That superior dominion of the sovereign power over property within the state that authorizes it to appropriate all or any part thereof to a necessary public use, reasonable compensation being made.

Erosion—Occurs when soil, usually bared of its natural cover, is carried away by wind and/or water at increasing rates, as the upper, more absorptive levels are removed.

Evapotranspiration—The natural process by which water is lost from a land area by the combined action of evaporation from free surfaces and transpiration by plants.

Flood Plain—Lowland that borders a river or creek, usually dry but subject to flooding during periods of high flow or high water.

Ground Water—Water that occurs in the pores and fissures in soil or rocks below the ground surface. (See Aquifer.)

Hydrologic Cycle—The total cycle by which water condenses from vapor in the air and by precipitation descends to the ground and into watercourses or into the ground and ultimately returns to the atmosphere by evapotranspiration.

Impoundment—The holding of water behind a structure such as a dam or dike.

Irrigation—The artificial watering of land by canals, ditches, flooding, or sprinklers.

Land Management (or forest or soil management)—Using the area to conserve available water, to protect soil from erosion, to restore and increase fertility and productivity of the soil.

Leaching—The process of removing water-soluble material from the soil by passing water through it.

Multiple-Purpose Development—Places major emphasis on the use of water for two or more of the following purposes: irrigation, power, flood control, domestic and industrial water supplies, pollution control, navigation, recreation, fish and wildlife. The first multiple-purpose project authorized and designed as such was the Boulder Canyon Project (Hoover Dam), 1928.

Overdraft of Ground Water—Removing from the underground supply of water more than is replenished naturally over the long-term average.

Photosynthesis—The formation of carbohydrates (from carbon dioxide and water) within chlorophyll-containing tissues of plants exposed to light.

Pollution—The introduction into a body of water of substances of such character, and in such quantity, that its natural quality is so altered as to impair its usefulness or render it offensive to the sight, taste, or smell.

Reasonable Use—The use of water for a beneficial purpose in a manner and in an amount that is not wasteful and does not injure the use or rights of others who have rights to use water from the same source of supply.

Riparian Rights—The legal rights of the owners of land abutting upon a stream or other body of water, including the use of such water. The definition of riparian rights has been modified considerably in the history of the United States, and one will find major differences in it as he travels from east to west. In the west, appropriation doctrine largely prevails.

River-Basin Concept—Recognizes the interrelation of resources elements in a single basin, and assumes that multiple-purpose measures can be undertaken in harmony. The river-basin concept is considered by many to be an opportunity to coordinate the tools of science, technology, and finance in unified developments. It extends the principle of ecological balance to the whole of the area and its occupants.

Runoff—That part of rainfall or other precipitation that reaches watercourses or drainage systems.

Saline Intrusion—Movement of sea water into fresh ground water deposits along coastal areas, due to overdraft.

Siltation—The process of depositing water-carried silt.

Stream Flow—The quantity of water flowing in a stream; also the velocity of the flow.

Transpiration—The emission or exhalation of moisture from plants.

Water District—A special-purpose district that has specified powers with respect to water, as a drainage district, a soil and water conservation district, a town sanitary district, or a multiple-purpose water conservancy district.

Water Rights—Whatever rights riparian owners, municipalities, or others may have in any stream or body of water by common law, statutes, or agreement.

Watershed—See "Drainage Basin."

Wetlands—Lands that have ground water or sea water at or near the surface, and which characteristically support types of vegetation that grow on wet soil.

APPENDIX C
Reading List

GENERAL

Ackerman, Edward A., and George O. G. Lof. *Technology in American Water Development.* Johns Hopkins Press, Baltimore, 1959.

Beauty for America: Proceedings of the White House Conference on Natural Beauty. U.S. Government Printing Office, Washington, D.C., 1965.

Kneese, Allen V. *National Water Policies and Problems.* Occasional Paper No. 1, Water Resources Center, The University of Wisconsin, April 1966.

Landsberg, Hans H., Leonard L. Fischman, and Joseph L. Fisher. *Resources in America's Future: Patterns of Requirements and Availabilities, 1960-2000.* Resources for the Future, Inc., Johns Hopkins Press, Baltimore, 1963.

Leopold, Luna B., Kenneth S. Davis, and the Editors of Life. *Water.* Life Science Library, Time Incorporated, New York, 1966.

Office of Science and Technology. *A Ten-Year Program of Federal Water Resources Research.* U.S. Government Printing Office, Washington, D.C., February 1966.

President's Science Advisory Committee. *Restoring the Quality of Our Environment.* U.S. Government Printing Office, Washington, D.C., 1965.

Senate Select Committee on National Water Resources. Print No. 29. *Report of the Committee.* 87th Congress, 1st Session. U.S. Government Printing Office, Washington, D.C., January 1961.

——. *Index to Committtee Prints Nos. 1-32.* December 1960.

Smith, Stephen C., and Emery N. Castle (editors). *Water Resources Development.* Iowa State University Press, 1964.

U.S. Department of Agriculture. *A Place to Live.* The Yearbook of Agriculture, Washington, D.C., 1963.

——. *Water.* The Yearbook of Agriculture, Washington, D.C., 1955.

——. Soil Conservation Service. *Water Facts.* (A pamphlet.) Washington, D.C., 1964.

U.S. Department of the Interior, Geological Survey. *Primer on Water.* Washington, D.C., 1960.

——. *Primer on Ground Water.* Washington, D.C., 1963.

Chapter 1: W A T E R   S U P P L Y

Fox, Irving K. *Water Supply, Demand and the Law.* Resources for the Future, Inc., Reprint No. 15, Washington, D.C., January 1960.

Hirshleifer, Jack, James C. DeHaven, and Jerome W. Milliman. *Water Supply: Economics, Technology and Policy.* University of Chicago Press, 1960.

National Academy of Sciences—National Research Council. *Water Resources.* Publication 1000B, Washington, D.C., 1962.

National Association of Manufacturers and The Chamber of Commerce of the U.S. *Water In Industry.* New York, January 1965.

Senate Select Committee on National Water Resources. Print No. 8. *Future Water Requirements of Principal Water-Using Industries.* U.S. Government Printing Office, Washington, D.C., 1960.

——. Print No. 26. *Saline Water Conversion.* U.S. Government Printing Office, Washington, D.C., 1959.

U.S. Department of the Interior, Geological Survey. *Has the United States Enough Water?* Washington, D.C., 1965.

——. *Water and Industry.* (A pamphlet.) Washington, D.C., 1962.

U.S. Department of the Interior, Office of Saline Water. *A B Seas of Desalting.* Washington, D.C., 1966.

——. *Saline Water Conversion—A Program to Develop a New Source of Fresh Water.* Washington, D.C., 1966.

Chapter 2: W A T E R   P O L L U T I O N

Carr, Donald E. *Death of the Sweet Waters.* W. W. Norton & Co., New York, 1966.

Dworsky, Leonard B. "Water Pollution Control," *Audubon Nature Bulletin.* Series 30, No. 3 Revised, New York, February 1966.

Graham, Frank, Jr. *Disaster by Default: Politics and Water Pollution.* M. Evans & Co., Inc., New York, 1966.

Herfindahl, Orris C. and Allen V. Kneese. *Quality of the Environment.* Resources for the Future, Inc., Washington, D.C., 1965.

Kneese, Allen V. *The Economics of Regional Water Quality Management.* Resources for the Future, Inc., Johns Hopkins Press, Baltimore, 1964.

League of Women Voters of the U.S. "Population + Production = Pollution," *Facts and Issues.* No. 309, Washington, D.C., 1965.

———. "Who Pays for a Clean Stream?", *Facts and Issues.* No. 313, Washington, D.C., 1966.

National Academy of Sciences—National Research Council. *Waste Management and Control.* Publication 1400, Washington, D.C., 1966.

National Association of Counties Research Foundation. *Community Action Program for Water Pollution Control.* Washington, D.C., 1965-66.

Proceedings: The National Conference on Water Pollution. U.S. Government Printing Office, Washington, D.C., 1961.

Senate Select Committee on National Water Resources. Print No. 9. *Pollution Abatement.* U.S. Government Printing Office, Washington, D.C., 1960.

———. Print No. 24. *Water Quality Management.* U.S. Government Printing Office, Washington, D.C., 1960.

Stein, Murray. "Problems and Programs in Water Pollution," *Natural Resources Journal.* University of New Mexico School of Law, Albuquerque, December 1962.

U.S. Department of the Interior, Geological Survey. *Primer on Water Quality.* Washington, D.C., 1965.

U.S. Public Health Service. *Acid Mine Drainage.* House Committee Print No. 18, 87th Congress, 2nd Session, April 19, 1962.

———. *Focus on Clean Water.* Publication No. 1184, 1964.

———. *Problems in Financing Sewage Treatment Facilities.* Publication No. 886, 1962.

CHAPTER 3: FLOODING

Hoyt, W. G., and W. B. Langbein. *Floods.* Princeton University Press, 1955.

Krutilla, John V. "An Economic Approach to Coping with Flood Damage," *Water Resources Research.* Vol. 2, Second Quarter, 1966.

Leopold, Luna B., and Thomas Maddock. *The Flood Control Controversy: Big Dams, Little Dams and Land Management.* Ronald

Press Co., New York, 1954.

Senate Select Committee on National Water Resources. Print No. 15. *Floods and Flood Control.* U.S. Government Printing Office, Washington, D.C., 1960.

——. Print No. 16. *Flood Problems and Management in the Tennessee River Basin.* 1959.

Tennessee Valley Authority, Technical Library. *Flood Damage Prevention; An Indexed Bibliography.* Knoxville, May 1965.

U.S. Army Corps of Engineers. *Water Resources Development in (State).* One for each state issued each year. Available from local district offices of the Corps.

White, Gilbert F. *Choice of Adjustment to Floods.* Department of Geography, University of Chicago, 1964.

——. (editor). *Papers on Flood Problems.* Department of Geography, University of Chicago, 1961.

CHAPTER 4: COORDINATION AND PLANNING

Advisory Commission on Intergovernmental Relations. *Intergovernmental Responsibilities for Water Supply and Sewage Disposal in Metropolitan Areas.* 1800 G Street, N.W., Washington, D.C., 20575, October 1962.

American Institute of Planners. *Background Paper: The Role of Metropolitan Planning.* Washington, D.C., September 1965.

Beckman, Norman, and Leonard Dworsky. "New Views on Public Responsibility for Resources Development—Jurisdictions, Consequences, and Remedies." Reprinted from *New Horizons for Resources Research: Issues and Methodology* (Papers of the 1964 Western Resources Conference). University of Colorado Press, 1965.

Fox, Irving K. *New Horizons in Water Resources Administration.* Resources for the Future, Inc., Reprint No. 51, Washington, D.C., April 1965.

Haveman, Robert H. *Water Resources Investment and the Public Interest.* Vanderbilt University Press, 1965.

Krutilla, John V., and Otto Eckstein. *Multiple Purpose River Development.* Johns Hopkins Press, Baltimore, 1958.

League of Women Voters of the U.S. *Planning in the Community.* No. 299, Washington, D.C., 1964.

National Academy of Sciences—National Research Council. *Alternatives in Water Management.* Publication 1408, Washington, D.C., July 1966.

Sears, Roebuck and Co. *A.B.C.'s of Community Planning.* Dept. 703, 925

S. Homan Ave., Chicago, Ill. 60607, 1962.

Strong, Ann Louise. *Open Space for Urban America.* Department of Housing and Urban Development, Washington, D.C., 1965.

CHAPTERS 5, 6, AND 7: RIVER BASIN PLANNING

Kindsvater, C. E. (editor). *Organization and Methodology for River Basin Planning.* Georgia Institute of Technology, Atlanta, 1965.

League of Women Voters of the U.S. *Know Your River Basin.* No. 256, Washington, D.C., 1958.

Leagues of Women Voters. *Lake Erie: Requiem or Reprieve?* (Prepared by Leagues in Indiana, Michigan, New York, Ohio, and Pennsylvania.) LWV Lake Erie Basin Committee, Marion Bldg., Room 425, 1276 West 3rd Street, Cleveland, Ohio 44113, July 1966.

——. *Man and the River.* (Prepared by Leagues of Delaware, New Jersey, New York, and Pennsylvania.) LWV of New Jersey, 460 Bloomfield Ave., Montclair, N. J., September 1959.

——. *The Ohio River Basin.* (Prepared by local Leagues in Indiana, Kentucky, New York, Ohio, Pennsylvania, and West Virginia.) LWV of Peters Township, 348 Bellwalt Drive, Bridgeville, Penna., April 1964.

——. *Red River of the North.* (Prepared by Leagues of Minnesota and North Dakota.) LWV of North Dakota, 433 8th Ave. South, Fargo, North Dakota, September 1959.

——. *Sudbury, Assabet, Concord River Basin Study.* (Prepared by local Leagues in Massachusetts.) Box 92, West Concord, Mass., December 1963.

——. *The Susquehanna.* (Prepared by local Leagues in Maryland, New York, and Pennsylvania.) LWV of Pennsylvania, Strowbridge and Clothier, 8th and Market Street, Philadelphia, Penna., May 1962.

Martin, R. C., and others. *River Basin Administration and the Delaware.* Syracuse University Press, 1960.

CHAPTERS 8 AND 9:

TOOLS AND THE EFFECTIVE CITIZEN

Conservation Foundation. *Action for Outdoor Recreation for America.* A digest of the Report of the Outdoor Resources Review Commission, with suggestions for citizen action. Washington, D.C., 1964.

League of Women Voters of New York State. *Getting Something Done: Political Effectiveness and Conference Techniques.* LWV Education Fund, Washington, D.C., 1966.

League of Women Voters of the U.S. "Federal Departments, Agencies,

and Commissions Concerned with Water and Land Resources,"
Current Review of Water Resources #1. Washington, D.C., March
1965.

——. "The 89th Congress Acts . . . on Water Resources Management,"
Current Review of Water Resources #2. Washington, D.C., November 1965.

——. *Do You Know the ABC's of Your Town's Government?* No. 297,
1963.

——. *Know Your County.* No. 80, 1962.

——. *Know Your Local Government.* No. 288, 1963.

——. *Recreation and Parks.* No. 286, 1962.

——. *Tips on Reaching the Public.* No. 277, 1962.

——. *Why Write Your Congressman and How.* 3 pp., 1965.

——. *You and Your National Government.* No. 273, 1962.

National Association of Counties and Conservation Foundation. *County
Action for Outdoor Recreation.* Washington, D.C., 1964.

National Wildlife Federation. *Conservation Directory.* Published annually.

——. *Conservation News.* Washington, D.C.

——. *Conservation Report.* Published weekly while Congress is in session.

Office of Economic Opportunity, Information Center. *Catalog of Federal
Programs for Individual and Community Improvement.* 1200 19th
Street, N.W., Washington, D.C. 20036, December 1965.

Young Women's Christian Association. *Community Action for Conservation and Outdoor Recreation.* 600 Lexington Avenue, New York,
N.Y. 10022, 1965.

For copies of federal legislation, write your Congressman.

Index

Names and addresses of federal departments, offices, and commissions most concerned with water and related land resources are listed in Appendix A, pp. 232-35. Nongovernmental organizations from which information is available appear on pp. 235-36.